Jossey-Bass Teacher

Jossey-Bass Teacher provides educators with practical knowledge and tools to create a positive and lifelong impact on student learning. We offer classroom-tested and research-based teaching resources for a variety of grade levels and subject areas. Whether you are an aspiring, new, or veteran teacher, we want to help you make every teaching day your best.

From ready-to-use classroom activities to the latest teaching framework, our value-packed books provide insightful, practical, and comprehensive materials on the topics that matter most to K–12 teachers. We hope to become your trusted source for the best ideas from the most experienced and respected experts in the field.

The Elementary Teacher's Book of Lists
Gary Robert Muschla, Judith A. Muschla, and Erin Muschla • ISBN 978-0-470-50198-6

The ADHD Book of Lists: A Practical Guide for Helping Children and Teens with Attention Deficit Disorders
Sandra F. Rief • ISBN 978-0-7879-6591-4

The Reading Teacher's Book of Lists, Fifth Edition
Edward B. Fry and Jacqueline E. Kress • ISBN 978-0-7879-8257-7

The Vocabulary Teacher's Book of Lists
Edward B. Fry • ISBN 978-0-7879-7101-4

The Art Teacher's Book of Lists, Second Edition, Grades K–12
Helen D. Hume • ISBN 978-0-470-48208-7

The Special Educator's Book of Lists, Second Edition
Roger Pierangelo • ISBN 978-0-7879-6593-8

The School Counselor's Book of Lists, Second Edition
Dorothy J. Blum and Tamara E. Davis • ISBN 978-0-470-45065-9

The ESL/ELL Teacher's Book of Lists, Second Edition
Jacqueline E. Kress • ISBN 978-0-470-22267-6

The American History Teacher's Book of Lists
Fay R. Hansen • ISBN 978-0-13-092572-5

The Homeschooling Book of Lists
Michael Leppert and Mary Leppert • ISBN 978-0-7879-9671-0

The Literature Teacher's Book of Lists, Second Edition
Judie L. H. Strouf • ISBN 978-0-7879-7550-0

The Math Teacher's Book of Lists, Second Edition
Judith A. Muschla and Gary Robert Muschla • ISBN 978-0-7879-7398-8

The Writing Teacher's Book of Lists, Second Edition
Gary Robert Muschla • ISBN 978-0-7879-7080-2

The Physical Education Teacher's Book of Lists
Marian D. Milliken • ISBN 978-0-7879-7887-7

The Health Teacher's Book of Lists
Patricia Rizzo-Toner and Marian Milliken Ziemba • ISBN 978-0-130-32017-9

The Differentiated Instruction
BOOK OF LISTS

JENIFER FOX
WHITNEY HOFFMAN

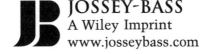
JOSSEY-BASS
A Wiley Imprint
www.josseybass.com

Published by Jossey-Bass
A Wiley Imprint
989 Market Street, San Francisco, CA 94103-1741—www.josseybass.com

Library of Congress Cataloging-in-Publication Data

Fox, Jenifer.
  The differentiated instruction book of lists / Jenifer Fox, Whitney Hoffman.
    p. cm.–(J-B ed : reach and teach ; 6)
  Includes bibliographical references and index.
  ISBN 978-0-470-95239-9 (pbk.)
  ISBN 978-1-118-09440-2 (ebk.)
  ISBN 978-1-118-09441-9 (ebk.)
  ISBN 978-1-118-09442-6 (ebk.)
  1. Individualized instruction–United States.   2. Inclusive education–United States.   3. Mainstreaming in education–United States.   4. Classroom management–United States.   I. Hoffman, Whitney, 1966-   II. Title.
  LC1201.F69 2011
  371.9'0460973—dc23
                                                                      2011017902

Printed in the United States of America
FIRST EDITION
PB Printing   10 9 8 7 6 5 4 3 2 1

The Authors

Jenifer Fox, author of *Your Child's Strengths* (Viking, 2008; Penguin, 2009) and *Stories of Excellence: Case Studies of Exemplary Teaching and Learning with Technology* (NAIS, 2008), is widely considered the international leader in developing strengths-based curriculum for youth. Ms. Fox is a school consultant, public speaker, and creator of Strong Planet, a media-driven interactive curriculum to help all kinds of learners discover their strengths. Ms. Fox served for twenty-five years as a public and independent school administrator and teacher. Her experience includes creating strengths-based teacher evaluation programs, teacher and parent partnerships, and sustainable professional growth programs. She is the head of school at the Clariden School, a progressive K–12 school in Southlake, Texas, that focuses on Montessori, strengths, and innovation and is truly a laboratory for differentiated instruction and personalized learning. Ms. Fox also moderates the Personalized Learning Group on Edutopia, is an expert blogger for the *National Journal,* and writes for the *Huffington Post*. She holds an undergraduate degree from the School of Education at the University of Wisconsin-Madison, a master of arts (MA) in Writing from Middlebury College's Breadloaf School of English, and a master of education (M.Ed.) from Harvard University. She is a certified public school teacher and principal who has been widely published and made numerous expert appearances on television, radio, and in print. She is often invited to speak before audiences of parents and educators throughout the world. Her growing platform crosses between public and independent schools, and she is the founder of the nonprofit organization The Strengths Movement in Schools (http://www.strengthsmovement.com).

Whitney Hoffman is the director of Hoffman Digital Media (http://www.whitney hoffman.com), which produces digital content for the Web, and has created and produced the LD Podcast (http://www.ldpodcast.com) for five years. The LD Podcast features interviews with educational experts including Dr. Robert Brooks, Dr. Russell Barkley, Dr. Tom Brown of Yale University, Dale Brown from LD Online, Jenifer Fox, Rich Weinfeld, Peter Wright, Dr. Stuart Brown from the National Institute of Play, Rick LaVoie, and various other professionals, educators, physicians, and parents. Over 100 podcasts have been produced, downloaded over 100,000 times. Ms. Hoffman also produces OB-GYN To Go, a podcast for medical resident education. Her work on OB-GYN To Go has resulted in publication of an academic paper showing the improvement in learning and retention in resident physicians who use podcasts as part of their education process. Ms. Hoffman is the mother of two children with learning disabilities, both of whom have attended both private and public schools. She has served as the chair of Community Education at the Centreville School in Wilmington, Delaware. With degrees in developmental biology from the University of Pennsylvania and a law degree from the Dickinson School of Law,

Ms. Hoffman delivers considerable knowledge and experience when it comes to making the complex world of special education understandable for parents and educators in online digital platforms. She speaks regularly before audiences on the use of social media platforms to create communities of learning in both the education and business worlds. She also holds a position on the Kennett Consolidated School District Technology Committee, advising about the integration of technology in the classroom, and with Jenifer Fox, moderates the Personalized Learning Group on Edutopia. Ms. Hoffman is also the director of operations for the Podcamp Foundation, which produces digital media community-based unconferences.

For more information on the authors, or to access additional exclusive Web-based resources, please go to their website located at http://www.differentiatedinstruction.co.

Acknowledgments

From Jenifer

Whitney, for thinking of me and bringing me into this project

Marjorie McAneny and everyone at Jossey-Bass for their support and direction

Amy, Paul, and Clay for a place to write and the accompanying support

The faculty of the University of Wisconsin-Madison School of Education for teaching me much of what I know about teaching

William Patterson and Wendy Moore, my first mentors

All the education reformers who tirelessly keep pushing the boulder up the hill

To Carl, thank you for everything

From Whitney

The first people we need to thank are Marjorie McAneny and Tracy Gallagher for being supportive and encouraging from the very start and to Dale Brown for recommending us in the first place.

Additional heartfelt thanks go to

My husband, Matt, and my two boys, James and John, for teaching me what learning, patience, and encouragement are about every day

Jenifer Fox for taking a leap with me on this project

My mother, Janet Schumacher, for her support and eagle-eyed copyediting skills

The teachers and educators in the Kennett Consolidated School District, especially Dan Maguire, Steve Mancini, Philip Reggio, Tamara Fellows, and Jeffra Leo, for giving me an inside look into what dedicated DI teaching looks like and how well a twelve-year-old boy can respond

Chris Lehmann and Gary Stager for showing me what great teaching can be and how school reform starts from each teacher making a child's life a little bit better at EdCon every year

Michelle Wolverton for Web design help; Chris Penn, Chris Brogan, C. C. Chapman, and Julien Smith for being incredibly supportive mentors through the whole writing process; and Christina Gorman, Elizabeth Stintson, and Kelly Figueroa for all the encouragement when needed most

All the guests, listeners, and readers of the LD Podcast and blog—you give me confidence every day

Contents

Section 10   Strategies for Differentiating Science   171

Section 11   Strategies for Differentiating Social Studies   181

Section 12   Strategies for Differentiating the Arts   199

Preface

At the heart of it, differentiated instruction is about empowering every student to learn and master the class objectives and standards to the highest level of his or her potential. The approach gives students multiple options for taking in information and making sense of ideas; it requires teachers to refocus their attention to the learners and modify the curriculum to meet their diverse needs. Ultimately, differentiated instruction offers both students and teachers greater opportunities for success and satisfaction.

Each student arrives in the classroom with a different set of skills and experiences and, still, we often treat instruction as "one size fits all." Teachers today are tasked with delivering instruction to meet the needs of each child with very little guidance. We wrote *The Differentiated Instruction Book of Lists* as the definitive reference tool for differentiated instruction from kindergarten through high school. Ready for immediate use, it offers over one hundred up-to-date lists for developing instructional materials and lesson planning. The book is organized into fifteen convenient sections full of practical examples, key words, teaching ideas, and activities that can be used as is or adapted to meet students' diverse needs. Our hope is that these lists will serve as the basis for discussion, planning, and collaboration among teachers as they commit to success for all students.

Almost half of the states have mandates requiring differentiated instruction for gifted students, and special education laws in the United States, including the Individuals with Disabilities Education Act (IDEA) and Section 504 of the Rehabilitation Act of 1973 (Section 504), along with the Americans with Disabilities Act, come together to help guarantee a free and appropriate public education for all children. Regardless of the locale, socioeconomic level, race, ability or disability, or other perceived advantages or disadvantages of the students or school district, all teachers need to come to terms with the fact that each child in the classroom has the right to learn. We understand that this mandate can appear daunting, and that is where *The Differentiated Instruction Book of Lists* comes in. It will help make this task a bit easier every day by providing you with references, tips, prompts, and guidance.

Now, more than ever before, we need creative problem solvers and thinkers. The strategies in this book will challenge teachers to think about *how* students learn as well as *what* students learn. We need young people to feel like they own the knowledge they gain through school rather than feeling bored and disengaged. Many suggestions in this book will point teachers in the direction of creating authentic, meaningful lessons that engage students on every level. This kind of learning is not new. There are new examples of successful teaching and learning popping up every day. Teachers who do not begin to engage students with these strategies and concepts will be left behind and regarded as ineffective.

Life requires us to find answers to new problems every day, and we need young people who are prepared to tackle these problems. As teachers, you have all the information at your fingertips that you need to be successful. All you have to do is begin to take these steps. We hope this guide will help spark your ideas and empower you as both a teacher and a learner.

To my husband, Matt, and my children, James and John.

For all the students who enriched my life.

The Differentiated Instruction
Book of Lists

Introduction

Maggie Kline teaches third grade in the Center School District. Every year the principal receives dozens of calls from parents requesting that their child be placed in Ms. Kline's classroom. Ms. Kline is known for her popularity with students and the high-quality work they consistently produce, as well as her positive relationships with parents, teachers, and administrators.

Jillian Hanson teaches across the hall from Maggie. Even though they both teach the same curriculum, to the same diverse population of students, Jillian's students don't consistently complete their assignments, pay attention in class, or produce the high-quality work Jillian expects.

At the end of the school day, Jillian is exhausted, but Maggie appears fresh and ready to return home and carry on with her personal life. What is the secret to Maggie's success?

Maggie understands how individualizing her classroom for success by using strategies to differentiate instruction ultimately gives her more stress-free time during the school day and allows her to feel confident and competent as a teacher. How does it give her more stress-free time? Differentiated instruction stresses planning in advance for lessons in which students are actively involved in classroom activities and teachers act more often than not as facilitators. When Maggie's students do well, she feels proud and content and enjoys teaching. All teachers can learn to use these techniques.

Differentiated instruction involves nothing more than looking at the total process of teaching and learning with an eye toward how to inspire each student to be successful. There are three places to implement differentiated strategies: when planning for class, when delivering the lessons, and when students demonstrate learning. Foundational to differentiated instruction is the belief that all students want to feel known, valued, and appreciated and they are more likely to be successful when school becomes a place where they feel these qualities.

On first glance, for many teachers this sounds like a tall order. Classrooms today are full of so many kinds of learners—everything from gifted students to students with documented learning disabilities. Some students can barely speak English; others can't sit still long enough to hear the instructions. Teachers are charged with returning higher test scores, covering a prescribed amount of content, writing reports, and mapping the curriculum. In addition, they are asked to be on committees, perform extra duties, and attend additional meetings. How in the world will they also be able to teach to each student as an individual?

This is a fair question and the answer may surprise you. You already *do* know each student as an individual. Teachers grade and report on every student they come into contact with, so they are already in a relationship with each student, and if they grade students, they already know them. When teachers differentiate, they not only grade students based on this knowledge, but they also plan lessons and deliver teaching with this knowledge in mind. Teachers already prepare lesson plans, create activities, and assess student work. Differentiated instruction is not more work; rather, it is different work.

So what is different about differentiated instruction? It involves making many decisions based on what is known about individual students and finding ways to build on that knowledge and share it with other teachers, parents, and the students themselves. Although many teachers believe they are focused on students as individuals, they are often at a loss for how to get all students to learn. This book provides tips, suggestions, and strategies for helping all students succeed.

Today's students are no longer content with sitting quietly all day, taking in information passively. In fact, that never felt good. Differentiated classrooms are alive with student engagement because people learn by doing. Where did you learn more—reading about driving a car or actually driving it? A peek through the window of Ms. Kline's class will show something new each time you look. Sometimes students are working busily in pairs in desks facing one another while Ms. Kline calmly circles the room answering questions or offering feedback. When the activity is well planned in advance, class time becomes less work for the teacher. The group work in which students are engaged is not frenetic, with some students doing the work while others socialize. Instead, groups are set up in advance of the class, the activities take into account the various interests of the students, and all students in the groups have important roles that only they can fulfill. Planning for these groups is not difficult. The discussion of student groupings in List 4.6 will provide several examples of how to bring effective group work to class.

Both Ms. Kline and Ms. Hanson teach their students how to locate similes. Ms. Hanson reads a passage with several similes in it aloud to the class while the students read along. As they read through the passages, some of the students are bored because they can easily identify the similes and the reading level is too low; other students have not yet grasped the concept of a simile and give up because they don't understand what is happening or what they are looking for in the passage. Ms. Hanson is teaching to the middle of the bell-shaped curve of students in her classroom, while the students on either end become frustrated. This teaching to the middle causes students to act out, and before Ms. Hanson knows it, the class is no longer paying attention. Time is lost, everyone feels frustrated.

Ms. Kline has the same objective for her class. She knows that some students will get the objective sooner than others and some won't understand it right off. She knows that by offering opportunities for all students to be learning, she must plan in advance for different kinds of learners. There are many options open to Ms. Kline and no one option is a magic bullet or a recommended approach. A teacher who is tuned into the different needs of her students will plan with them in mind and save time and energy for this. Ms. Kline decides to offer students three opportunities for working with similes. She provides a worksheet with definitions and examples, a short assignment that has students choose a book from the book center and identify two similes, and finally invites students to write their own similes in a paragraph, a poem, or a short story. She allows the students to choose which activity they feel most comfortable with. As students make their choices, Ms. Kline observes, and as students work through the chosen activities on their own, she circulates and spot checks for understanding by asking questions.

Differentiated classrooms are student-centered. This means the focus of the lesson and the time on task is more centered on student activity than direct teacher guidance. Traditional class instruction involves a great deal of time in which the teacher stands in front of the class delivering content in the form of a lecture or by using the board to demonstrate how to solve math problems or writing concepts that students copy as notes. In a traditional class, teachers read one book to the whole class, or hold discussions asking the same kind of questions to the entire group, providing most of the answers themselves. In traditional classrooms, teachers are "on stage" most of the day. No wonder they are exhausted at the end of the day! They do most of the work while students take in information.

In differentiated classrooms, it is not unusual to see students moving around the room to learning stations, leading discussions, giving presentations, and working on teams to solve creative problems. Because students are involved, they are more invested in the learning. Because teachers have planned the lessons with the students' interests and varying abilities in mind, each student is provided an opportunity for success and has an opportunity to become engaged in the activities on the level where they can experience both challenge and success.

Differentiated classrooms tend to have very few behavioral problems. Many students act out when they are bored, frustrated, or feel alienated. In this book teachers will learn, among other things, how to use interest inventories and strengths discovery techniques to connect to students on a personal level. Through simple questioning techniques and ongoing checks for understanding, teachers will gradually learn how to teach to different ability levels in the classroom. Teachers will learn how to use a technique called *scaffolding* to provide students the challenges necessary for new learning to occur no matter what level they are on.

What you will find in this book are suggestions and strategies that have worked for generations of successful teachers. Differentiated instruction is a very broad-based term that refers to planning, teaching, and assessment methods that accommodate differences in student knowledge, preferences, cultural backgrounds, and physical and social needs. In short, differentiated instruction is a flexible, equitable, and intelligent way to approach teaching and learning. Rooted in the research on multiple intelligences, learning styles, critical thinking, cognitive development, and hierarchical planning, differentiation is not simply a buzzword but a mandate for student success.

Bonus Web Material Available!

Note that we've included additional materials on Differentiated Instruction on this book's website. You can access them at: www.differentiatedinstruction.co.

Join the Twitter conversation: #DIBOL

Section One

Understanding Differentiated Instruction

In this section, the lists offer teachers insight into understanding how differentiated instruction differs from traditional classroom instruction. Teachers will discover that teaching to the individual is methodical yet open for an infinite number of ideas and creativity.

List 1.1. A Vision for the Differentiated Instruction Classroom

Here are some characteristics of a differentiated instruction classroom:

- Students are engaged in learning; they are focused and on task 80 percent of the time.

- Teachers have a clear plan for the time spent in class. There is little wasted time or confusion over materials and protocols; instead, there is a sense of shared purpose.

- Students ask many questions and feel safe questioning.

- Everyone belongs. There is evidence of diverse personalities in the classroom through personalized materials, spaces, or use of nicknames.

- Time is divided into small learning chunks with checks for understanding in between concepts.

- Students hold one another accountable for rules and respect. The class agreements are posted on the wall and there are visual reminders of the class and school values.

- Quality work is valued and displayed in the classroom.

- Students know what is expected of their work by viewing examples of excellence and using rubrics to guide them toward mastery.

- Teachers are not at the front of the class all the time; they are learning alongside the students. When students write poetry, teachers do too and share their work with students.

- Students move from whole class discussion to group work with ease because training was provided and they understand the roles they take on during the group work.

List 1.2. One-Size-Fits-All Teaching Versus Differentiated Teaching

Differentiated instruction (DI) offers students a more responsive and personalized learning experience, and can be an alternative to the frustration and failure many students experience when learning is presented and assessed in the same way for each student. This list compares DI with the one-size-fits-all approach to teaching by providing examples so teachers can begin to see some key differences.

One-Size-Fits-All Teaching	Differentiated Instruction
Teachers answer all the questions.	Teachers redirect questions to students.
Every student writes on the same topic.	Students choose from a variety of topics.
Tests are all multiple-choice questions.	Tests have different sections that offer multiple ways to demonstrate learning.
Everyone reads the same book.	Students choose books according to their interests and reading levels.
For most class time, teachers are at the front of the room directly teaching all students the same materials.	Teachers guide students through activities rather than spend most of the time delivering content.
Teachers give only verbal directions.	Teachers give both oral and written directions; teachers may provide a sample of a project so students can see an expected outcome.
Class time is spent doing one kind of activity the entire time.	Class is broken down into seven- to ten-minute chunks with new activities for each chunk.
Teachers are viewed as the authority on all knowledge.	Teachers ask for student input on lessons, topics, and projects.
Students read in class and work on projects outside of class.	Students work with others in class and do things they can do on their own when they are not in class.
Students have one opportunity to perform, usually in the form of some kind of cumulative test at the end of a unit.	Students are provided examples of what quality work looks like, and their work is checked along the way with many opportunities for revision.

List 1.3. Small Things That Make a Big Difference

Differentiating instruction can seem like an overwhelming task. Teachers worry that given all the roles and responsibilities they must take on, the call to differentiate is simply too difficult. This list gives examples of small things teachers can do that will make a big difference in their classrooms.

- **When deciding where to begin, start with broad categories in mind and then work backward to the actual lesson plan.** As in "reverse engineering," take the big idea or point of the unit and lesson and start working backward to design a pathway toward that goal, including all the steps students will need to take to reach it. Start thinking about differentiating at the following four points: content (what is taught); process (how it's taught); product (how students demonstrate knowledge); and environment (where students learn). See List 3.1 for more help on backward design.

- **By making minor adjustments, such as supplementing oral instructions with written instructions or using diagrams to explain complex points, you can better reach a variety of learners and augment the learning of every student.** Teachers do not have to differentiate to meet the needs of every student, all the time. A common frustration occurs when teachers believe they have to provide more than twenty styles of assignments or assessments in every class. This would be impossible and create chaos. Instead, simple adjustments such as providing instructions in several formats—oral, written, diagram—helps students, regardless of learning style, have a better idea of what the teacher wants them to do and why.

- **Frequent simple knowledge checks—such as "thumbs up/thumbs down"—help ensure students are not left confused or lost in the middle of a lesson.** A teacher who realizes in the moment that students don't quite grasp certain points will save time from having to reteach material and diagnose students' misunderstandings in a subsequent class period.

- **Get to know all the students' names as quickly as possible.** When teachers know all the students' names, and one personal fact about each of them, students feel valued for the unique individual they are. Feeling known and valued is a key ingredient to success in school. Students perform better for teachers with whom they have a relationship than if they feel like they are a mere cog in the educational machine, just as teachers perform better when they feel valued by administrators rather than as someone sent to keep a desk or seat warm.

- **Partner with other teachers to share information and ideas.** Not all teachers have to do interest inventories on students. These can be shared. In fact, DI works best when partnerships occur across content areas and grade levels. When teachers work on teams or with partners to share ideas about what works, the process becomes easier. Likewise, finding areas where content overlaps helps students make concept connections between subject areas, thus making all their learning more meaningful.

List 1.3. (continued)

- **Provide choices to students about how to demonstrate learning rather than creating multiple standard assessments.** Students can demonstrate mastery of learning in many ways beyond a typical multiple-choice, fill-in-the-blank kind of test. In addition, this approach gives teachers a better picture of student mastery and understanding than typical end-of-unit tests. Choice also allows students to take advantage of the best way to present their ideas.

  Example: Culture study. Students compare and contrast two versions of a fairy tale from different cultures. Students can draw pictures of similarities and differences or discuss and prepare an oral presentation or create thirty-second reenactments representing similarities and differences.

- **Write the class objective on the board and point students' attention toward it.** Each day, and unit by unit, write the objective, big idea, or point of the lesson on the board. Let students know what the class is working toward, and check that the objective is met.

  Example: Fraction to decimal conversion (lesson/unit goal). By the end of the unit, students should be able to convert fractions into decimals; understand decimals and their relationship to percentages; and comprehend how common fractions, decimals, and percentages are related.

- **Prepare questions in advance of discussions and be sure that there are questions that are recall for the struggling students as well as evaluative for those more advanced.** When teachers run discussions with questions at every level of the cognitive hierarchy, students stay engaged and do not experience frustration. Questions might ask not only for factual recall, but also about implications and relevance of the lesson, especially relating to the big ideas or goal of the lesson. (See List 3.3 for more on differentiating questions and Bloom's taxonomy.)

- **Believe the research that supports DI—these methods work.** Teachers are sometimes skeptical of new initiatives in schools. The research supporting student success when DI methods are employed is vast and time tested. (For a complete list of articles and research on differentiated instruction with links, see our website: http://www.differentiatedinstruction.co.) These are not new ideas; they are practices that have worked for years. Think of this as finally translating bench-top science into bedside practice in education.

List 1.4. Common Misconceptions

Despite commonly held misconceptions, differentiated instruction (DI) is actually *not*

- **A fad.** The suggestions in this book are not new. They are time-tested hallmarks of good teaching. With today's students becoming increasingly disengaged with school, it is more important than ever before that teachers adopt these techniques and strategies.

- **Only for struggling students.** The main idea behind differentiated instruction is that all learners need individual attention paid to their learning styles and interests. All students, from those with diagnosed learning disabilities to those in advanced placement courses, will benefit from these strategies.

- **A customized learning plan for each student in every lesson.** There are some simple techniques that can be applied to the entire class for the benefit of all. Teachers do not have to do everything at once. Nor will every student require the same DI strategy for every lesson. As content varies and changes, so will each student's level of interest and individual need for support.

- **A perfect science.** There are hundreds of ways to differentiate instruction. The main point is that teachers are mindful of the individuals who make up their classrooms and work to help each student get the education he or she deserves.

- **Costly.** Implementing these strategies does not involve costly materials, new text-books, or specialized technology. Often teachers already have all of the necessary teaching tools in place; they only need to alter their presentation, the interactivity of the lesson, and how students demonstrate their mastery of the material.

- **Optional.** Teachers today must embrace the fact that students need certain kinds of relationships and instruction to succeed. Any teacher who doesn't want to embrace these strategies, even if it is only a little at a time, is not doing his or her job.

- **Something a teacher does every once in awhile and then is finished.** DI is a philosophy that is backed up by practice and becomes the cornerstone for effective teaching. It is a set of tools and ingredients that can be combined and recombined endlessly to meet the ever-changing needs of students.

List 1.4. (continued)

- **Adding more work to students who finish early.** Students should be able to remain challenged within the normal class time alongside the rest of the students. The message that "more" is challenging is wrong. Quality is stressed over quantity. Often this means providing optional challenge assignments and opportunities to explore content more thoroughly for those who have early mastery.

- **One-size-fits-all instruction.** Differentiated instruction takes all students and their learning needs into consideration, but it does not provide a completely individualized lesson each day for each student. We know already that individualized instruction is challenging, so rather than trying to make specialized lessons for each student, a teacher needs to include students with Individualized Education Plans (IEPs) and 504 Plans in the general instruction while making alterations or accommodations as needed. Often the accommodations for students with learning disabilities helps other students in the class better understand and master the material as well, thus helping all students succeed.

- **Difficult.** DI takes planning and a new way of thinking, but there is nothing esoteric or too difficult about it. There are many simple strategies that work with groups of students to allow them to discover success, and we present many of them to you throughout this book.

List 1.5. Differentiate the Materials

Learning materials can be differentiated by student interest or ability level, and also by format, such as incorporating audio and video resources into lessons. Teachers can assign different materials or provide student choice. Many of the lists in this book offer tips on how to do this most effectively. This list provides examples of what it looks like in the classroom.

- In some classes, especially in the arts, the materials are differentiated by nature. For example, in music, students sing different parts according to their abilities or play different instruments according to their abilities and interests.

  Example: Allowing students some choice in choosing instruments or switching instruments each class period exposes students to different experiences while making sure any one student isn't stuck with an instrument that he or she has more difficulty playing.

- In any grade, literature teachers can teach the entire class the same literature concepts and objectives while each student reads a book suited to his or her ability level and interest. For example, when teachers focus on the elements of setting and how they inform the story, students can write about or discuss this concept in terms of the books they chose. The teacher does not have to know each book to determine whether a student has demonstrated understanding.

  Example: Ms. D uses the "Reading Olympics" and Newbery Award book lists as two lists from which students can select books for the unit at hand. There are many reading levels represented, but students have some choice about the book they read.

- In a foreign language class, students can participate in a simulation (such as two old friends meet in a restaurant to discuss their past and dream about the future). Each student is assigned different vocabulary words and different tenses to practice.

  Example: Mr. S has students in small groups write out brief lines of a typical conversation that might take place in a restaurant or in a classroom. While performing these scenarios, Mr. S records the students on audio-video. The recordings are later watched so students can hear themselves and review their own performance as part of the assessment and as a test of fluency.

- A social studies teacher approaches a class about Martin Luther King Jr. with an assignment that every student become familiar with the "I Have a Dream" speech. A copy of the text of the speech, an audio recording, and video are available for students, and the teacher asks that students both read and watch or read and listen to the speech. A worksheet is provided to compare the experiences of reading and seeing or listening.

List 1.5. (continued)

- In an elementary unit on the solar system, the class is arranged with a book station that has three books about the planets (the three books are geared to different reading abilities). Another station has a chart with the planets that students fill in, naming the planets and coloring them; then they cut the planets out and paste them onto another paper. A third station has an experiment about gravity for the students to perform. The teacher is stationed at the experiment because this needs teacher guidance. Students move in groups through the stations.

Further Reading

Online Book Lists

Association for Library Service to Children. Newbery Medal and Honor Books, 1922–Present. http://www.ala.org/ala/mgrps/divs/alsc/awardsgrants/bookmedia/newberymedal/newberyhonors /newberymedal.cfm. Retrieved January 2011.
Association for Library Service to Children. Caldecott Medal and Honor Books, 1938–Present. http://www.ala.org/ala/mgrps/divs/alsc/awardsgrants/bookmedia/caldecottmedal/caldecotthonors /caldecottmedal.cfm. Retrieved January 2011.

Reading Olympics

Book lists for Reading Olympics vary frequently by school district and reading level. Please consult with your district or school librarian for current lists of books. A sample list of Reading Olympics books is included in this book's bonus Web material.

List 1.6. Differentiate the Task

Differentiation happens when students are able to practice learning in ways that allow for their optimal success and mastery. Teachers can differentiate tasks according to learning styles, interests, or readiness. There are lists in later sections of this book that specifically guide teachers on how to differentiate along these lines most effectively. This list is designed to give teachers a feel for what differentiating the task may look like in class.

- In an elementary math class, one student works independently with headphones on to block out noise, while a group of three works together to solve the same problems. At the same time, the teacher is working with a pair of students while some students work at their seats. One boy is sitting on the floor doing the work. This section of working on problems doesn't become chaotic because it only lasts for ten or fifteen minutes, and students are engaged in the task in a way that best suits their individual needs.

- A middle school math teacher partners with a social studies teacher to create a unit on transportation and the economy. The teachers determine which objectives to cover and where they can combine content. The math teacher adds ratios, measurements, and percentages. They create a lesson with five activities for students to determine how products are shipped across the country.

- In a social studies unit, the objective is to demonstrate mastery of the electoral process. Some students create a pamphlet explaining this process to potential voters, while others write a paper about it and another student creates a PowerPoint and classroom presentation to explain the process to the class. Another group of students decides to make an analogy of the steps and stages of the electoral process to other common processes, such as building a house or joining a club. Same objective, different tasks.

- In an arts class, the students are taught about the color wheel and how some colors are complementary whereas others are not. Students have a choice from several different projects to give side-by-side examples of complementary colors versus those that create excitement because of their noncomplementary nature.

- A middle school language arts teacher has students pick a monthly independent reading book. Each week, the teacher asks students to write a paragraph about the book on their classroom blog or their individual wiki, picking from a selection of appropriate writing prompts. Each student performs a similar task, but individual choice from the list of prompts helps students select a level of challenge that is appropriate.

List 1.7. Differentiate the Homework

All homework assignments do not have to be the same for every child. However, differentiation is about more than simply assigning different problems. Some children may work better in groups, and a teacher may suggest they form a study group to review content while suggesting that five other students read an interesting article that evening. In the differentiated classroom, homework can be viewed as an extension of learning. Students can both extend and practice in multiple ways. Here are some examples of how homework can be differentiated.

- When working on projects, students can each have a different task, performing acts that cannot be done in school. For example, one student interviews an elderly person, while another takes photos of the home where the person grew up, or finds or draws pictures of what the home was like based on the person's description.
- Have students practice only as much as they need to practice. In math, if a student has failed to grasp the concepts, doing another twenty problems is not useful. Instead, ask the student to spend time in the evening looking over the process and problems, and write a few sentences about where he or she is getting confused or what is not making sense. This not only helps the teacher and student to better understand what is causing the confusion, but it may also help the teacher enhance his or her teaching of this skill in the future. (See List 9.1: Using Reading and Writing to Differentiate Math Instruction.) Other students may be assigned a book to read about useful math applications, given challenge problems, or asked whether they can find an example from real life where a particular math application is useful.
- Rather than assign the total reading for the whole class, assign small groups different sections to report on in class. This way, students will be responsible for sharing knowledge, as well as listening and cooperating.
- Provide assessments as homework. All homework does not have to be a practice exercise or formative. Some homework can be summative. This is a concept commonly referred to as the "take home test."
- Everyone does not have to do homework every night. You can assign some of the class at-home responsibilities one day and the rest of the class another day.
- Don't use homework as a punishment. All work done at home should be considered a chance for greater learning. Differentiating homework works when the teacher and the students buy into this concept.
- Try to occasionally assign homework about making broader connections of the material to real life. For example, a science unit on taste receptors offers opportunities for students to have friends and family try different condiments, salt, sugar, and more at home by applying them with a Q-tip directly to areas of the tongue to test and demonstrate the formal lesson. This can be fun and also put the student in the role of teacher at home, which almost every student enjoys.
- Make homework interactive. Post an article or question to a classroom blog or wiki, and ask students to comment on the blog, adding additional information and resources in the comment as appropriate. Students will have the opportunity not only to leave their own feedback, but also to review and comment on the information left by others. This also serves as a great launching point for subsequent classroom discussions the next day.

List 1.8. Differentiate Checking for Understanding

To customize learning and differentiate instruction, teachers must continuously check for student understanding throughout the lesson. Does this mean stopping and quizzing students? No, quizzes are a traditional, anxiety-evoking method that usually gets in the way of differentiated instruction. This list provides some examples of what checks for understanding look like in the classroom on a day-to-day basis. Additional lists on designing differentiated assessments are included in subsequent subject-specific sections.

- In math class, instruct students to choose which problem they most enjoy solving, and explain why to a partner. Then with the same partner, have students find a problem they dislike, and explain why. Circulate the room while they are sharing, listening for what challenges students.
- Ask students to repeat back what they just heard.
- When presenting a lesson, ask students for a simple "thumbs up/thumbs down" as to whether they are getting what you are saying. If there are thumbs down, ask students to ask you a question or two to see whether you can identify what might be causing confusion in the moment. Chances are, many students may be having the same difficulty, and it's easier to correct misunderstanding or confusion in the moment rather than feel you have to reteach the lesson later.
- Have students teach each other what they just learned. The classic "see one, do one, teach one" is a great way for students to apply what they've learned and demonstrate mastery.
- In an elementary language arts class where all students are reading different books, have each student explain his or her book to another. Having students give mini–book reviews or even discuss what they think may happen next gives them a great opportunity not only to share, but also to use preview and reflection skills.
- Use these questions:

    Why?
    What do you mean by _____?
    How do you know?
    Could you give an example?
    Do you agree?
    Tell me more.

- Asking open-ended questions allows students to demonstrate their understanding and requires development of critical-thinking skills. Since most open-ended questions don't have a strict right or wrong answer, students gradually lose the fear of pass/fail in participating in class because they learn that their opinions and thought processes are valued.
- Some classrooms are starting to use audience response systems in class, which allow teachers to take small sample quizzes during class to see what percentage of the class understands and what percentage is still struggling. This helps the teacher modify the lesson on the fly, while also testing for common errors or mistakes that might need clarification.

List 1.9. Differentiate the Outcome

Not all students have to demonstrate learning the same way as long as they demonstrate mastery of the class objectives. Here are some examples of class objectives and how they may look with differentiated outcomes.

- **Middle school literature objective:** Understand how plot, conflict, resolution, character, setting, theme, and point of view work within a piece of fiction.

  Differentiated outcomes: Assign the whole class one short story and divide into groups to build poster walk-arounds (see List 11.1: Gallery Walks), one for each literary device. Digital posters may also be created with Glogster (http://edu.glogster.com).

- **Third-grade science objective:** Describe the movement of Earth and the moon and the apparent movement of other bodies through the sky.

  Differentiated outcomes: One student may create a 3-D model, another will draw it on paper, and another will write in a narrative how it works.

- **High school algebra objective:** Use linear functions or inequalities to solve problems from graphs or algebraic properties.

  Differentiated outcomes: Students each take a real-world application of this and show how it works. Provide three levels of problems and let them choose.

- **First- and second-grade writing objective:** Students will be introduced to the mechanics involved in writing sentences.

  Differentiated outcomes: Some students will practice with worksheets, while others write original sentences.

List 1.10. Are You Ready for Differentiated Instruction? A Few More Examples of What Is Expected

Becoming an expert teacher takes many small adjustments, made consistently over time. This doesn't mean that every existing lesson has to be rewritten from scratch, or that every teaching skill or strategy must be relearned and revamped. In fact, there are many things teachers do already that can be considered differentiation and they are not even aware of it. This list of pertinent questions offers examples from various sections of the book of some of the techniques involved in differentiated instruction (DI). When you ask yourself these questions while planning lessons, you will be able to see where DI can begin to fit in with your existing teaching style.

- **Is the lesson plan for tomorrow about me, or is it about the student?** Look at the lesson plan for tomorrow and decide whether it describes what the teacher does or what the students are going to do. DI lessons focus on what *students* do and learn. (See List 3.3: How to Create Differentiated Lesson Plans with Bloom's Taxonomy.)

- **Is there time planned into the lesson to check and see whether students understand the instruction?** It's never effective to ask the whole group whether or not they understand. DI teachers have specific checkpoints mapped into the lesson; these may be as simple as asking individual students to paraphrase what they have heard or understand. (See List 3.4: Differentiated Assessments.)

- **Do I know what the students should take away after the lesson?** Before each lesson, consider exactly what the students are supposed to know at the end. Share this with the students at the start of the lesson. At the end of the lesson, remind them and see whether they accomplished what was asked. (See List 3.1: Where to Begin and What to Do.)

- **Can I make a student feel valued today?** Each day, give special attention to one student. This is a way to get to know students incrementally in a conscious way. It doesn't mean teachers ignore other students; it simply means that each day, they turn their attention, like a laser, on a different student. Find out something new about the student, direct questions to this student, share a fact about yourself, such as your favorite book. This strategy will give you five deeper relationships with students by the end of the week. DI is about knowing students. When students feel known, they want to do better. (See List 2.1: Building Relationships.)

List 1.10. (continued)

- **Can I help students focus without calling them out?** Small, subtle things can help students refocus without formal correction or discipline, and without disrupting the flow of the class. Keep a squeeze ball in the classroom and when a student begins to get fidgety, calmly walk over and without saying anything, hand the student the ball. This acknowledges an individual's attention span and provides a tool to help the student stay focused without devaluing the student. (See List 5.4: Discipline Strategies.)

- **Can I help parents understand the importance of learning over just grades and test scores?** When talking to parents, stress mastery of learning objectives over the importance of grades. This is an ongoing conversation that won't be understood the first time it is raised. (See List 5.7: Classroom Management and Parental Communication Tips.)

- **Do I feel comfortable asking for help and giving help to colleagues?** Working with other teachers in this way can be extremely valuable in helping discover which lessons are working and not working for students. One way to do this and "test" whether the lesson is working is to ask a colleague to review a student's finished project and ask whether he or she can tell from the end point what the assignment was and what the process may have been to get there. Ideally, the product should be a reflection of both the assignment and the learning that occurred to produce it. (See List 3.4: Differentiated Assessments.)

List 1.11. Definitions of Concepts Commonly Associated with Differentiated Instruction

The following are definitions that educators and researchers commonly use in conjunction with differentiated instruction (DI). The list is by no means exhaustive, but it offers a general guide to the terms used throughout this book and elsewhere in discussions of differentiation. The concepts listed here are used throughout the book to describe methods and practices.

Authentic assessment. Evaluating student work based on the student's collective abilities rather than one isolated skill tested in a uniform, standardized manner. Simply testing an isolated skill or a retained fact does not effectively measure a student's capabilities. For example, in science class, a test that has every student choosing answers from a list of multiple-choice questions is a traditional assessment method, whereas an authentic assessment may require students to create their own hypothesis and work toward creating a science experiment using the scientific method.

Authentic projects, authentic learning. Authentic projects are those in which students take what they've learned in class and use it to do something useful or meaningful. Also known as experiential learning, or learning by doing, authentic learning helps students transfer the knowledge into practical experience. For example, in a kindergarten class, students can play cooking or they can actually cook. In high school, students can learn about the ecology from a textbook (traditional) or they can go out and conduct projects such as cleaning up a polluted estuary.

Backward design. Grant Wiggins, educator and coauthor of *Understanding by Design* (2005), first introduced the concept of backward design, whereby the teacher plans backward from product or assessment to the daily lesson plan. For example, when deciding to read a Shakespeare play, the teacher begins by deciding what the goal of this is and how the students will be assessed to demonstrate if they achieved the goal.

Bloom's Taxonomy. Developed by Benjamin Bloom (1956), the taxonomy is a classification system for cognition. The model guides teachers to develop lesson plans that move students from the simplest forms of thinking to the most complex, as represented by a hierarchy of skills beginning with knowledge and advancing through comprehension, application, analysis, synthesis, and evaluation. At each level, the amount of interaction or application of base knowledge is extended from the previous level, until students are able to apply the learned knowledge in new, novel situations. This taxonomy is important for differentiating learning because it gives teachers ways to teach to multiple cognitive levels at the same time.

Constructivism. An educational philosophy that holds that students learn best and generate the most knowledge when they can use their experiences and ideas to make meaning and solve problems. Constructivist theory was put forth by James Bruner (1961) and states that instruction should be based on four basic principles: (1) a learner

List 1.11. (continued)

should have an interest or a predisposition for learning; (2) the curriculum taught should be structured in a way that is most accessible to the student; (3) there should be an overlying sequence or order to the curriculum; and (4) there should be a nature and pacing of rewards and punishments (largely based on behavioral cognitive theory). Many DI strategies are constructivist, since they call for structuring the curriculum in a way that is accessible to all learners.

Cooperative learning. Also known as collaborative, group, or team learning, it generally refers to small groups of students with different levels of expertise and performance who are working together toward educational objectives. Learners are not only responsible for their own learning, but also for assisting and contributing to the learning of others in the group.

Differentiated assessments. Assessments designed to check students' progress and understanding during learning, in contrast to the usual end-of-unit summary test. By having intermittent, low-stake opportunities for students to demonstrate their learning and understanding, educators can assess students' understanding and mastery of concepts long before a cumulative exam is given. Although these intermittent assessments can take many forms (such as allowing students to choose methods of expression, e.g., multimedia presentations, written papers, or tests), they should give instructors the feedback they need about their students' progress and serve as a guide for further instruction.

Differentiated instruction (DI). An educational practice that provides learners with multiple ways to master the objectives. Students of all ability levels and learning styles gain equal access and opportunities to acquire and demonstrate mastery. All DI strategies are geared toward personalizing the learning experience to reach all students in a classroom.

Executive functions. Executive functions include attention controls, decision making, planning, sequencing, and problem solving, along with regulation of action and self-control. Many students who struggle in school have low executive functioning. This presents as inability to remain organized, on time, or on task for any sustained period. Executive functions are also developmentally linked, with many of the higher-order functions developing during mid to late adolescence.

Homogeneous and heterogeneous groupings. Homogeneous groupings place similarly situated students together, whereas heterogeneous groupings, also known as mixed-ability groupings, allow students of different abilities to work together in the classroom.

Inclusion. Under the Individuals with Disabilities Education Act (IDEA), all students with disabilities are to be taught in the "least restrictive environment" possible, with the regular classroom usually being that least restrictive environment. Inclusion presupposes that every student, regardless of ability, belongs in a normal classroom first, with his or her peer group, and that, to the extent possible, services should be brought to the student rather than removing the student from the classroom.

List 1.11. (continued)

Interdisciplinary learning. Merging content from several traditionally segregated disciplines into one blended content experience. For example, combining art and history in one unit.

Learning contracts. An agreement between a teacher and student (and sometimes parents) about the responsibilities for learning. All parties are held, in writing, to their responsibilities, thus helping make them more accountable for their portion of the learning process.

Learning profile. Based on work by both Lev Vygotsky (Moll, 1990) on scaffolding and Howard Gardner's (2006) theory of multiple intelligences, learning profiles delineate how individual students learn best. A learning profile includes a student's learning style (kinesthetic, tactile, visual, or auditory), grouping preferences, and environmental preferences.

Mastery. Achieving a percentage of performance ability that signals success and the ability to move on to new and higher levels of cognition. Based on the work of Madeline Hunter (2004), the concept of mastery includes the ability to repeat performance. Teachers are to repeat instruction until students achieve mastery.

Modeling. Differentiated instruction encourages educators to model successful strategies and endpoints to help students "see" the end point, goal, or pathway toward mastery. As in role modeling, teachers help students visualize what they need to do by providing examples and guidelines.

Outcomes. Outcomes may include a range of skills and knowledge. Generally, outcomes are expected to be measurable in concrete terms, that is, "Student can run fifty meters in less than one minute," instead of "Student enjoys physical education class."

Processing. The ability for a student to take in information and manipulate it so as to make the information useful in future problem solving, also referred to as acquisition of knowledge. Some students may have a naturally faster processing rate, allowing them to acquire and master knowledge, or stated more simply, to "catch on," faster than other students.

Readiness. The point at which a student is ready, willing, and able to learn concepts and curriculum. Readiness is tied in closely with a child's developmental process and ability to grasp concepts. For example, most kindergarteners are not yet developmentally ready to read middle-school-level textbooks. Readiness is also closely tied to Lev Vygotsky's (Moll, 1990) concept of the zone of proximal development, that is, the time or window in which students are most able to grasp information and make leaps in understanding.

Response to intervention (RTI). In the latest version of the Individuals with Disabilities Education Act, RTI was incorporated as a way to try to implement early intervention with research-proven educational strategies and to reduce the number of students requiring

List 1.11. (continued)

special education services, when early intervention and intensive instruction, delivered when necessary, could prevent later academic complications. The goal of RTI is to provide the additional help students may need as early and as often as possible to make sure students master key academic skills before determining that trusted interventions are failing, and more intensive special education services, such as resource rooms, are required. RTI and differentiated instruction work well together, because DI helps teachers identify struggling students and use research-based interventions to help them master material. There will still be students who will need special education services and more intensive interventions outside the classroom, but DI and RTI serve to bridge the achievement gap.

Rubrics. Rubrics are basic scoring tools for what may be traditionally subjective assignments, such as essays, projects, posters, and more. Rubrics delineate the assessment criteria and the number of points assigned to each element, so students have a list of what elements must be included in the final project, along with the grading metrics and standards. Rubrics, when shared with students at the time the assignment is given, make the grading parameters transparent and place more control and responsibility on the students for their final grade. Rubrics help maintain consistent and fair grading while helping students understand the basis and standards for evaluation.

Scaffolding. Introduced in the 1950s by cognitive psychologist James Bruner (1961), instructional scaffolding describes the process in which parents and teachers support a child's learning by assisting them at their instructional level until such a point at which they become independent at the particular skill or task in question. Scaffolding is closely related to Lev Vygotsky's (Moll, 1990) concept of the zone of proximal development, the point at which a student is the most ready and able to learn new skills with adult-mediated support.

Student centered. This term refers to instructional methods and classroom cultures that take individual students and their interests, needs, and experiences into consideration when teaching and testing for understanding.

Zone of proximal development (ZPD). First described by Russian psychologist Lev Vygotsky (Moll, 1990), it is the point at which a student is the most ready and able to learn new skills with adult-mediated support. Students cannot learn when the task is too easy because they become bored. Students need challenge, but not too much challenge, or anxiety prevents optimal learning. The ZPD is the point at which a child is pushed beyond the comfort level but not so far beyond as to feel threatened.

Section Two

Teaching with the Individual in Mind

Personalized learning with attention to the class as a group of individuals with different learning needs is the backbone of differentiated instruction. Research has proved that individuals do not learn in the same way (Fischer & Rose, 2001; Green, 1999; Guild, 2001; Mulroy & Eddinger, 2003). This section provides a variety of lists with suggestions to understand the different ways students learn and how to accommodate the variety of learning preferences through varying instruction during the lesson. It is necessary to take into account the vast differences among students in a classroom, acknowledging each student's strengths while accommodating their limitations (Guild, 2001; Mulroy & Eddinger, 2003; Tomlinson, 2001, 2002). Teachers will find many tips and suggestions for how to build trusting, personal relationships with all students.

List 2.1. Building Relationships

One of the most important aspects of effective teaching is building strong rapport and trusting relationships between the students and the teacher. Differentiated instruction (DI) teachers ask their students to step out of their comfort zones and face challenges; this is difficult without establishing the requisite trust levels first. Because each student is different, every teacher-student relationship will be different. This list provides some general tips for building strong teacher-student relationships.

- **Build trust over time.** In the beginning of the year, a classroom is like any new group—people need to get to know each other to be able to form strong relationships. Trust begins with small steps, so consider starting out the year with a few easier, but not trivial, assignments that students feel capable of doing before moving on to more challenging material. (See List 2.8: Tips for Motivating All Students.)

- **Call students by their names**. When responding to their questions and comments, for example, say, "Yes, Carl, I see what you mean by that statement. I think the part about the migratory birds is interesting. Can you tell me more?"

- **Refer back to students' previous work and contributions.** Doing so shows that you remember and take them seriously.

  Examples: "Carl, remember the point you made earlier this week about the migratory birds? I thought about it a lot and shared that comment with a friend of mine." "Allie, isn't *Green Eggs and Ham* your favorite book?"

- **Share some appropriate personal information with students.** Information such as middle names, favorite colors, pastimes, childhood memories, or favorite foods are all bits of information that will show students the authenticity of their teachers. This authenticity is necessary if the teacher wants to build the kinds of relationships where students feel comfortable taking risks.

- **Complete the work expected of the students.** Nothing builds a teacher's credibility in the classroom more quickly than students' seeing the teacher doing the same performance tasks as they are. This modeling shows students that the work is serious and real.

- **Inquire when students are absent, appear distressed, or late for class.** Show genuine concern for what life is like outside the classroom.

List 2.1. (continued)

- **Return student work in a timely fashion.** If teachers expect students to turn in work on certain dates, it follows that teachers should return the work with comments in a timely fashion. This reciprocity builds trust and respect.

- **Consider using nicknames.** This practice builds camaraderie among students and with the teacher.

- **Admit mistakes.** Nobody is perfect. When students see teachers own and admit mistakes, they develop great admiration and trust.

- **Find something to like about every student.** There are lots of children who drive teachers crazy, and rightly so. Teachers don't have to like every child all the time. But it is the teacher's job to rise above emotionalism and embrace each student's potential.

- **Discover students' interests and hobbies.** This knowledge not only helps you get to know students, but it can also serve as a way to help leverage student interest during lessons. A student who loves skateboarding might become more engaged and interested if the teacher uses skateboarding as an example in science when talking about physics or in math when discussing the dimensions and area needed for building a skateboard ramp, how to calculate costs, or the relationship between speed, acceleration, and distance. (See List 2.3: Interest Inventories.)

List 2.2. Strategies to Determine Individual Strengths

The strengths we're talking about here are the activities, relationships, and ways of learning that energize people. They are the inner qualities that make students feel most alive, and because of that, they are central to students' greatest potential to remain attentive and invested in learning. When activities energize students, they stay working at the lesson longer. *Everyone* has different strengths. Strengths are things like feeling energized when asked to organize something, come up with ideas, or interact with people. They are specific actions that allow the student to become engaged in the activity. When teachers discover students' strengths, they are more likely to engage their students in learning. Strengths are different from interests because strengths are innate and children will be drawn to them for their entire lives, whereas interests (such as playing guitar or using a computer) may be fleeting. But combining strengths and interests creates a synergy that allows children to remain focused longer on learning. Here is a list of ways to determine students' strengths.

- **Use play and cultivate the imagination.** During imaginative play, young people are free to unleash and exercise their strengths. Watch students at play and you will learn a great deal about what they prefer, how they socialize, and the unique ways they view themselves. Play encourages cognitive enrichment and emotional growth.
- **Seek out what makes each student unique.** Little quirks can be clues to strengths. What initially may look like "showing-off" might be an early sign of a child who has strength for entertaining.
- **Listen to students.** Individuals know their strengths better than anyone else. In order to listen effectively, ask many questions. Avoid questions that can be answered with a simple yes or no. Likewise, consider asking parents to write a paragraph describing their child and their best qualities. This can help you start to identify a student's unique abilities.
- **Show interest in students' perspectives through active listening.** For every answer you receive, follow up with another question, "Why do you think that?" Genuinely listen and reflect back to students what you believe you heard them say. If a student says he no longer wants to play soccer, rather than saying he should, try saying, "I hear you saying soccer no longer interests you. Can you tell me why?"
- **Reinforce the curiosity and the attention the students display when discovering their interests.** Help all students feel they have special roles in the classroom. Make it as important to be a good listener or leader as it is to be a good writer. Make a list of strengths and have all students choose what they believe best describes them.
- **Don't compare students with their older siblings.** There is nothing more hampering to students' abilities to discover their strengths than when they feel they are constantly being compared with their "perfect" siblings. Every student will be unique and different. The differences are causes for celebration, not reasons for feeling *not good enough.*

List 2.2. (continued)

- **Give students as many choices about what to do as possible.** Are there students who want to help around the classroom? Use it as an opportunity to discover their preferences and let them choose among the jobs you have for them to do. Provide multiple opportunities for engagement and encourage them to choose between a variety of things to do; support their choices even if they could do better at something else.

- **Recognize children's uniqueness, even if the unique qualities seem bothersome.** A child who asks too many questions can be seen as inquisitive. A child who talks out of turn can be seen as an eager participant. When students perform behaviors that are disruptive, validate the strength first, then correct the behavior. Say, "Julie, I see you are very inquisitive, and that is a good thing, but you have to raise your hand to speak so everyone gets a fair turn."

Understanding strengths is a matter of self-reflection. Nobody can tell another person what energizes him. Every person must figure this out for himself because nobody can tell someone how he feels when engaged in an activity. The following questions will help students begin to reflect on what they feel energized by and will help teachers begin to note students' strengths.

1. If you could spend all day on a Saturday doing whatever you want, what would you do and why?
2. What is the favorite memory you have with your family? Why? Be specific.
3. If you could do any job in the world, what would it be? Why?
4. What would you rather do, lead a discussion or take notes?
5. What is the first thing you do in the morning when you get up and the last thing you do before you go to bed?
6. Whom do you admire and why? What are that person's qualities?
7. If you were working in the theater or on a major sports event, which jobs would you prefer?
8. Have you ever felt so involved in an activity that time slipped away from you?
9. When people say good things about you, what are they likely to say? Do you agree?
10. What do you like best about yourself?

Further Reading

Devereaux Student Strengths Assessment. [http://www.devereux.org/site]

Fox, J. (2008). *Your child's strengths: Discover them, develop them, use them—A guide for parents and teachers.* New York: Viking. [http://www.strengthsmovement.com/ht/d/sp/i/191/pid/191]

Sternberg, R. J. (2006, Sept.) Recognizing neglected strengths. *Educational Leadership: Teaching to Student Strengths* (special issue) *64*(1). [http://www.ascd.org/publications/educational-leadership/sept06/vol64/num01/Recognizing-Neglected-Strengths.aspx]

Strengths Checklist for Parents. [www.able-differently.org/PDF_forms/handouts/StrengthChecklist.pdf]

Strengthsquest: Online paid strengths assessments. [http://www.strengthsquest.com/home.aspx]

List 2.3. Interest Inventories

The key to differentiated instruction lies in how well a teacher knows the students. In order to effectively accommodate all students, it is essential to know them and understand where they are coming from in a variety of genres, such as home life, preferences, interests, and learning styles. Interest inventories are a quick and fun way to gather a plethora of information about students. This list shows samples of questions teachers can ask of students, as well as how to use the inventories.

Uses of Student Interest Inventories

- Using the inventory as a guide, have each student give a presentation on someone else in the class, reporting on his or her strengths, interests, and little known facts.
- Begin one-on-one interviews with students. Have at least one interview a day, reviewing the interest inventory, with the student answering simple follow-up questions to the answers that especially interest the teacher.
- Use the interest inventories for assignments such as writing letters to people, creating characters in creative writing, or starting a memoir.
- Share interest inventories with other teachers so nobody has to reinvent the wheel.
- Refer to interest inventories when creating lessons, planning units, and selecting materials.
- There are some published inventories that can be helpful. One is *My Book of Things and Stuff* (McGreevy, 1982), written for primary and intermediate students. Another is *The Interest-a-lyzer* (Renzulli, 1977), appropriate for middle and secondary school students.

The following can be used as a reflection guide for teachers to determine how well they know their students.

Inventory Questions for Teachers to Ask About Their Students

- How well do they read? Write?
- How well do they understand when they listen?
- What's hardest for them in school?
- What's most engaging for them in school?
- How do they feel about their peers?
- How do their peers regard them?
- How does their culture affect their learning?
- How does gender affect them?
- What gaps do they have in their knowledge?
- What do they already know that I'm planning to teach?
- What are their interests?
- What are their dreams?
- How do they work best?
- What kind of adult support do they have outside of school?
- What kind of adult support do they need in class?

List 2.3. (continued)

The following questions can be used to determine information about students. These questions can be used at the beginning of the year as "getting to know you" strategies.

Inventory Questions for Teachers to Ask Their Students Directly

- What is your favorite subject in school?
- What is your least favorite subject in school?
- What do you plan to do when you graduate high school?
- How do you view homework?
- What do you want to be when you grow up?
- Do you expect to go to college?
- What do you like to read?
- What kind of music do you like?
- What are your favorite movies?
- What television shows do you enjoy?
- What kinds of things do you and your family do together?
- What do you do in your free time?
- Do you participate in sports?
- Are you musical? Do you play any instruments?
- How many brothers and sisters do you have?
- Do you go to church or any other spiritual function?
- What do your parents do for a living?
- Do you collect anything?
- Do you have any pets?
- Where have you traveled? What is your favorite place?
- What is your earliest childhood memory?
- What do you think your strengths are?

Bonus Round: Think about sharing your own interest inventory with students to help them get to know you better, as may be appropriate.

List 2.4. Planning with Learning Styles in Mind

Differentiating instruction means creating lessons that engage as many learning styles as possible. Most teachers are aware of the three types of learning styles: visual, auditory, and kinesthetic. This list provides pointers for how to arrange a lesson to meet multiple student needs. Remember, every lesson does not need to accommodate every style all the time. The point is to begin building awareness of differences and planning with these in mind. Also be aware that sometimes students will learn well through multiple modalities—don't expect students to fit neatly into only one of these categories.

Qualities of Visual Learners

- Think in words
- Learn through reading and writing
- Remember what has been read
- Learn from taking notes and from reading assignments
- Learn sequentially (step-by-step)

Examples of Visual Learning Strategies

- Use flash cards to recall information needed at the knowledge level.
- Use pictures and photographs to illustrate key ideas.
- Find cartoons that depict the ideas in the lessons.
- Create or demonstrate ideas by using graphs, charts, and outlines.
- Show maps to explain anything to do with places.
- Provide written instructions to complement verbal instructions.
- Let books explain concepts, as these learners are often readers.
- Allow films to teach new ideas.
- Encourage underlining with colored highlighters as a means to assimilate knowledge.
- Use or teach color-coding as a method of organization.
- Create and use graphic organizers to teach complex ideas.
- Hang posters that outline important processes.
- Use time lines as a means to learn history.

Qualities of Auditory Learners

- Learn best by hearing
- Notice sounds
- Are distracted by background noise
- Need to hear things in order for them to sink in

Examples of Aural Learning Strategies

- Use books on tape.
- Integrate music into the lesson.
- Take time for discussions.
- Read all instructions aloud.

List 2.4. (continued)

- Use cooperative or group learning in which students interact.
- Integrate videos and CDs into classes.
- Repeat all key points verbally.
- Allow reading aloud in pairs.
- Encourage oral presentations over written as assessment of mastery.
- Use interactive computer games and websites.
- Allow studying with music.

Qualities of Kinesthetic Learners

- Learn through physical experience
- Explore through movement
- Like to touch things
- Enjoy putting things together and taking them apart
- Have trouble sitting still

Examples of Kinesthetic Learning Strategies

- Give child clay or squeeze ball to hold when having to sit still for longer periods.
- Allow to doodle or draw while listening.
- Construct models to illustrate complex ideas.
- Provide opportunity for dramatized reports rather than just written work.
- Use games and puzzles to lead to understanding.
- Provide manipulatives to generate math understanding.
- Offer many opportunities for experiments and group work.
- Plan field trips.
- Allow role-playing for understanding scenes from literature, characterization of math, and science processes.

Further Reading

Learning styles information and free online quizzes and inventories for use in assessing styles:

A to Z Home's Cool Homeschooling. Links to many learning styles articles and resources on the Web. [http://homeschooling.gomilpitas.com/weblinks/assets.htm] Retrieved January 2011.

What's Your Learning Style? Online inventory quiz and explanation of different learning styles—appropriate for students in middle school or above. [http://people.usd.edu/~bwjames/tut/learning-style/] Retrieved January 2011.

Fleming, G. Learning Styles: Know and Use Your Personal Learning Style. [http://homeworktips.about.com/od/homeworkhelp/a/learningstyle.htm] Retrieved January 2011.

List 2.5. Multiple Intelligences and Differentiated Instruction

Professor of education Howard Gardner (2006) devised a way to think about differentiating between types of learners when he introduced the concept of multiple intelligences. The following table gives teachers practical strategies that will reach each type of learner. It is not necessary to have each intelligence engaged in every lesson, rather, refer to this table as a resource to determine whether over time you are varying activities to reach different types of learners.

Types of Intelligence	Thinks by	Finds Success with
Linguistic	Words, sentences	Lectures, debates, large- and small-group discussions, brainstorming, writing activities, word games, speeches, reading to class, talking books and cassettes, journal keeping, choral reading, news, print, interview
Logical, mathematical	By reasoning	Manipulatives, formulas, labs, problems with numerical solutions, experiments, puzzles, inquiry, calculations, patterns, sequences, organizing mathematical problems on the board, Socratic questioning, scientific demonstrations, problem-solving exercises, logic puzzles and games, quantifications and calculations, computer programming, logical-sequential exercises
Spatial	Images and pictures	Models, manipulatives, computers, charts, graphs, diagrams, maps, visualization techniques, photography, slides, puzzles and mazes, metaphors, painting, collage, visual arts, mind-maps, telescopes, microscopes, binoculars
Bodily, kinesthetic	Sensations and physical reactions	Sports, games, group activities, creative movement, mime, field trips, competitive and cooperative games, crafts, cooking, gardening, manipulatives, computers, projects
Musical	Melodies and rhythms	Songs, instruments, recordings, singing, humming, whistling, playing recorded music, rhythms, raps, chants
Interpersonal	Communication with others	Interviews, relationships, cooperative groups, conflict mediation, peer teaching, board games, brainstorming, mentorships, volunteering, community service, clubs, simulations, parties
Intrapersonal	Personal ideas and thoughts	Meditation, reading, reflective processes, independent study, self-paced instruction, individualized projects, private spaces for study, one-minute reflection periods, inspirational/motivational curricula, self-esteem activities, journal keeping

Source: Adapted from *Multiple Intelligences: New Horizons in Theory and Practice* by Howard Gardner (New York: Basic Books, 2006).

List 2.6. Tips for Raising Students' Comfort Level

Schools are filled with all kinds of students with varying degrees of comfort in a classroom situation. Depending on their cultural background, gender, personality type, and learning challenges, students will need a variety of interpersonal responses to feel secure enough to perform well and take intellectual risks. The following suggestions help teachers begin to think of how to raise the comfort level in their classes.

- **Enforce classroom rules consistently for all students.** Nothing makes a student more uncomfortable than be held to a standard different from the others.
- **Do not ask Latino or Asian students to display their knowledge in front of the class if they appear uncomfortable.** Some cultural norms teach children in the home at an early age that speaking up or looking an adult in the eyes is disrespectful. Respect this trait by praising them for being good listeners and allow them to display knowledge in smaller settings or one-on-one with the teacher.
- **Allow bicultural students to embrace their duo cultures by treating their language and ethnicity with respect.** Never use negative comparisons or try to correct their accents.
- **Monitor behavior frequently—if a student is behaving inappropriately, immediately direct the student to an appropriate behavior rather than calling out the poor behavior in front of classmates.** Behavioral change of any sort requires repeated positive reinforcement, so try to make a point of noticing when the student makes a more positive choice in the future.
- **Avoid sarcasm.** Often teachers try to diffuse tense environments with humor. Although humor is fine, sarcasm and anything with a mean or mocking edge can be humiliating and demeaning. This approach rarely works and tends to shame students.
- **Use nonverbal cues to connect with students.** Take time to give nonverbal cues, such as smiling and nodding, when students are talking. Small positive reinforcements like these go a long way to helping students feel as though they are making positive steps forward.
- **Increase the wait time when asking questions so students, especially girls, have time to gain confidence to speak.** In general, girls are often more hesitant to speak with boys in the room. Call on girls. Don't wait for them to raise their hands.
- **Use examples that both boys and girls can relate to.** Give interest inventories (List 2.3) to discover what they are interested in before creating examples.
- **Speak up.** Research shows that girls can hear better than boys. Therefore, boys in the back row may not hear a soft-spoken teacher or have more difficulty tuning in on the voice from the background noise and distractions in the classroom.
- **When students say things that other students find immature or unintelligent, find a way to support them through redirection.** For example, say, "I see what you mean and in a different context that is a very good thought."
- **Let students know that failure can be a good thing, that everyone fails sometimes, and that failure in a particular subject area is not failure as a person.** Be sure to show less capable students that their grades do not interfere with the personal relationship they have with the teacher. For example, if a child fails an assignment, let the child know he or she is still valued.

List 2.6. (continued)

- **Don't believe the adage "Don't smile until Christmas."** Smile often and show students they belong. Consider what it would be like if your principal or administrator never smiled at you. How would that affect your opinion of that person and where you stood? Treat students the way you would like to be treated. We all work harder for people we like and respect than for people we feel we can never please.
- **Celebrate birthdays.** All students should have a special day, no matter what age they are. Pick a day or several days to celebrate birthdays that occur when school is not session.
- **Rather than give a list of rules that explains only what students should *not* do, let them know what they *should* do.** For example, say, "Rule number 3, Have fun learning!" Some teachers allow students the opportunity on the first day of class to help form or tweak the standard classroom rules so students feel involved and engaged with the classroom procedures.
- **Call students at home who have experienced bad days at school or who were absent.** Let them know that you are concerned for their well-being or that they were missed.
- **Even better, call students or parents when a student has a good day in school or has made real progress**. Most people consider a call or a note home as signaling bad news. Change the dynamic: making a call when a student does well will be something the student and their parents will remember, and it is much more likely to help that student strive to do better, especially if the reinforcement comes after a time when the student was struggling. For example, say, "I just wanted to let you know how happy I was when I saw Sarah's report she turned in today. She is making tremendous progress in her writing. I wanted to make sure you know how hard she is working and how proud of her I am."
- **Engage students in discussions about their home life.** Appear interested in what they do outside of school. These personal interactions will increase students' sense of comfort and trust.
- **Remember, it all begins with being human.** The more you can help students accept that learning requires experimentation and mistakes, as well as success, the more likely they are to take chances and challenge themselves. The more you can model the "Let's try this and see what happens" approach yourself, letting students in on the experiment, the more likely they are to try something new as well.

Further Reading

Goleman, D. (1996). *Emotional intelligence: Why it can matter more than IQ*. London: Bloomsbury.

Pomerantz, E. M., Altermatt, E. R., & Saxon, J. L. (2002). Making the grade but feeling distressed: Gender differences in academic performance and internal distress. *Journal of Educational Psychology, 94*(2), 396–404.

Valdés, G. (1996). *Con respeto: Bridging the distances between culturally diverse families and schools: An ethnographic portrait*. New York: Teachers College, Columbia University.

List 2.7. Tips to Help Struggling Students

Despite any teacher's best effort, some students will struggle with learning. Some may have learning disabilities or other cognitive challenges; others may not yet be developmentally ready to learn certain concepts. Some students may not have perfected previous skills now required for the current lesson. This list provides some ideas on how to accommodate struggling students in the classroom while building skills or identifying underlying challenges.

- **Provide audiobooks to struggling readers.** Audiobooks can help kids appreciate material beyond their normal instructional level, enrich vocabulary, and bring a story to life. For more academic material such as textbooks, built-in text-to-speech software can help students access material they might otherwise struggle with on their own.

- **Use testing results as a diagnostic tool** to determine where students are struggling rather than just as an assessment of current level of performance. Are there any patterns that indicate specific areas of weakness? Do these patterns affect multiple students in the classroom? These results can help you define students who will be more responsive to specific interventions.

- **As much as possible, use high-interest materials** at their instructional level to engage students. Where there is a clear gap between comprehension and reading ability, supplement with more advanced materials in audio form to maintain engagement.

- **Help struggling younger readers predict what might happen next** in the story before turning the page or to talk about what just happened. This helps them engage in the story and build critical-thinking skills at the same time.

- **Allow struggling students to sit near the teacher when possible.** Struggling students will be more in need of support, and are at greater risk for tuning out, if the material seems constantly beyond their ability. Sitting nearby will make keeping them on track easier.

- **Be specific in providing feedback.** Avoid telling students their work is "good." Let them know exactly what is and isn't good about their performance.

- **Help struggling students to see where they are succeeding,** as well as where they need a bit more help, and provide guidance as to different approaches they may want to try on the next assignment. Students who just see a paper swimming in red ink are more likely to toss it aside than examine it to see what they can do better next time.

- **Be sure to praise and recognize all efforts and attempts at improving.** Give lots of verbal and nonverbal reinforcements such as smiling and nodding. Make sure the verbal praise is specific to the work or task and that it is authentic.

- **Give students opportunities to provide feedback.** Let them say why they are struggling or what they find confusing. Often students are able to articulate what they feel when they feel safe and trust the teacher.

- **Ask others for help.** Tutors, learning specialists, or good supplemental materials can provide insight and ideas for helping struggling students. Teachers are not expected to have all the answers for every child. Use your colleagues and resources. Don't forget to ask parents to help reinforce good study habits at home, as well.

List 2.7. (continued)

- **Don't assume disinterest.** Some students may need glasses or their hearing may be poor due to prior ear infections. Check out these issues before diagnosing the struggles.
- **Create small opportunities throughout the day for the students to experience success.** Reward behaviors such as being patient, listening attentively, sharing, and having positive attitudes.
- **Be patient.** Not all students develop at the same rate. Some take a little longer. Keep encouraging these students and assure them that their successes are noticed. Sometimes a goal chart will help them recognize their progress and stay motivated.
- **Don't be afraid to discuss observations with students.** Perhaps they are not experiencing struggles that you think they are. There may be outside influences such as home or health that are temporarily interfering with a student's ability to focus. When teachers have trusting relationships with students, these conversations may be helpful to both the teacher and the student.
- **Remember that all students want to learn.**
- **Everyone wants to be successful.**
- **Try to avoid a "cycle of blame"** for struggling students. Making a statement such as "I know you could do it if you just tried harder . . . put your mind to it . . . [insert classic phrase here]" may not only be untrue, but may add additional insult to injury for students who struggle. A little understanding and encouragement often go a long way.
- **Encourage students to use a tape recorder, software** such as Dragon Naturally Speaking, **or other recording and dictation programs** to brainstorm ideas before assignments in which they must come up with original ideas. This will allow them to remember what they are thinking and organize it later.
- **Create a memory-friendly classroom.** Post assignments and due dates, written steps for multistep tasks, and other things they should remember.
- **Allow students to word-process and even e-mail assignments** as appropriate. This helps students who have trouble organizing and keeping track of papers.

List 2.8. Tips for Motivating All Students

Motivating students is an essential part of differentiating because differentiated instruction is about finding ways for all students to be successful and master the material. In order for students to learn, they must be motivated. Every teacher has sometimes felt frustrated by a disinterested student. Educators know that students are rarely truly motivated by threats of punishment or poor grades. Rather, they respond when they feel competent and in control of their learning, and have positive connections with their classmates and teachers. The following list provides ideas about how to motivate all students.

- **Look for intrinsic rather than extrinsic motivators.** Intrinsic motivators are feelings of self-worth, competency, and well-being. Extrinsic motivators, such as grades, rewards, punishments, and prizes, come from outside the learner. Having too many extrinsic rewards decreases true motivation.

- **Give frequent, early, positive feedback that supports students' beliefs that they can do well.** Make the feedback as specific as possible and about the students' work rather than their personalities.

- **Make sure students are ready to learn.** Do they have all the necessary materials? Have they eaten well and had enough sleep? Sometimes lack of motivation has to do with conditions outside the class. Don't assume their lack of motivation is due to the class. Ask direct questions about eating, rest, and home life to determine if something is interfering.

- **Show students how their learning can enhance their lives.** Make learning relevant to their experiences. Providing students with a context or reason for learning helps students see the "point" to what they're doing and keeps them interested.

- **Reduce or remove components of the learning environment that lead to failure or fear.** This includes warnings about poor grades or threats of losing privileges if they don't learn. Remember that threats may cut off bad behavior in the moment, but they do little toward building positive, gradual behavior change over time.

- **Allow students to participate in as much of the class decision making as possible.** Seek their input about what they enjoy and why, and which things they feel depleted by and why. Use student concerns and suggestions to organize content and develop themes and teaching procedures.

- **Validate student suggestions by giving credit when implementing.** For example, say, "We are going to have small groups today because Lisa and Kevin suggested these work well. Thanks, Lisa and Kevin, for these helpful suggestions."

List 2.8. (continued)

- **Be prepared to teach.** A common reason students disengage is because the teacher has not planned well for class. Planning is the most important thing a teacher can do to be a success.

- **Provide three positive interactions with students for every "negative" interaction.** Just as you would begin to balk or feel picked on if all your principal did was criticize you at every turn, remember that students are constantly being evaluated at home and at school at every turn. Provide as many opportunities as possible for students to feel successful and valued.

Further Reading

Ames, R., & Ames, C. (1990). Motivation and effective teaching. In B. F. Jones & L. Idol (Eds.), *Dimensions of thinking and cognitive instruction*. Hillsdale, NJ: Erlbaum.
Davis, B. G. (1993). *Tools for teaching*. San Francisco: Jossey-Bass.
Davis, B. G. (2009). *Tools for teaching* (2nd ed.). San Francisco: Jossey-Bass.

List 2.9. Class Discussion Strategies

Class discussion is a very important aspect of differentiated instruction because it encourages all learners to contribute at their own level of participation. This is the first and most effective place teachers can begin to implement the knowledge gained from Lists 2.1–2.8 where the students will notice a difference. Teachers who routinely employ these strategies will reach all students, build positive student-teacher relationships, have more lively classes that are satisfying to both the teacher and the students, and build a learning culture. This list gives you some strategies to help you lead more productive and successful classroom discussions.

- **Plan your questions in advance of a class discussion.** There is no better way to run a great discussion than by first planning what questions students will be asked. Plan for multiple-level questions and call on students according to their ability. For example, ask one student to describe the setting and another one to interpret why it matters to the story. Even better, post the questions in advance to the classroom website or wiki, so students have some time to think about the questions and how they might respond.

- **Redirect student questions** so other students are answering the questions rather than the teacher. This creates a more active and participatory environment where the students feel they also have knowledge to share.

- **Ask students to comment on one another's responses** rather than the teacher responding to every question.

- **If possible, arrange chairs in a circle or U** or have students seated in fixed seating in such a way to foster eye contact with each other.

- **Sit among the students** during the discussion part of the class so as to place the community of students, rather than the teacher, in the center of the discussion.

- **If one student is dominating** the discussion at the expense of the others, then break eye contact with that student and look at others.

- **Choose open-ended questions** rather than closed-ended ones that only call for a yes or no response. For example, "What would you do in the character's place?" is much better than "Did the character go to the store?"

- **Challenge thinking,** ask follow-up questions, or request clarification to probe for deeper thinking. Reflecting what a student said while following up will also help students clarify their points or thinking.

- **Apply appropriate wait time.** Sometimes waiting as long as a full minute will allow students to get their thoughts organized before speaking.

- **Listen fully to your students' questions and answers**; avoid interrupting. Even if the student is going down the wrong path, allow her to finish her full response without interrupting.

- **Provide examples of how students might answer difficult questions**. Give specific, varied examples.

- **Point out what is helpful or interesting about student contributions.** Pick up on comments that were made but not discussed. Consider extending the discussion beyond the class period on a classroom-based website or blog.

List 2.9. (continued)

- **To help students focus on the question, put the question on an overhead, the board, or a slide.** Give the students all the questions in advance of the discussion and let them read them over and think before starting the discussion.
- **Praise students for their responses,** being sure to tell them exactly what was good about it rather than simply applying a generic "Great answer."
- **Ask other students to repeat what has been said**, summarizing main points from another student's response. This can take the form of "What I heard Joan say was that . . . and I think . . . "
- **Do not answer your own questions.** Instead, rephrase and follow up until students begin to chime in. If you answer all your own questions, you will reinforce the idea that your opinion and thoughts are most important, or that if they wait you out, they won't have to take the risk inherent in participation.
- **Have students prepare questions** for discussion and appoint students as discussion leaders.
- **Give out a list of questions** and ask students to write answers on a piece of paper, then share the responses in pairs. Alternatively, have students write their questions and respond to questions posed by other students online on a classroom blog or wiki.
- **Have students make up the questions,** given a primary source document, and then pass them to other students to answer.
- **Consider using alternate platforms for discussions.** Using a classroom blog or wiki to conduct discussions, for example, may allow students to be more open and take more risks in a discussion than they would within the classroom. Also consider trying a Socratic discussion, in which the teacher leads the discussion by asking questions and follow-up questions, thus guiding students toward conclusions or to rethink their positions.
- **When more than one student wants to participate**, let students know in advance when they will be asked to participate. Say, "I am going to call on John, then Sarah." This encourages them to stay in the conversation.

Section Three

Planning the Differentiated Curriculum

The single most important way to make differentiating instruction successful is careful planning. Everything from the overall course to the unit plans to daily instruction involves careful planning to meet the needs of all students. Although the best plans allow for built-in flexibility, the fact is that no class instruction can be truly successful without conscientious and dedicated forethought.

Even though planning is the cornerstone of good teaching and necessary for differentiating instruction, many teachers simply do not know when they can find the time to plan effectively. The lists in this section provide suggestions for when and how to plan courses, units, and daily lesson plans.

List 3.1. Where to Begin and What to Do

Educator and author Grant Wiggins promotes the concept of "backward by design" (Wiggins & McTighe, 2005). The best plans begin with the end in mind, so all planning for lessons should proceed with an understanding of what the students should learn and do. First, though, here are some tips for how to begin.

- **Begin with an annual calendar.** Look at all the months school is in session and begin by blocking out the days that are devoted to district or schoolwide meetings, in-services, and days before holidays when students are less likely to focus on learning.
- **Plan one course fully at a time.** Review the overall curriculum and block out units according to what product the students are to produce at the end of the unit. For example, in an English class, first choose whether it will be a genre study or theme based. If it is a genre study, determine a logical order according to which unit will take longest. Perhaps a novel will take two weeks and culminate in a written paper; poetry will take three weeks and result in a multimedia presentation.
- **Make choices about the form of assessment** and place these due dates on the calendar, then plan the instruction backward from these dates. Map out the whole year according to this overarching concept.
- **Share annual plans with other teachers** to determine when students are expected to produce high volumes of work. Avoid placing all major assessments at the same time.
- **After units, then assessments.** After units are anchored on the calendar, look at the assessments. Review the lists on assessments and commit to incorporating a variety of types of assessments, rather than ending each unit with a traditional test or a paper. The more kinds of assessments used, the more the course becomes differentiated.
- **Plan for frequent, low-level assessments as well as cumulative assessments.** Keep in mind that frequent, low-level assessments may be better for keeping students on track than one major test or project alone at the end of the unit. Frequent "thumbs up, thumbs down" knowledge checks, use of online quizzes and "games" with Quia (http://www.quia.com) or other online tools, or other intermittent assessments will give you a better idea of which students are keeping up and which may need additional support along the way. (See List 3.4: Differentiated Assessments.)
- **Make course objectives clear.** Review course objectives and determine which objectives will be covered in each unit. Write these down in the unit document.
- **Create a "cheat sheet" for learning style and interest inventories for quick reference.** Review class lists and after giving interest and learning style inventories, create a chart dividing students according to general interests and learning styles. See the following examples.

Sports	Animals	Investigation	Performance	Reading
Mary	Kyle	Joseph	Jake	Kevin
Trevor	Lucy	Lamont	Karla	Matthew
Lucas	Mike	Kellie	Ayanna	Justine
Annette	Maria	Anna	Lyle	Marla

List 3.1. (continued)

Visual	Auditory	Kinesthetic
Kevin	Mark	Kyla
Maria	Kellie	Justine
Linda	Anna	Matthew

- **Use student learning chart when planning lessons.** Use the chart when creating daily lesson plans to come up with differentiated examples, assigned reading, and assessment or questions. There is no precise way or exact science for doing this, but a little forethought will guide your thinking about the individuals in the class and serve as a beginning.
- **Don't forget to check readiness.** As daily lessons are planned from the unit plans, think about student readiness for each objective. Begin by planning questions to reach a wider variety of Bloom's Taxonomy (see List 3.3).
- **Bloom's Taxonomy will help.** The single best way to begin differentiating daily lessons is to refer to the Bloom's Taxonomy chart in List 3.3 and choose from the levels of readiness and moving various students from one level to the next throughout the lesson.
- **Use planning time to plan for classes.** Often teachers eat up planning time with socializing or simply wandering around. This causes teachers to leave planning until the end of the day, at home, when personal responsibilities get in the way of effective planning. Some of the best teachers make it a rule to not leave school until the next day's plans are complete.
- **Don't feel as though planning needs to be perfect.** Good planning becomes a habit, and what seems tedious at first becomes second nature in time. Plus, we all know that plans will need to be modified based on the unexpected, so think of your plan as a living, breathing document, not written in stone.
- **It's better to overplan than to underplan.** Teachers can always modify on the fly, but it is difficult to come up with more material during class. The more material you have available, the easier it will be to adjust your pace to the needs of the students.
- **Planning should be student focused.** Think of planning in terms of what the *students* will be doing, not what the teacher will do.

List 3.2. Tips for Keeping Records for Differentiated Lesson Plans

The information teachers gather about individual learners is valuable and can be used to create an overall learning profile for students. This profile can help teachers, parents, and students monitor progress. It can also help students come to better understand their own learning; this is invaluable for self-advocacy as students grow into lifelong learners. This list provides a few quick tips for keeping these records viable.

- **Keep the records simple.** Interest inventories, rubrics, sample work, work in progress, and learning profiles are all useful to keep in the database. But when there is too much information or too many samples, the record of learning becomes lost.

- **Allow students to see and even comment on the records.** When students are allowed to interact with their learning, they take greater ownership in it and can see how they are able to contribute.

- **Collaborate with other teachers.** Share the records and information you gather about students.

- **Get everyone involved.** See whether the school can create an online database for profiling student strengths, interests, and challenges. This will help all teachers access and share student learning information easily.

- **Learning portfolios can help.** Consider creating a portfolio method that includes samples of student work. The samples can be both completed work and work in progress. Some school districts create individual wiki pages for each student. These wiki pages act as their ongoing student profile and learning portfolio, following them from year to year and school to school within the district.

- **Make the records longitudinal.** Pass them up to the next-level teacher as students move to the next grade. Longitudinal snapshots of students can give a great deal of information about how someone learns.

- **Create easy ways to share information.** Try to collaborate with other teachers on a standard or uniform way to collect, share, and store data. The data will be more easily accessible and therefore more likely to be used. Sometimes a simple form created through Google Docs or even Microsoft Word can serve as a template to make sure each teacher is looking at similar data points.

List 3.2. (continued)

- **Share information.** Collecting information about student interests, strengths, and challenges is a time-consuming process. Save time by keeping these records on hand for students and their parents. Placing these records in a secure, online database accessible from home and school will ensure the information can be used as needed by all interested parties. This information can even be helpful for students when applying for summer jobs, internships, or college.

- **Records can be helpful for response to intervention strategies.** Use records and portfolios when discussing plans for struggling students. Anecdotal evidence backed up by actual documents will help make finding solutions easier, as well as keeping track of steps taken in the event of a referral for services.

- **Use the records to plan for daily instruction.** Think of the records as an aggregate. What are the commonalities among the students? What are the differences? Do the differences fall along gender or cultural lines? Does age play a factor in how students learn? In short, use the records to understand the class as a whole and then make lessons based on the knowledge in the whole set.

List 3.3. How to Create Differentiated Lesson Plans with Bloom's Taxonomy

Over fifty years ago, Benjamin Bloom (1956) devised a hierarchical arrangement for understanding thinking skills commonly referred to as Bloom's Taxonomy.

This taxonomy offers a framework for teachers to plan lessons that move students sequentially from the most basic kind of learning (knowledge) into the most complex (evaluation). Today the taxonomy is the foundation of lesson planning that pays attention to developing cognition. Bloom's Taxonomy is a staple in planning for differentiated instruction.

When using this taxonomy, teachers can differentiate their instruction according to student readiness. If a student has not mastered the most basic levels of the taxonomy, he will be frustrated if asked to move too quickly to more complex levels. Likewise, should a student have mastered the lower levels on the taxonomy, she will become bored and disinterested if forced to remain in performance too long at these levels.

Bloom's Taxonomy in Action

Readiness Level	Common Verbs	Types of Questions
Knowledge: Exhibiting previously learned material by recalling facts, terms, basic concepts, and answers.	Tell, define, locate, circle, name, recall, list, point to, select	Who, what, when, where, how . . . ? Describe.
Comprehension: Demonstrating understanding of facts and ideas by organizing, comparing, translating, interpreting, giving descriptions, and stating main ideas.	Summarize, explain, interpret, describe, compare, classify, paraphrase, differentiate, demonstrate	Retell . . . write in your own words. What do you think could have happened next? What do you think about the passage? What was the main idea? Can you distinguish between . . . ? What differences exist between . . . ? Provide an example of what you mean.
Application: Solving problems by applying acquired knowledge, facts, techniques, and rules in a different way.	Solve, illustrate, calculate, use, interpret, relate, manipulate, apply, modify	How is . . . an example of . . . ? How is . . . related to? Why is . . . significant?
Analysis: Examining and breaking information into parts by identifying motives or causes; making inferences and finding evidence to support generalizations.	Analyze, organize, deduce, contrast, compare, discuss, distinguish, plan, devise	What are the parts or features of . . . ? Classify . . . according to . . . Outline/diagram . . . How does . . . compare/contrast with . . . ? What evidence can you list for . . . ?

(*continued*)

List 3.3. (continued)

Bloom's Taxonomy in Action (*continued*)

Readiness Level	Common Verbs	Types of Questions
Synthesis: Compiling information together in a different way by combining elements in a new pattern or proposing alternative solutions.	Design, hypothesize, support, schematize, write, report, justify	What would you predict/infer from . . . ? What ideas can you add to . . . ? How would you create/design a new . . . ? What might happen if you combined . . . ? What solutions would you suggest for . . . ?
Evaluation: Presenting and defending opinions by making judgments about information, validity of ideas, or quality of work based on a set of criteria.	Evaluate, choose, estimate, judge, defend, criticize	Do you agree . . . ? What do you think about . . . ? What is the most important . . . ? Place the following in order of priority. How would you decide about . . . ? What criteria would you use to assess . . . ?

Tips for Using Bloom's Taxonomy

- Search the Internet for posters on the verbs associated with Bloom's Taxonomy and keep them on hand for lesson planning or refer to the charts in List 3.1.
- Memorize the taxonomy and refer to it whenever planning. When it becomes an integral part of thinking about lesson and unit planning, this tool alone will improve teaching greatly.
- Use when creating multiple groupings. Students can work with the same content at different levels.
- Ensure mastery of the basic skills before moving to the higher-order skills.
- Plan lessons to move past knowledge-level tasks (most lessons do not get past this level) because this is the level that most students forget, since it is based on short-term memory. Moving past will ensure long-term retention.
- Use the taxonomy to diagnose lack of ability to perform. Students who don't understand what is being taught may have skipped a level.
- Try to employ as many verbs in one category as possible in your planning. Don't overrely on one method, such as listing or discussing.
- Review current plans to discover the levels to which tasks are matched and determine whether students are moving past more than one level. Don't get stuck in the lower levels.
- Don't expect all students to move through the hierarchy at the same speed.

List 3.4. Differentiated Assessments

Assessments are an ongoing, necessary part of the learning process. They are used to guide teachers about what should be taught, as well as to track and direct student progress. Many teachers only use assessments at the end of a unit to determine a grade. To truly differentiate instruction, teachers must assess student work, readiness, and mastery throughout the learning process. Teachers will be successful at differentiated instruction when they incorporate assessments into the planning phase. This list provides suggestions for how to use assessments to get effective feedback on individual progress.

Assessments can be used to pretest for formative understanding, and as summative or posttests.

- **Pretesting:** used to determine what students know before they begin working on an objective. Methods include formal testing, quizzing, questionnaires, and anecdotes.
- **Formative testing:** used to check for understanding along the way so teachers can ensure whether or not students are learning. Formative assessments can be check-ins, questions and answers, quizzes, and discussion.
- **Posttesting:** used to determine how well students have mastered the objectives of the class or met the standards set out by the curriculum.

Understanding and Creating Differentiated Assessments

- **There are many ways to differentiate assessments.** Many schools have offered students only traditional tests to prove mastery; however, traditional tests are ineffective because all students do not perform the same on these measures, and the tests are often incapable of measuring everything students know.
- **Teachers can use both formal and informal assessments.** Informal assessments are reading nonverbal cues, asking questions, and listening in on student conversations. Formal assessments are presentations, portfolios, quizzes, and tests.
- **Variety is key.** The differentiated classroom will provide a variety of formal and informal assessments, pretests, formative and post-instructional assessments, and opportunities for students to choose different ways to be assessed, as in opting to give an oral presentation over a written assignment
- **Effective assessments set up students for success.** Many times students ask teachers, "What is going to be on the test?" and teachers respond as though the test is some kind of mystery. Students will learn more and perform better when they have a solid sense of what they are supposed to learn and exactly how that learning will be assessed. Tests are not assessments, and grades can be determined by assessments, not just tests.
- **Assessment format may drive depth of learning.** Objective assessments (usually multiple choice, true/false, short answer) have correct answers. These are good for testing recall of facts and can be automated. Objective tests assume that there are true answers and assume that all students should learn the same thing. Objective assessments frequently ask students to recognize the right answer, not understand why it is right. When teachers test students by using recall information questions, they are not actually discovering what students know, but learning how well they recall information (they test memory, not content) or how well they take tests. Also, traditional testing at the end of a unit does not allow for relearning, which is essential for mastery of concepts.

List 3.4. (continued)

- **Differentiated assessments require deeper thinking and application of knowledge.** Differentiated assessments will give all learners opportunities to move past the knowledge-and-recall level and toward synthesis and evaluation. Students who "ace" tests are often not challenged at the higher end of Bloom's Taxonomy.
- **Assessments demonstrate steps toward mastery.** Assessments should be lined up with learning objectives and then used to determine whether students have mastered the concepts. Assessments are not the end of learning but the beginning of relearning or a guide toward further learning. Assessments focus on learning whereas tests focus on achievement.

Performance-based assessments allow a variety of types of learners to demonstrate mastery of subject matter if the teacher has worked to closely align the assessments with the course, unit, or lesson objectives.

Examples of Differentiated Performance-Based Assessments

- **Portfolios.** A collection of student work. These can be used to showcase the best work, show works in progress, or highlight work and mastery over time. Portfolios can be used to start conversation between teachers, between student and teacher, between parent and teachers, and between student and student. Portfolios can be kept in folders or online. They can include artifacts or papers, comments, and rubrics. Subject-specific portfolios can be developed.
- **Rubrics.** Quality rating assessment tools. Rubrics define levels of success and assign points for areas of mastery. In short, they are rating scales that allow students to know exactly what they will be rated on and what needs to be accomplished to receive a certain grade. Rubrics give students insights into what needs to be improved, as well as what is expected. Provide rubrics as soon as you hand out the assignment. Walk students through the rubrics, and whenever possible show real examples of work that corresponds to each level on the rubric.
- **Presentations.** In individual or group presentations, students get up before an audience, usually the class, and present what they know. Presentations can be in the form of a play, a talk, or a demonstration. They can be multimedia, as in PowerPoint presentations and slide shows. Rubrics greatly assist in getting students to give high-quality presentations.
- **Projects.** Ongoing learning experiences in which students must complete a variety of activities resulting in a product of the learning. Projects can
  - Be both Web-based and classroom based
  - Come after the initial instruction and demand a great deal of student input
  - Work best when there are formative assessments built in and multiple deadlines given for completion of parts rather than giving one cumulative deadline
  - Be hands-on and experience-based, thus making them highly engaging for all kinds of learners

List 3.4. (continued)

- **Essays.** Teachers tend to think of essays as something left to English class. However, essays can be used in any subject area. They are especially effective in classrooms in which writing is not the norm, such as science or math. Essays provide a differentiated alternative for students who are linguistically focused, and they can be used as an option to a project or a presentation.

- **Experiments.** An easy way to assess what students are learning is to observe them performing an experiment. Experiments are not limited to science class. Students can perform social experiments in psychology or social studies. Although many experiments are available in the curriculum, students can also be challenged to come up with their own.

- **Quick checks.** A way to assess formative understanding is to ask the class questions for understanding. Quick-check examples: "Everyone who feels ready to move on, put your thumbs up." "On a scale of one to five, put up your fingers to indicate how comfortable you are with the concept we just learned."

- **Exhibitions.** These can be set up as museums or galleries where students display the results of an experiment or a study on posterboard. They can gather and explain artifacts, such as photographs and letters from the Civil War or illuminate students' understanding about a topic that has great depth.

- **Contracts.** Students and teachers make agreements on the objectives and timetable for mastery. Contracts can be effective when students need more guidance and motivation to stay on task. They work well for the linear thinker, as they lay out time lines for completion of tasks.

- **Journals.** A wide variety of journals can be used to help students reflect on their learning and serve as formative assessment tools. These journals are not to be considered private, but shared as a classroom tool.

- **Graphs and charts.** Visual students can often explain concepts via graphs or charts. These can be student- or teacher-generated. Using the chart or graph, a student is asked a series of questions and uses the image to begin a verbal explanation of concepts.

- **Poster demonstrations.** Posters can be used for students to explain concepts. Posters can have pictures, drawings, or photographs. They can be made by individuals or groups.

- **Online interactive assessments.** Many schools are now using online tools like Quia to create study and assessment tools for their classrooms (http://www.quia.com), or implementing "audience response" systems that allow teachers to ask questions and get immediate feedback on what students understand and where they may be getting confused. It can be a quick way to identify students who need more reinforcement while also allowing others to advance as needed.

List 3.5. Curriculum Compacting: Why and How

Curriculum compacting is a differentiation strategy developed by Joseph Renzulli and Linda Smith in 1978 (Renzulli & Reis, 2008). This method was developed to

- Create a challenging learning environment while ensuring all students meet proficiency in basic curriculum
- Modify the grade-level curriculum by allowing students to bypass material they have previously learned
- Avoid wasting time and risking loss of motivation in teaching material that the students have already mastered
- Provide learning opportunities that are adapted to the needs, rates, and interests of students

Renzulli and Smith's curriculum-compacting model includes the following steps:

1. **Pre-select the learning objectives** for a given subject for all students in the class. Determine how these will be assessed. Ask which objectives cannot be learned without formal or sustained instruction, and which objectives reflect the priorities of the school district/state department of education.

2. **Pre-assess** all students to determine which objectives they have already mastered. Point out that some students will already be familiar with the material. Ask whether any students would like to demonstrate what they already know about the objectives being taught.

   Examples of performance-based pretests:
   - Students write and submit a persuasive essay that the teacher reads and analyzes for content.
   - Students create portfolios and work samples that show their mastery of the learning objectives.
   - Teachers observe students taking notes, tracing thought patterns, and posing open-ended questions.

3. **Identify students** based on the pre-assessment. Choose who may have potential to move through the curriculum at a faster pace than the majority of the students in the class, or who may benefit from a challenge or independent learning assignment.

4. **Allow students who have learned the objectives to move directly into comprehension and higher-order thinking skills.** In some cases, this will mean providing more complex problems to work on. In others, such as in literature classes, it may mean having a variety of writing topics, some of which ask for higher-order thinking skills. A choice of several advanced projects from which students can choose will give these students an opportunity to select a meaningful opportunity to extend their learning.

5. **Curriculum compacting should not mean greater amounts of work for students who move more quickly.** Instead, it will mean designing lessons in which students work simultaneously on different levels of problems. This strategy will not work effectively in classrooms where direct instruction is the main mode of teaching.

List 3.5. (continued)

6. **Compact by unit, chapter, or topic rather than by time (marking period or quarter).** By choosing smaller units, more students will probably get an opportunity for challenging work. Students are less likely to be overwhelmed by projects of a larger scope, in which time management and organization may pose potential problems, especially for middle school students.

7. **Decide in advance what each pre-assessment score means.** For example, students who demonstrate complete mastery should be compacted out of the entire unit. Standard criteria for demonstrating mastery to determine compacting = 90 percent or higher on the pretest. Criteria for demonstrating partial mastery = 80 percent or higher on the pretest.

8. **Start the compacting process by targeting a small group of students for whom compacting seems especially appropriate.** When students who move quickly through lessons are assigned additional work, more problems, and longer reading assignments, they may resent having to do more and intentionally slow down their output to appear to be moving more slowly. It's important to challenge within the framework of the lesson rather than simply assign extra work.

9. **Keep trying; reflect on what has worked and field-test new ideas.** Sometimes additional challenge may be welcomed, but other times it may prove stressful for students as they balance the requirements of other courses, outside activities, and home life. Keep a flexible attitude toward compacting and don't forget to ask students for their feedback after the lesson or unit is over. A final grade itself may not be the sole marker for success—sometimes it may be students' perception of trying something new and how they felt about the experience.

Examples of curriculum compacting may include

- Setting up several different labs in a science class. Direct the students to the lab where their skills can best be challenged.
- Designing projects where each member in the group has a different task with varying complexity. For example, some students do the research, while others may complete original drafts and still others proofread the final document.
- Design class discussions with Bloom's Taxonomy in mind. For example, if students have read a poem, ask one student who the speaker is and another to discuss the theme.
- Set up math class in stations. Have students move through the stations as they complete the assignments.
- Offer a choice between several kinds of books to read, some more complex than others.

List 3.6. What Are Authentic Choices? How to Plan with Them

Authentic learning is a pedagogical approach that allows students to explore, discuss, and meaningfully construct concepts and relationships in contexts that involve real-world problems and projects that are relevant to the learner (Donovan, Bransford, & Pellegrino, 1999). When teachers choose authentic ways to instruct and assess students, they are differentiating the curriculum because, by nature, authentic assignments and assessments involve choice. Student choice is one of the cornerstone concepts in a successful differentiated instruction classroom. This list provides a rationale and ideas for creating lessons that use authentic learning as a basis to deliver the curriculum.

- **Authentic learning is meaningful learning.** When learning is authentic, it is centered on tasks, projects, and activities that are real. For example, instead of students making up letters to write to pretend people, they write to real people such as politicians, newspaper personnel, or pen pals.

- **Collaborative projects get everyone involved.** Students are presented with problem-solving activities that encourage collaborative effort; for instance, painting a mural in a public place rather than simply painting for their own sake with no audience except the teacher. Some schools have even had students work on art that is offered up for auction at PTA/PTO events, thus helping the students make a tangible contribution to their school community.

- **Ask an expert.** When learning about science, students may dialogue with informed expert sources to make hypotheses about real-life science, such as what occurs in the natural environment. For example, rather than studying about food from a book, students may visit a store and trace the food backward from the shelf to how it got in the store to where and how it was produced, including asking questions of the people involved in each stage of the process.

- **Students are engaged in exploration and inquiry.** The hallmark of authentic lessons are that they are inquiry-based, forcing students to engage in real-world research that results in a product that is useful (such as writing a newspaper article, submitting an argument before the local government, solving local water-pollution problems, or entertaining seniors in an assisted-living home).

- **Learning, most often, is interdisciplinary.** The real world is not divided into neat topics and separately defined boxes, unlike the traditional curriculum. When students interact in the real world, they explore across and between academic disciplines. For instance, in the previous example of the mural, students not only plan and create the art, they must also engage in local politics to gain permission to create a public display.

- **Learning is closely connected to the world beyond the walls of the classroom.** Since the classroom is limited to resources that can be brought into the school, authentic learning guarantees that students get out and make applications in the real world.

List 3.6. (continued)

- **Authentic learning requires advanced problem solving.** Students become engaged in complex tasks and higher-order thinking skills, such as analyzing, synthesizing, designing, manipulating, and evaluating information. By solving real-world problems, students get a chance to practice these skills with a meaningful outcome to show for their work.

- **Students produce a product that can be shared with an audience outside the classroom.** When students create things like newsletters and blogs or assist in community projects, they have real audiences and their work is held to a higher level of accountability. This naturally ensures greater effort on the part of the students, because the stakes for success are raised.

- **Learning is student driven** with teachers, parents, and outside experts all assisting and coaching in the learning process.

- **Learners employ scaffolding techniques.**

- **Authentic learning applies knowledge.** Although knowledge of facts is important, facts must be learned within the context of authentic experience. Teachers must rethink their traditional role as "knowledge deliverer" and accept a new responsibility as facilitator, coach, and coordinator of experiences.

- **Classroom curriculum guides instruction.** Classroom curriculum will always guide authentic instruction, matching objectives to new methodologies for learning. Students say solving real-world problems motivates them. They often express a preference for doing rather than listening. Most educators consider learning-by-doing the most effective way to learn.

- **Authentic learning provides context and meaning.** Authentic learning typically focuses on real-world, complex problems and their solutions, using role-playing exercises, problem-based activities, case studies, and participation in virtual communities of practice.

Features of authentic instruction include

- **Ill-defined problems:** Authentic activities are relatively undefined and open to multiple interpretations, thus requiring students to identify the tasks needed to complete the project.

- **Collaboration:** Authentic activities make collaboration necessary to successfully accomplish the goals.

- **Sustained investigation:** Problems are considered over a sustained period, thus requiring significant dedication to the process and the result.

- **Multiple sources and perspectives:** Authentic activities offer students the opportunity to use a variety of resources, forcing students to distinguish relevant from irrelevant information in the process.

- **Reflection (metacognition):** Authentic activities enable learners to make choices and reflect on their learning.

- **Polished products:** Authentic activities culminate in the creation of a whole product, valuable in its own right.

List 3.6. (continued)

Examples of authentic lessons:

○ **Create flyers:** Students created thousands of flyers inviting local community members to attend a town meeting on turning an open space into a public garden. Students learned the local government process, honed their public speaking skills, researched local laws, planned for implementation, prepared diagrams, and created budgets, among other activities, to reach their goal.

○ **Television advertisement:** Students created a thirty-second ad for local access television outlining the reasons for having a new cross light put in a busy intersection where a fellow student was killed by a speeding car.

○ **Create a new product:** Students were challenged to invent a new soft drink by using their knowledge of chemistry. They designed the bottle label, named the drink, and developed marketing plans. Local businessmen were pitched in product development. The final winning product was bought by one of the businessmen and sold in the local grocery store.

○ **Engage in civic duty:** Students in a rural area tested water in a local pond and found the water too toxic for the surrounding plant life. They did water analysis, met with environmentalists, and developed a plan to clean up the pond. With the plan in hand, they approached local businesses for funding needed to complete the project.

Further Reading

Herrington, J., & Oliver, R. (2000) An instructional design framework for authentic learning environments. *Educational Technology Research and Development, 48*(3), 23–48. http://ro.uow.edu .au/edupapers/31.

List 3.7. General Planning Tips for the Differentiated Classroom

Teachers can use differentiated instruction in planning lessons that can meet the needs of all the students. In general, all state and local standards can and should be met through planning; the differentiation should happen in the classroom units, projects, and through day-to-day instruction.

- **Keep it simple.** When planning for differentiated instruction, the first rule of thumb is to keep it simple. Teachers do not have to do everything at once.

- **Know your students.** Determine the ability level of your students. You can do this by surveying past records of student performance to determine capabilities, prior learning, past experiences with learning, and so forth.

- **Same activity, different tasks.** One way to approach planning is to plan different tasks for the same activity. After the initial teacher instruction, offer two main options for finishing tasks. For example, with a science investigation, offer the option to write a lab report or give a presentation explaining findings.

- **Survey student interests.** Get to know your students informally. You can do this by an interest inventory (List 2.3), an interview or conference, or asking students to respond to an open-ended questionnaire with key questions about their learning preferences (depending on the age group).

- **Offer both structured and unstructured alternatives.** A structured alternative is working in a small group with a very specific task. An unstructured option is having students go off on their own to research. Different students will do well in each of these alternatives. The unstructured alternative will need more monitoring for time on task.

- **Develop a wide repertoire of teaching strategies.** Because "one size does *not* fit all," it is imperative that a variety of teaching strategies be used in a differentiated classroom. It is a professional responsibility of teachers to keep developing their strategies. In the digital age, this means becoming familiar with the various kinds of and uses for technology.

- **Know when to use direct instruction.** This is the most widely used and most traditional teaching strategy. It is the most teacher centered and can be used to cover material that students need to get going. Once they have the knowledge needed, it is time to turn to more student-centered activities to prevent boredom and disengagement.

List 3.7. (continued)

- **Try inquiry-based learning.** Inquiry-based learning has become very popular in teaching today. It is based on the scientific method and works very well in developing critical-thinking and problem-solving skills. It is student centered and requires students to conduct investigations independent of the teacher, unless otherwise directed or guided through the process of discovery. For more information, do a search online for *inquiry-based learning*.

- **Plan your assessments before you begin teaching.** Having a sense of where you are going and how you will get there is a strategy that educator Grant Wiggins calls "backward by design" (Wiggins & McTighe, 2005). Once teachers know what students will need to demonstrate, the next step is to determine how it might be demonstrated. Select different methods and backload these into the daily lesson plan.

- **Invite students into the planning process.** Seek suggestions for activities that have worked well for them in the past. When students feel a part of the process, they buy in more readily and feel responsibility for their learning. They are often quite good at identifying their needs. Make clear from the beginning your expectation that students will participate.

Most Commonly Used Differentiated Instruction Techniques and How to Use Them

Differentiated instruction and personalizing learning for students uses teaching strategies and tools you probably know already, and maybe even use regularly now. These tools fall under the name *differentiated instruction* because they help students with different learning styles understand and master the material they might not understand as thoroughly otherwise.

Good teaching, at its heart, is like good jazz. Teachers need to be well versed in their teaching "instruments" and tools at hand and be able to improvise when needed by pulling out new tools and giving them a try. Each class of students may need something a little different from the one before. Although the basic format of the lessons may be the same, teachers will be most successful when flexible and willing to meet the needs of the students. The differentiated instruction techniques and suggestions contained in this section are most commonly used and prove to be most helpful in the differentiation process.

List 4.1. Tiered Lessons

A tiered lesson has the same learning objective(s) for all students yet becomes differentiated through the tiers or groupings, which provide different learning activities for the various groups of students. Lessons can be tiered based on readiness, interests, or learning styles. This list offers definitions of the different ways to tier a lesson, followed by an example lesson of each.

Readiness Tier

Tier or group students according to readiness to master the objective: divide the students into groups based on ability level and provide each level with an appropriate task. This will involve pre-assessment.

Sample Readiness Tiered Lesson Plan

Subject: Reading
Grade: Second
Standard: Students will demonstrate ability to comprehend main points in a reading passage.
Resource: All students read the same high-quality grade-level short story.
Preparation: Divide students into three groups according to reading comprehension readiness: (A) those who read below grade level, (B) those who read at grade level, (C) those who read above grade level.

Tier A (below-grade-level learners, refer to Bloom's Taxonomy knowledge and comprehension activities in List 3.3). This group will work on comprehension activities in the story. Students should answer the following questions:

1. Who is the main character? Describe him.
2. What kind of things does this character like to do?
3. What do the other characters think of him? Find the passage that shows this.
4. What is the character's problem?

Students need to answer these factual questions. Create an activity such as a discussion group or a worksheet to complete.

Tier B (grade-level learners, refer to Bloom's Taxonomy application and analysis activities in List 3.3). Present the following three-step approach to problem solving first:

1. Identify the problem: What is the main character's problem?
2. How does he solve the problem? Explain the process.
3. Was this a good solution? What evidence is there to support this?

After students analyze the problem using these three steps, discuss the people in the story who helped him solve his problem. How important are the other characters to his solving of the problem?

List 4.1. (continued)

Tier C (above-grade-level learners, Bloom's Taxonomy synthesis activities in List 3.3).
1. Write what you think happens next in the story.
2. Do you think the character acted in a manner that was helpful to him?
3. How do think he could have done things differently?

Assessment: Once the small groups have worked on their questions, bring the entire class back for a whole-group discussion about the story.

Interest Tier

While all students are working on the same objective, they are given different options to accomplish the object based on their individual interests.

Sample Interest Tiered Lesson Plan

Subject: Science
Grade: Seventh
Objective: Students will be able to identify and comprehend the circulatory, respiratory, and digestive systems of the human body and the impact of those systems on health.
Preparation: Have students choose which system (circulatory, respiratory, digestive) they have the most interest in studying.
Activity: Once students have chosen their preferred system, have students work individually to create a diagram of the system that labels the parts and functions of each system. Once the diagrams are complete, divide the class into small groups based on the interests they chose. Have each group come up with three to five health concerns for each system, describe the problem, and explain how it effects the system and why it is a threat to overall health.
Assessment: Have each group choose the best diagram in the group and assess it for accuracy, adding anything that may be missing. Then each group will present their findings to the whole class.

Learning Style Tier

Given the same objective, provide three options, each relating to a different learning style.

Sample Learning Style Tiered Lesson Plan

Subject: Mathematics—Calculus
Grade: Twelfth
Objective: Students will create a representation of the mean value theorem.

List 4.1. (continued)

Preparation: Introduce the mean value theorem. Each student will create a representation of their interpretation of the meaning, use of the mean value theorem based on the information provided in the introduction, or both. Assess student learning styles and offer the following four ways for students to complete the assignment.

Tier A: Logical-mathematical learners in this tier are to create a problem that illustrates the meaning and/or use of the mean value theorem.

Tier B: Visual/spatial learners in this tier create a visual design that illustrates the meaning and/or use of the mean value theorem.

Tier C: Musical/rhythmic learners in this tier create a melody or rap song that illustrates the meaning and/or use of the mean value theorem.

Tier D: Bodily/kinesthetic learners in this tier create a model that illustrates the meaning and/or use of the mean value theorem.

Assessment: Have several students present their creations and use them as a basis to further discuss the mean value theorem.

General Tips for Tiered Lesson Plans

- **Not everything needs tiers.** Choose lessons in which the tiering and the type of tiering seem natural to the task.
- **Choose the best fit with the lesson.** Choose the type of tier that makes the most sense. In general, math and reading are good subjects to tier for readiness. Language arts and social studies are good for tiering to interest level and learning style.
- **Integrate tiers gradually; plan in advance.** When starting out, review all your lessons for an upcoming unit and try to add one type of tiering a week. Each week try a new type.
- **Make the objectives for each tier the same.** Focus on having students complete the same objective as illustrated in the sample lessons. Tiering should not lower standards or expectations for the students.
- **Use the Internet to help; adapt lesson plans from others.** Look for sample lesson plans on the Internet. The Indiana Department of Education has a great page on their site with examples.
- **Give students a choice.** Don't guess at students' interests, learning styles, or readiness. Let students choose, given the options.
- **Advance all students through tiers.** Advance all students through the different tiers in the readiness lessons. Students who reach the upper levels of Bloom's Taxonomy can always expand at this level while the other students advance toward mastery.
- **Use tiers in conjunction with other objectives and guidelines.** Use tiering in conjunction with Bloom's Taxonomy objectives, school curriculum standards, interest inventories, and learning styles knowledge.

List 4.2. Scaffolding Tools

Scaffolding is an instructional support strategy whereby teachers incrementally shift the building of knowledge to the students. Lev Vygotsky (Moll, 1990) developed the concept of scaffolding in the early twentieth century when he defined the zone of proximal development. The zone of proximal development (ZPD) is the level of difficulty at which a student can succeed with some support while still feeling challenged by the task. If the student is not challenged by the task, she may feel it's too easy and she may not enhance her learning, but if no support is offered, the task may seem too challenging for the student to succeed. The ZPD is what you probably know as simply the best "instructional level" for the student. Optimal scaffolding occurs when the student feels challenged but has enough support to be successful. This list offers examples of when and how to use scaffolding.

- **Use scaffolding to challenge students** and as students are coming to understand new concepts at greater levels of complexity. Plan units and projects with this in mind. As students get further into the materials, the scaffolding should become less and less.
- **Use visual components to help aid understanding.** Use diagrams, hand gestures, pictures, and other visual components when explaining to students to scaffold understanding. A great book aimed primarily at business, *The Back of the Napkin: Solving Problems and Selling Ideas with Pictures* by Dan Roam (2008), shows how simple stick pictures and diagrams can be useful in getting complex ideas across to others and in learning how to support complex ideas with simple drawings and diagrams.
- **Use models** to explain abstract concepts in subjects such as math and science.
- **Use visual cues and gestures.** Provide pointing gestures to show students where in the text you want them to focus.
- **Stay close.** Sit beside students who are having trouble working through concepts.
- **Provide new vocabulary in advance.** When introducing new reading, provide vocabulary lists in any subject.
- **Break it down into bite-sized chunks.** Break complex tasks into easier, smaller pieces to facilitate achievement. For example, when writing papers, have students begin by writing an introduction and having it approved before you assign the whole paper.
- **Show examples of completed work.** Give students examples of what completed tasks look like prior to beginning. This gives students something to emulate, as well as a more concrete idea of your expectations.
- **Ask students to verbalize.** Ask students to think aloud as they work through problems.
- **Provide the big picture and context for the lesson.** Give time lines or visual overviews when studying history or literature.
- **Help students look ahead.** Guide students to make predictions about what will happen next in science experiments and when reading.
- **Help by giving clues and signposts along the way.** Provide hints or clues as to what to expect. For example, say, "If the water isn't changing color by now, you may have to go back and repeat a step."

List 4.2. (continued)

- **The "two-minute warning"—help with pacing.** Whenever something is timed, provide clues as to how much time is left and where students should be by the time listed.
- **Share strategies with colleagues.** Let other teachers know that students understand how to use a specific strategy. Share copies of the strategy steps with these instructors and invite them to provide students opportunities to use the same strategy in their classrooms.
- **Partner with parents to reinforce skills.** Send a note home to parents outlining the steps of the strategy. If appropriate, encourage parents to help the child use the strategy on a homework assignment.
- **Help students help each other.** Enlist students who are proficient in using the strategy to serve as peer tutors, available to train other students to use the skill. Students can often take direction from peers more easily than from an authority figure.
- **Don't forget Bloom's.** Use Bloom's Taxonomy as a companion for scaffolding; teachers will see how differentiating the classroom is not a matter of using different techniques for the sake of technique but to ensure student cognitive advancement.
- **Don't overdo it—let students experiment and stretch.** Sometimes teachers over-scaffold, providing too much structure and filling so many blanks for students that they are not able to explore and learn on their own.

Types of Scaffolding

Reception. Reception scaffolds are used to draw the student's attention to the important or necessary information in the resources provided by the teacher. This is used most effectively at the beginning of teaching new concepts. Examples include

- **Reading guides.** These can be anything from a handout pointing students to main ideas by listing the page numbers where to look for them or a list of the least-known vocabulary words found in the text with the definitions to an outline of each of the characters and their character traits. Anything that helps the student receive the information in the text more easily falls into this category.
- **Glossaries.** Lists of most important words in the text and their meanings. These are most useful with very unfamiliar information.
- **Time lines.** A visual representation of the important events surrounding or leading up to a studied event, era, or historical period. They can be depicted with pictures, photos, or drawings for greater memory effect.

Transformation. Transformation scaffolds assist learners in transforming the information they've received into some other form when they need to sort out similarities and differences among two or more ideas or generate new ideas. Anything that assists in moving students from receiving the information as knowledge to analyzing it (see

List 4.2. (continued)

Bloom's Taxonomy, List 3.3) can be considered this type of scaffold, if it's a tool the teacher has specifically provided to help students move to the next level. Some examples of these include

- ○ **Brainstorming.** When having students brainstorm, this is considered a scaffolding technique when teachers model the technique, provide guidance with appropriate examples before turning the students loose on the activity, and lay the ground rules.
- ○ **Features chart.** Any graphic representation of the features of the concept, thing, or idea being analyzed. For example, in comparing the features of the agrarian age with the industrial age, students may first look at a features chart as a guide to making the comparisons. For less advanced students or to save time, the teacher may have filled this in beforehand. For more advanced scaffolding, the students may fill in the chart in small groups if they are knowledgeable.
- ○ **Graphic organizers.** These are used to organize information in a wide variety of ways to provide students with visual representations of ideas for the purpose of comparing, interpreting, or analyzing. As with the features chart, these will be scaffolded according to student readiness. There are many kinds of graphic organizers. (See List 4.5.)

Production. Production scaffolds assist learners in producing something tangible. These are best used as examples with guidelines. They are most often used when the form of the product follows a particular standard style. The common production scaffolds are

- ○ **Templates.** These are standardized outlines such as the precise formatting found in a script or a blank laboratory report write-up. A to-do list may be considered a template when all the student has to do is fill in the blanks. There are many templates for newsletters, yearbooks, and other publications in which the only thing the learner must do is supply the missing information.
- ○ **Outlines.** An outline can be thought of as a recipe. It provides a graphic representation and instructions for how to complete the new product.

Further Reading

A Scaffolding Strategy. (n.d.). http://projects.edtech.sandi.net/staffdev/presentation/scaffolding.htm. Retrieved August 15, 2010.

List 4.3. Project-Based Learning

Project-based learning is an instructional approach that is based on developing inter-disciplinary projects that engage students' interest and motivation. The activities in the projects are designed to meet content area standards in the pursuit of solving an authentic problem or creating a real product. Project-based learning is focused on higher-order thinking and developing critical-thinking skills. Projects are intended to stretch students' thinking and inspire their active involvement while covering all the standard goals and outcomes of the curriculum.

Projects can be created for a single teacher to implement or they can be interdisciplinary, involving collaboration between several teachers. Project-based learning as a collaborative event takes a great deal of planning, but the time is well spent because it allows teachers to learn from each other, share information about students, and participate in a highly engaging teaching experience.

Steps in Planning for Successful Collaborative Projects

- **Start with a team.** Assemble a team of content area teachers in an extended planning period.
- **Check those standards.** Identify the standards for each subject area in which students need to demonstrate mastery. Teachers should explain the nature of the standards for their content area to teacher colleagues both within and outside their content areas.
- **Use backward design to plan assessments first.** Create assessments in each content area that are tied to the standards. By starting with what you want the students to have mastered, it will be easier to make sure all aspects are covered within the project itself. This is called working backward.
- **One task serves many masters.** Identify and look for natural overlap in the standards and assessments. One task is likely to serve many goals.
- **Work collaboratively to develop a project.** What is the real-world problem that students will be asked to solve? Some examples include cleaning up a natural waterway that has been polluted, creating a public art space, organizing a campaign, inventing a product for sale, developing a system for better transportation, designing a school. The examples are endless but share the common theme that they are all real-world work.
- **Create a reasonable time frame for carrying out the project.** This step takes coordination of when students will receive content-specific direct instruction to meet standards.
- **Choose the goals for standards wisely.** Choose which standards the project will cover, and be careful not to choose too many but pick enough to make it worth the time commitment. Place all the standards in one project document and then make notes as to how students demonstrate mastery of the standards. Note that mastery of many standards will be accomplished during the process of the project rather than all at the end in the culminating activity or product.
- **Begin with the end in mind.** Consider the central question or problem students are to develop and determine what the end product will be. Plan backward from

List 4.3. (continued)

the completion to the actual lessons; use rubrics as guideposts where appropriate. Knowing the end result will guide the project assembly.

- **Start small and build on success.** Teachers do not have to re-invent the wheel. There are many schools that have successfully created and carried out projects at every level.
- **Real life means flexibility, too.** Plan projects well but allow for flexibility in case the project takes an unexpected turn, such as students becoming extremely engaged in something unanticipated but worth following through. Clear time lines with due dates for parts of the project along the way will ensure all students are on track.
- **Be a mentor and facilitator.** The teacher's role is one of coach, facilitator, guide, advisor, or mentor; it is not one of directing and managing all student work.
- **Keep the eye on the prize.** Share the project goals and expectations with students. Provide any examples that are available so students can see what a final product looks like and thereby know what they are aiming for.
- **Make sure they're ready.** Before initiating the project, pre-assess student knowledge and experience to avoid re-teaching and to gauge student interest levels. Solicit student feedback at the beginning of and throughout the project. Don't be afraid to change direction based on this feedback.

Some Examples to Guide Your Research

Elementary Projects

Explorer Elementary Charter School lists over twenty elementary school projects on their website with in-depth descriptions. Search this school's website, and if more information is needed, they are open to contact.

Middle School Projects

Salvadori Center is an educational center devoted to real-world construction and design projects for middle-level students. On their website under the resources tab are projects listed for each content area of the middle school curriculum.

High School Projects

The Virtual School House is an Internet site that has a number of projects for high school students.

Collaborative projects on the Internet. Many projects are taking place over the Internet that teachers and students can join and participate in with students from other schools in the United States and around the world. Many of these projects can be accessed through an organization called the Global SchoolNet Foundation. Their website has

List 4.3. (continued)

collaborative projects for every grade level. Here is an example of a project from the Global SchoolNet, used with permission from the Global SchoolNet Projects Registry.

Example of Project-Based Learning Plan

Project Level: Basic project

Curriculum Fit: Arts; English as foreign language; international relations; language; multicultural studies; social studies

Technologies Used: Discussion forum; Web-published; **Audio:** files; clips; CDs; tapes; **Text:** stories; essays; letters; **Video:** files; clips; CDs; tapes

Collaboration Styles Used: Intercultural exchange; social action

Full Project Description: Magical Moment Around the World is a global educational project dedicated to inspiring global coexistence, compassion, mutual care, understanding, and a reverence of life by fostering awareness that we are all connected by one human spirit. Magical Moments Around the World is dedicated to showing that all humans share a unique spirit connecting us all. It is also dedicated to spreading light in others and us. Envision a world that is guided by compassion and respect. By reading other people's magical moments we become aware that our happiness is connected to other people's happiness. We see that others' desires for happiness are the same as mine. In its essence the project aims to provide youth the right to be aware that we are all connected by one human spirit. This is done by writing magical moments in a global online book that will be presented in a multilingual website. The writing of the book will be on an ongoing basis for generations to come. In this way the people for the people create one big book. A book that depicts the human spirit.

Objectives

- Give inspiration, hope and a sense of well-being. Spreading light in others and ourselves. Raising awareness in our ability to summon up good feelings. A reverence of life.
- Creating a new awareness/spirit of coexistence among the various peoples, religions and cultures within a single interconnected civilization.
- Showing that we are all part of one big human family sharing a unique human spirit connecting us all.
- Deepen pro-social values such as kindness, helpfulness, personal responsibility, and respect for others.

List 4.3. (continued)

Outcomes
- A dossier is given to each participant that contains project material
- Magical Moment booklet for that year

For other sites for online collaborative projects, see the References section and the book's bonus Web material.

Further Reading

Center for Innovation in Engineering and Science Education. This organization can be found online and provides students the opportunity to collaborate by contributing local information to ongoing online collaborative projects ranging from monitoring weather and pollution to plate tectonics. See the Human Genetics Project, the Noonday Project, and the Square of Life Project. http://www.k12science.org. Retrieved January 2011.

Flat Stanley. This is a global literacy project connecting students and classrooms in many countries. The Flat Stanley website provides a wealth of resources for teachers about developing geography and cross-cultural projects. http://www.flatstanley.com. Retrieved January 2011.

Journey North. These collaborative projects for K–12 focus on seasonal changes such as real-time migrations and weather patterns. Teacher resources and data are available. http://www.learner.org/jnorth. Retrieved January 2011.

Web-Based Inquiry Science Environment. This site provides real-world evidence for students to research and make hypotheses about a variety of scientific topics that are current and relevant to today's world. http://wise.berkeley.edu. Retrieved January 2011.

List 4.4. Learning Contracts

Learning contracts are agreements made between students and teachers about what students will learn in a particular unit. Traditionally these have been created when students engage in independent study or when the compacting of the curriculum has placed the student outside of the aggregate of students for a short time to complete work independently. Although these purposes are useful, the truly differentiated classroom will not isolate advanced students, but instead bear a design that will address the needs of all students in the classroom community. Learning contracts can be used to help all students understand what they have to accomplish, as well as the time frame for meeting the objectives. This list is presented with the idea that all students in the classroom will be working on a learning contract. Learning contracts can be used at the start of a new project, activity, or unit of study.

Basic Components of a Learning Contract

- **Learning objectives.** The contract will include a statement of the learning objectives for the activity, project, or unit. The objectives should be the same for all students in the classroom. Individual contracts will modify the pacing, assessment, and methods for individuals or small groups.
- **Activities.** Steps, assignments, and activities needed to complete the objectives and a reasonable time line for their completion. Activities include such things as researching, conducting experiments, completing a problem, and writing stories. The teacher may fill this section in advance, but a learning contract works best when the student is presented with choices and has input into the process.
- **Time line.** The contract should include a time line for the completion of each step on the contract.
- **Materials and resources.** The contract should include a list of all the materials needed to complete each step of the assignment or unit. Specifics are necessary. Complete bibliographies and references, including any proposed community-based resources and organizations used, should be identified and recorded. Print materials and websites may also be included.
- **Statements of commitment.** Both the teacher and the student should include a statement of their commitment to the contract, so that they understand what is intended and expected of each other. These may be written as personal goals. The personal goal is a brief statement of what the learner intends to accomplish via an independent project. *Example:* "By the end of the semester, I will design and develop *[name of your course, topic for study, video, script, or other]*." The teacher's commitment statement may include, for example, being available for the student, ensuring resources are available when needed, and providing consistent check-ins toward completion.
- **Methods of evaluation.** Describe exactly how the project should be evaluated to determine how the goal has been accomplished. This may be a rubric or other form of benchmark the student should meet in the end-product and as mile-markers along the way during the process.

List 4.4. (continued)

The Basic Four Questions of Learning Contracts

- What are you going to learn?
- How are you going to learn it?
- How are you going to know that you learned it?
- How are you going to prove that you learned it?

General Tips for Using Learning Contracts to Differentiate Learning

- **It's all about the learning.** Don't be intimidated by the term *learning contract.* The emphasis is on *learning,* not *contract.* Contracts are really just an exchange of promises between two parties, even in the real world, so keep that in mind.
- **Involve the students.** Get students intimately involved in the process of developing their unit of study.
- **Make contracts mutual.** Like real-world contracts, the best ones have obligations for both parties to live up to and are not a simple "to-do" list handed to students to sign. Make sure the student knows what your obligations and promises are to them as well.
- **Be specific.** Make the contract specific and concrete with clear time lines. Vague terms and conditions only serve to confuse everyone.
- **Keep on track.** Schedule regular meetings with the students to go over contracts and check progress so no one gets too far off track or risks missing deadlines.
- **Keep parents in the loop.** Share the contracts with parents and get them to sign off on them.
- **Frequent feedback helps.** Provide continuous feedback about progress made, and give pointers to what could be beefed up or altered while the contract is in progress.
- **Use all resources available.** Encourage use of a variety of resources to complete objectives. Rather than just books, articles, or Internet resources, encourage students to interview relatives, neighbors, or other informational sources if appropriate.
- **Keep it simple and straightforward (KISS).** Don't make the contracts too long. Keep them simple and tracking toward goals.
- **Contracts work for groups.** Consider differentiating by providing small-group contracts.
- **Be consistent.** Find a time every week to have students review the contracts.
- **Contracts help everyone.** Assign learning contracts for all students, not only the ones struggling to meet deadlines. By making the learning objectives clear, learning contracts can help all students see the big picture of projects, as well as the day-to-day steps needed to get them to the end goal.

List 4.4. (continued)

- **Contracts should be helpful and encouraging.** Keep the process of using contracts positive rather than punitive, not as a means to trap students who are behind. Learning contracts are great for almost any project, and they work best when they include responsibilities to be met by both teacher and student.
- **Keep colleagues informed.** Share contracts with other teachers to avoid overloading students.

Sample Learning Contract

Student: Kelly Callaghan, Class: Fourth-Grade Reading, Teacher: Mr. Kline

Learning Objectives	Activities	Time Line
1. To identify story plot.	Read two books from the fourth-grade reading list.	9/12
2. To understand characters' personalities, qualities, feelings.	Draw storyboards showing the basic plots of each book.	9/14
3. To comprehend setting and apply its effect on story.	Create a poster for each main character showing how he or she feels and thinks.	9/15
4. To compare characters and their relationships.	Find people in real life who are like the main characters in the chosen books. Compare the real-life person to the book character and create a PowerPoint presentation showing this.	9/20
5. To evaluate characters and their motives.	Find a real-life news story that relates to the actions of the main character of one of your books. Explain in a PowerPoint presentation.	9/22

Materials and Resources

Fourth-grade reading list, paper, posterboard, markers, pens, glue, magazines, PowerPoint and computer, search engines

Statement of Commitment

Teacher: I, Mr. Kline, will help you brainstorm activities numbers 4 and 5 and will work with you until you find an appropriate match for these activities. If we cannot find people who make this work, we will switch to another activity and ensure you have the time to complete it. I will provide you with a rubric for the posterboard and check in to make sure you are completing the subdeadlines.

List 4.4. (continued)

Student: I, Kelly Callaghan, will come to class prepared to work on these assignments and not waste time in class talking with my friends. When I am researching on the Internet, I will maintain focus on the task at hand and not surf to other places. I will give each assignment my best effort.

Evaluation

Each product will be evaluated according to a rubric. At the completion of the unit, there will be a short quiz on the learning objectives. Effort and classroom behavior will also be evaluated based on a rubric. This portion of the evaluation will be shared ongoing.

Further Reading

Egg Harbor Township Schools. Differentiated Instruction: Learning Contracts. http://www.eht.k12.nj .us/~jonesj/differentiated%20instruction/learning%20contracts.htm. Retrieved January 2011.

Teachnology Learning Contract Maker. http://www.teach-nology.com/web_tools/contract. Retrieved January 2011.

List 4.5. Graphic Organizers

Graphic organizers help students organize information. In many classrooms, teachers are very likely to use a process of lecture and note taking to transfer information to students. Graphic organizers are a type of scaffolding tool that is highly effective in helping students visualize information and organize content. This list provides useful information about using graphic organizers, their benefits, and the types of organizers available. Many students are successful with graphic organizers, and organizers can be helpful throughout their education. Even law students still use outline techniques to study for their exams.

Who Benefits from Graphic Organizers?

- **Students who process information visually rather than orally.** Visual learners don't usually perform well on sequential or linear tasks (such as following multistep instructions or long division problems). They learn information in chunks in a holistic way. They learn much better by demonstration than by explanation. And they are naturally creative problem solvers. Graphic organizers help both chunk information and present it holistically.
- **Students with limited English language skills.** Content materials present text that is too dense for English language learners (ELLs). Visual tools help them understand and organize information. They promote active learning, develop higher-level thinking skills, and promote creativity.
- **Students who are challenged by the material.** Graphic organizers help students with language processing demands by visually presenting the most important information and eliminating information that is not so critical. This helps students focus and place information into a mental framework without excess language processing demands.
- **Students who relate to concepts conceptually rather than through narrative.** Most young readers are presented stories in a linear narrative. Students who think conceptually, who relate to pictures better than words, can better understand the story when it is presented in a graphic depiction. A type of graphic organizer known as a *story board* can help students keep track of characters, plot, and themes, thus assisting them in learning to read.

Why Graphic Organizers Work

- They help students see connections between concepts.
- They make conceptual patterns more visible.
- They encourage creativity.
- They help students organize information during the planning phase.
- They provide tools for recognizing inconsistencies.
- They help students organize information.
- They push students to using higher-order thinking skills.
- They allow students of different abilities to participate together in groups.
- They reduce stress for some students.
- They make students more engaged in the learning process.
- They allow students to effectively discuss points that they don't initially comprehend.

List 4.5. (continued)

Tips for Effective Use of Graphic Organizers

- Become familiar with the variety of graphic organizers available by doing an Internet search on the topic. The Education Place has a great selection to get you started (http://www.eduplace.com/graphicorganizer).
- Allow students to work with the graphic organizer by filling in the information alone or in groups.
- Explain to students the benefits of graphic organizers:
  - They help visual learners.
  - They organize information in an easily accessible format.
  - They assist in generating new ideas.
  - They can help students identify patterns and connections between concepts and information in a creative way.
- When possible, provide choices for different organizers.
- Use the Internet as well. Many simple programs are available, ranging from Kidspiration to OmniGiraffe to Personal Brain (http://www.thebrain.com/c/personalbrain/?c=69). They can be used to create mind maps and decision trees to help students organize information, plan projects, and more.

Which One Should You Use or Recommend?

The type of organizer a student might use or create is determined by the content and the organization of the material. The learning or cognitive style of the student or teacher creating the organizer also factors into the decision. Individuals usually have a preference for one type of graphic organizer or another. For example, big picture, creative thinkers seem to gravitate toward a conceptual organizer, with its nonlinear, open-ended quality. The hierarchical organizer, with its chronological structure, usually appeals to the more concrete, sequential learner. Having knowledge and experiences with several types of organizers allows teachers and students to choose the type most appropriate for the subject and the purpose (Bromley, DeVitis, & Modio, 1999).

Basic Examples of Graphic Organizers

Compare and Contrast Matrix

Compare	Contrast

The compare and contrast matrix shows similarities and differences between two concepts. The Venn diagram in Figure 4.1 shows features common among several ideas. The hierarchy in Figure 4.2 shows dominance relationships or a hierarchy of ideas. Relationship organizers like the one in Figure 4.3 show how concepts relate to one another. Fishbone

List 4.5. (continued)

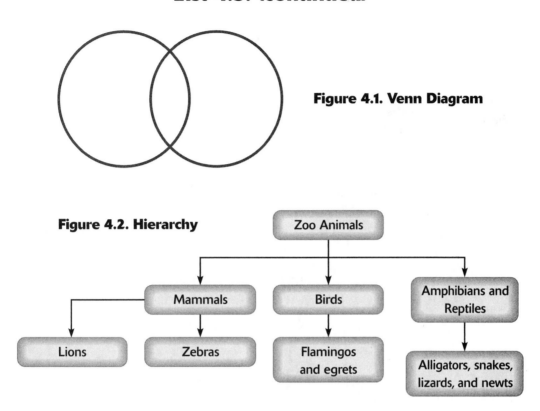

Figure 4.1. Venn Diagram

Figure 4.2. Hierarchy

organizers (see Figure 4.4) show parts of a whole or interactions between events. Process organizers (see Figure 4.5) show the steps in a process. Cycle organizers (see Figure 4.6) can be used to organize information that has no definitive beginning or ending. Pyramid organizers (see Figure 4.7) show interrelatedness of concepts. Spider maps (see Figure 4.8) can be used when information relating to the main idea does not fit into a hierarchy.

Graphic organizers can also be creative, using pictures and words to make the concepts come alive. Many software programs can generate these lively graphic organizers.

Applications of Graphic Organizers Across Content Areas

Graphic organizers have been applied across a range of curriculum subject areas. Although reading is by far the most well-studied application, science, social studies, language arts, and math are also content areas that are represented in the research base on graphic organizers. Operations such as mapping cause and effect, note taking, comparing and contrasting concepts, organizing problems and solutions, and relating information to main ideas or themes can be beneficial to many subject areas. The observed benefits in these subject areas go beyond those known to occur in reading comprehension (Bulgren, Schumaker, & Deshler, 1988; Darch, Carnine, & Kammeenui, 1986; Herl, O'Neil, Chung, & Schacter, 1999; Willerman & Mac Harg, 1991).

List 4.5. (continued)

Figure 4.3. Relationships

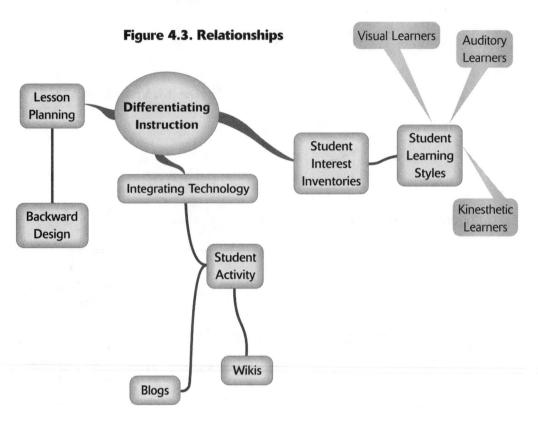

Figure 4.4. Fishbone

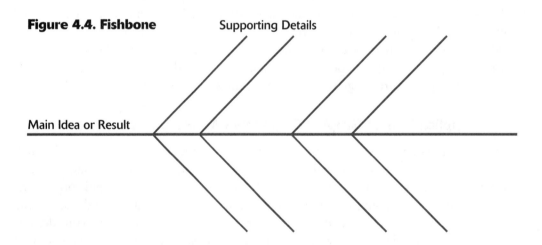

List 4.5. (continued)

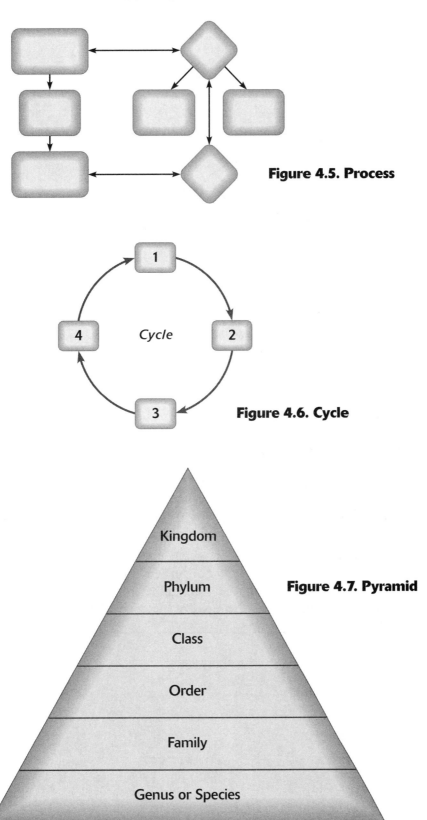

Figure 4.5. Process

Figure 4.6. Cycle

Figure 4.7. Pyramid

List 4.5. (continued)

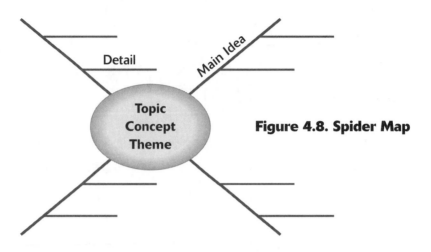

Figure 4.8. Spider Map

Further Reading

Graphic Organizer Software

Commercial software can be found at

> www.inspiration.com
>
> www.enchantedlearning.com

Free Online Graphic Organizers

Freeology: http://freeology.com/graphicorgs

The Education Place: http://www.eduplace.com/graphicorganizer

The Graphic Organizer: http://www.graphic.org/index.html
This site is a rich resource for learning about graphic organizers; it offers links, lists of references and books about graphic organizers, information about using graphic organizers for writing, guidelines for designing graphic organizers and assisting students in designing them, and samples of student work with graphic organizers.

List 4.6. Flexible Grouping

When grouping is aligned with instructional objectives and goals, it can be an effective way to reach a variety of learners in a classroom. This list gives suggestions for when to use a particular type of grouping.

- **Pairing (two to three students).** Pairing works best when the task has a short turnaround time, such as in a short discussion. Pairs allow students to get limited outside input that may help move their ideas from one level to the next. Pairs often work well to allow students to debrief information, check one another for understanding, and share anecdotal experiences. Random pairs for short periods work well in the context of a break from whole-group instruction. This is best used without shifting seating.

- **Small groups (three to five students).** Small groups work best when each student within the group is assigned a role. Roles may include leader, scribe, summarizer, and task-master. When each student in a group is given a specific role, it minimizes time spent off task or the possibility of one student carrying all the weight. Small groups work best for objectives that result in creating a product. Multiple inputs will yield a higher-quality product while introducing students to teamwork. Consider implementing online tools such as wikis or Google groups to help students communicate, share and keep track of information and deadlines, and allow teachers to monitor progress.

- **Large group (teacher led).** This most practiced method of student grouping is most effective when the teacher has instruction that all students must receive in the same way at the same time. This method (whole-class instruction) affords the teacher the most control over student behavior but the least control over student engagement. This method should be used sparingly and for no longer than thirty minutes at a time.

- **Large group (student led).** This method can be used with a single student leading a class as a means to demonstrate and reinforce knowledge or with a small group of students giving a presentation and involving the rest of students through question and answer. Students must be cued with instructions for effectiveness. Give students presentation rubrics. Find these online.

- **Multiple age groups.** Not all lessons must be taught to the same age group. Look for opportunities for young students and older students to learn something together. Some schools have multiple-age grouping in school performances, as in sporting teams. There is no reason that regular curricular activities cannot be considered in this light as well.

List 4.6. (continued)

General Ideas to Make Flexible Grouping Successful

- Combine flexible groupings with tiered lesson plans to challenge students at all ability levels.

- Provide students working in groups with roles and tasks. Typical group roles and their functions include
  - **Leader.** The leader makes sure everyone has an opportunity to participate and learn and keeps the group focused on the task at hand. The leader may also want to check to make sure that all of the group members have mastered activities of the exercise.
  - **Monitor.** The monitor acts as a timekeeper, ensuring that the activity is on track for completion whether it is a short or longer-term activity.
  - **Recorder.** The recorder takes notes of the activities and discussions, especially when there is to be a group presentation. The teacher is responsible for letting the group know what they will be reporting on.
  - **Reporter.** The reporter gives oral responses to the class about the group's activities or conclusions.

- Teachers should work among and between the small groups, checking for understanding and motivating students to stay on task. Teachers should never be seated at their desks doing "other" work while students are working in groups because that is the best way to guarantee failure.

- Avoid allowing students to form randomly selected groups in which they join up with their friends. Every student will benefit from trying out each role within the group structure with a variety of students. Try mixing up the groups for each cooperative learning session, thus giving students an opportunity to learn what it is like to work with all kinds of students in varying roles. Do not leave this grouping to random chance. It will not be effective.

- Establish, model, and practice clear routines for students to follow. Rehearse the expectations and review expectations frequently.

- Calmly and quickly approach and redirect students who are off task by using proximity control. This means standing near students who are off task.

- Use groups for a variety of purposes. There are several structures teachers can employ for conducting the business of the group. Spencer Kagan (1989/1990), an expert on cooperative learning, has come up with the following sample:
  - **Round robin.** This is a discussion technique and best used when there are several ideas in one lesson that will be discussed. Research has proven that this is *not* an effective model for reading groups. Starting with one participant, each person gets one to three minutes to present his or her point of view. There is no commentary in between and no cross talking. The recorder takes notes. This structure can be used in a variety of ways, including as a warm-up or an evaluation.

List 4.6. (continued)

- ○ **Think-pair-share.** This strategy is designed to encourage student involvement. First participants listen to the teacher's question. Then they think of a response. They pair up with someone and discuss their responses. In a group of four students, this can be done three times.
- ○ **Three-step interview.** This structure is used to further develop a simple concept. It works best in groups of four but can be adapted for larger groups. First, participants pair up within their group. One interviews the other with a question such as, "What did you find most interesting about the lesson on the planets?" Then they reverse roles. When they are finished gathering all the ideas, they can put them together to form a platform for their opinions. At this point they are ready to go onto more complex questions. The group uses the collective knowledge to build out ideas.

- Ask the expert; use the "Three Before Me" rule. If a student has a question, he asks three friends for assistance. If he still has a question, he can come and get a question card and set it on his desk. The question cards are tent-shaped cards with big question marks on them.

- Avoid using worksheets as the primary focus of small-group work. Worksheets should be kept to a minimum, if not eliminated altogether.

Further Reading

Kagan, S. (1989/1990). The structural approach to cooperative learning. *Educational Leadership, 47*(4), 12–15.

List 4.7. Learning Stations

Learning stations provide opportunities for students to interact with peers and chances to work on their own. They also cater to different learning styles, and students enjoy working on multiple activities set up in the classroom. Learning stations are typically considered elementary-level strategies, but they also work well in the upper grades. Although setting up learning stations requires extra planning and organizing, the teacher is then free to observe and monitor the learning during class time. This list offers some suggestions and information about different types of learning stations.

Things to Keep in Mind When Setting Up Learning Stations

- Stations can be permanent, set up to be visited when giving students choices, or rotational, set up to have students cycle through them in a class period.
- Use an anchor activity center to manage students who finish early, get stuck, or don't need to visit any of the stations that day.
- Teachers should circulate the room while students visit stations to monitor progress and answer questions.
- Spend time modeling the expectations and the types of tasks students will encounter at each station.
- Collaborate with colleagues to develop tasks for review, practice, enrichment, and acceleration.

Types of Stations

- **Permanent stations.** Some classrooms have permanent centers set up for students to use when they are finished with one activity before others. For example, a permanent science station may have a microscope and dozens of slides to review. Other permanent stations may be used for remediation, as in having a grammar station set with a box of files. In each file there is a different grammar lesson and the teacher can refer individual students to the files they need to work on. This makes it so the entire class is working on one writing assignment but choosing different lessons to improve their writing.
- **Changing stations.** Impermanent stations may set up to accommodate a particular unit. They may take up the entire class time, with students moving from station to station performing various tasks. An example of this is a class in fractions in which one station has food measuring, a second has currency, and a third has clay to cut into sections.
- **Listening stations.** Listening stations can be set up with a desk in a corner of the room where there are headphones and a listening device such as a tape, a cassette, or an equivalent. Students can use these for foreign language study or books on tape.
- **Art stations.** These can be permanent places where a daily or weekly project is set up for students to circulate through in times of choice. Place an assignment and the materials at this center and let students complete them independently. This can also be a place for the art portion of an interdisciplinary project. An example is a science project in which students must insert drawings of their ideas. While one student is at the researching station, another can be working on the art segment of the assignment.

List 4.7. (continued)

- **Computer station.** Bookmark pages that direct students to pages for research. Leave assignments at the station such as finding five facts about the solar system on three different webpages. Have students cite the facts. Computer stations are good for classrooms that have access to limited numbers of computers. While one or several students are on the computers, others can be at different stations; this avoids students hovering over each other's shoulders while looking for information. Teachers can also bookmark online activities and games they want students to try.

- **Math station.** Here students play math games, work with manipulatives, and learn through hands-on discovery. The activities allow the teacher to work one-on-one with students. Provide the students who need the most math assistance or tutoring with math learning stations that contain hands-on materials, including plastic counters, play money, base-10 blocks, and pattern blocks with which to work out math problems. Set up a math art station where students can draw pictures to help work out word problems.

- **Science station.** This is the place for science experiments to take place and for students to explore. The center can include a variety of books, microscopes, slides, and natural elements such as animal skins, feathers, shells, rocks, magnifying glasses, and discovery bottles. Have these centers change as themes or units change. For example, in a unit on the ocean, put out shells, horseshoe crabs, and vials of salt and fresh water to compare. Give students tasks such as comparing the water or testing it. Place books and articles about the ocean at the station.

- **Investigation drawers.** Fill the drawers of an old file cabinet or dresser with different objects. For example, in one drawer place rocks and minerals, in another place all circular objects such as bottle caps, coins, and buttons. Have another drawer for things that are all the same color. These drawers can be used for a variety of purposes, such as sequencing activities, comparing and contrasting, and recording observations.

- **Letter station.** In this center, students work with a variety of alphabet activities. Sometimes students get to play several different games. Other times, there is a required assignment for the child to complete. For a first-grade classroom, you may wish to change this center into a word-building center. Students can spell sight words, weekly spelling words, word wall words, and so on.

- **Puppet station.** Here students re-tell stories, poems, or nursery rhymes using puppets. This can also be a place to learn character virtues. Invite students to have the puppets act out a situation where they are sharing or comforting a friend.

- **Social studies station.** This station is a great place for children to discover and learn about cultures around the world. Maps, globes, atlases, travel brochures, and historical artifacts are some things that can be placed at this station. Again, change the station as different themes and units are created for interdisciplinary instruction.

- **Independent reading station.** Create an inviting reading station with beanbag chairs or floor pillows and baskets of books in all genres and all reading levels. Place a book-rating journal near this station where students can rate the books they read as great, good, or boring.

List 4.8. Rubrics

Rubrics are quality-rating assessment tools. Rubrics define levels of success and assign points for areas of mastery. In short, they are rating scales that allow students to know exactly what they will be rated on and what needs to be accomplished to receive a certain grade. Rubrics give students insight into what needs to be improved, as well as what is expected. As teachers move past traditional forms of assessment in an effort to engage all learners in the classroom, rubrics are a high-quality assessment tool, guiding students toward examples of mastery and setting expectations before the student begins work This list provides tips for creating effective rubrics.

- **Rubrics should be a road map to successful completion.** Although rubrics can be used to assure uniform grading criteria on what might otherwise seem to be subjective assessment of student work, they are most useful when given to students in advance to help them see the road map of the assignment and what the teacher's expectations are for completed work.
- **Avoid generic comments.** Comments that are specific to the work are the backbone of effective rubrics. Try not to simply circle numbers and hand back to students without comments. Rubrics need to provide students with specific feedback so they can incorporate this assessment into their next attempt or project.
- **Rubrics should be interactive.** The most effective use of rubrics is when they are accompanied by ongoing feedback and discussion. Invite students to create and discuss the criteria used to evaluate work.
- **Rubrics as "ground rules."** Rubrics can be used between teachers and students as well as between students to discuss work before it is completed. They can also be used as self-evaluation tools.
- **Examples help provide concrete goals.** When possible, provide examples of work that correspond with each category on the rubric. Show what an exemplary product looks like. Describe and demonstrate the difference between average rated work and exemplary work.
- **Review a variety of types of rubrics online.** There are hundreds of examples. Not all rubrics are created equal. Some will give students the feedback needed for improvement; others won't. Be sure to read them carefully. There are hundreds online, so if one doesn't seem to accomplish the task, search for another.
- **Use rubrics strategically.** Sometimes students push aside rubrics, especially when they are overused and undervalued as an assessment tool. Sometimes teachers use rubrics carelessly and students begin to devalue them. Be sure to explain the rubric and answer any questions before and after an assignment that has been assessed by using a rubric.
- **Create a library or resource of rubrics and share.** Keep a bank of rubrics that have worked well and share these with other teachers. Share work and rubrics with teachers across content areas to get a better understanding of students' abilities.
- **Rubrics as progress records.** Keep rubrics in student portfolios as records of student progress. Have students review and reflect on their rubrics over time. In addition,

List 4.8. (continued)

bring rubrics to parent-teacher conferences along with examples of student work to demonstrate progress and explain grades.

- **Tie grades to rubrics.** Any final grade should reflect a variety of types of assessments. Rubrics, when used effectively, will be a defense of a letter grade. Back up the rubric with an example of student work.
- **Rubrics and assessment should closely reflect work.** Rubrics should always be defensible against the actual work. If students feel that their work is being unfairly evaluated or penalized, the rubric provides the neutral framework against which teachers and students can discuss any perceived problems and make corrections as necessary.
- **Rubrics as guidelines for improvement.** Discuss with students how to effectively improve and move the work from level of assessment on the rubric to the next.
- **Give points for work as well as results.** Award points or grades for the process as well as the product. Class participation grades can reflect whether students showed up and worked well in a group, finished assignments on time, or contributed a great deal to the research.
- **Rubrics as group project checklist.** Assign group rubrics for not only the product but also for the group work. This will help students divide up and share tasks more effectively, as well as take responsibility for their contributions to the end product.

Further Reading

Rubistar: http://rubistar.4teachers.org. Retrieved January 2011.
Teacher Planet: Rubrics for Teachers: http://www.rubrics4teachers.com. Retrieved January 2011.
Teachnology: http://www.teachnology.com/web_tools/rubrics. Retrieved January 2011.

Section Five

Differentiated Classroom Management

Moving to a differentiated instruction model in the classroom can make many students uncomfortable at first as they experience change in the processes and expectations. Just as planning, instruction, and assessments can be differentiated, so can the way teachers manage their classrooms. A differentiated management approach will motivate students to learn more because it shows them that the course is focused on them and their needs as individuals, thus making learning personalized rather than institutional (see Figure 5.1).

Teachers' shifting routines need new ways to conduct classroom management. The most basic change a teacher makes with this approach involves moving into a facilitator and coaching role that involves establishing a new order and sharing expectations with students. The result of the new order is a more productive, work-focused class. The lists in this section provide tips for making that shift so students understand their roles and responsibilities in the classroom.

Figure 5.1. Maslow's Hierarchy of Needs in the DI Classroom

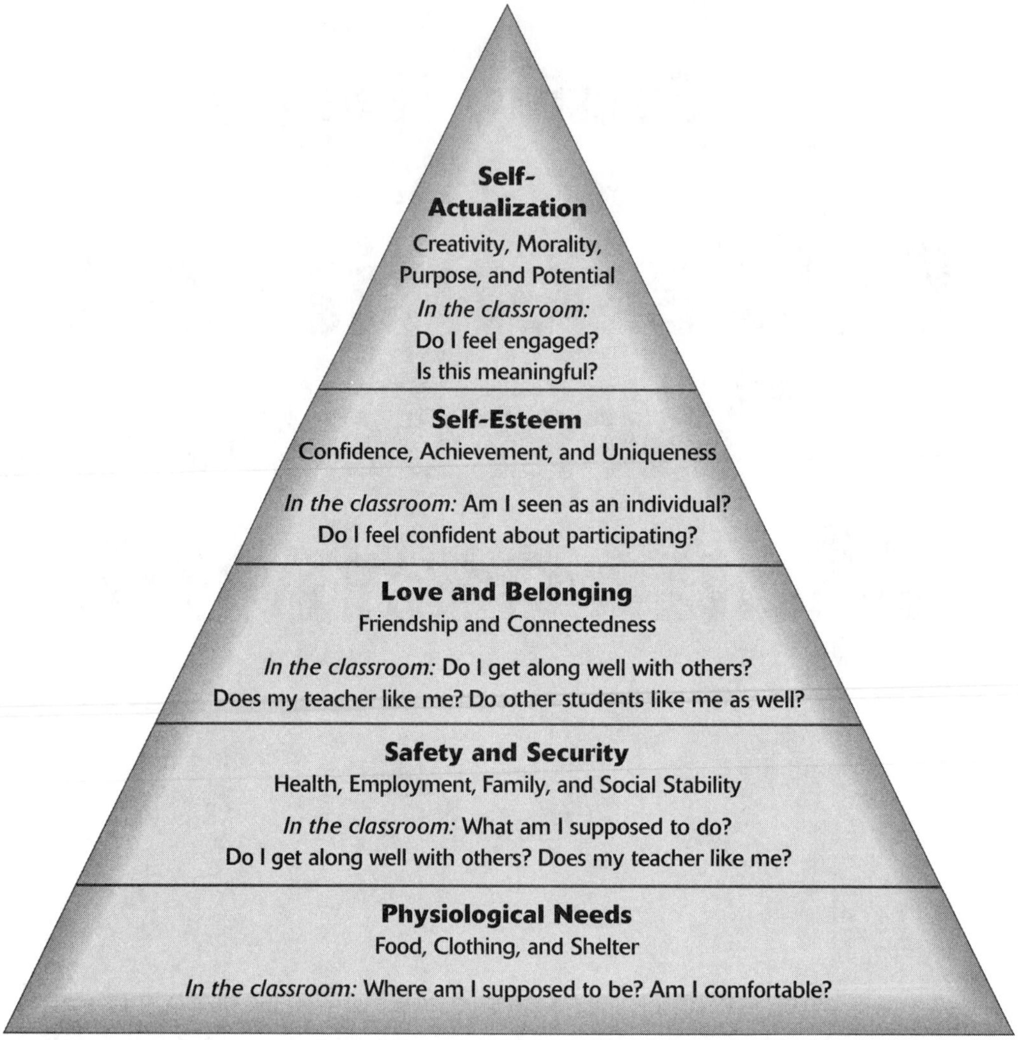

Self-Actualization
Creativity, Morality, Purpose, and Potential
In the classroom:
Do I feel engaged?
Is this meaningful?

Self-Esteem
Confidence, Achievement, and Uniqueness
In the classroom: Am I seen as an individual?
Do I feel confident about participating?

Love and Belonging
Friendship and Connectedness
In the classroom: Do I get along well with others?
Does my teacher like me? Do other students like me as well?

Safety and Security
Health, Employment, Family, and Social Stability
In the classroom: What am I supposed to do?
Do I get along well with others? Does my teacher like me?

Physiological Needs
Food, Clothing, and Shelter
In the classroom: Where am I supposed to be? Am I comfortable?

List 5.1. Arranging the Classroom for Optimal Differentiated Instruction Management

An important consideration when managing the differentiated classroom is how the environment is arranged. There is not a single best way to arrange the environment. Instead, the type of students, how they relate to one another, and what tasks are required will all dictate which arrangement will best serve the class. This list offers examples of things to consider when creating a space that facilitates a variety of types of learners, along with tasks and lessons geared toward them.

Environmental Considerations Supporting Differentiated Instruction

- **Minimize distractions (visual, tangible, and auditory).** A classroom that differentiates among varying learning styles will have a variety of learning cues that are visual and auditory. These things should not be crowded out or confused by a lot of other decorative stimuli.

- **Post rules and expectations where all students can see them.** Some students need visual cues and reminders, especially when it is important to their success. Posting the rules will reinforce their importance while also aiding a wider variety of students.

- **Post and review the daily and class schedules.** Many learners struggle with sequencing. Visual reminders and review will help these learners understand what is coming next and prepare their minds for greater participation because their anxiety will be reduced.

- **Provide students with personal spaces to place belongings.** Students feel comfortable learning when the space takes into consideration their needs and the fact that they bring personal possessions into the room. When each student has a place to call his or her own, the classroom generates a sense of "home" and belonging for the student. When students are able to personalize this space, they are more likely to buy into the learning culture. This can mean something as small as a space on the wall to hang a photo of their choosing.

- **Arrange furniture to allow for easy student movement.** In a classroom where a variety of learning styles are considered, there tend to be multiple activities that call for student movement. Consider the flow from one activity to the next as you arrange the classroom for learning.

- **Seat students in areas that allow for them to see instruction.** Classrooms are like theaters: teachers should consider the sight lines of all students from each angle.

List 5.1. (continued)

- **Arrange seating before students come to class.** When forming groups or moving furniture, do it prior to the students' arrival in class to save important instructional time and minimize distraction from lesson objectives.

- **Keep extra sweaters on hand.** Some students are especially sensitive to cool temperatures either from the outside air or air conditioning. Cold students will have trouble participating. Keep an extra sweater or jacket on hand to offer students who appear cold.

- **Don't break your own classroom rules.** On the one hand, if students are not allowed to drink during class, the teacher should not do it either. On the other hand, consider the time of day for class and whether or not blood sugars are low. Perhaps allowing a drink or a snack is not such a bad idea. Some schools have experimented successfully with allowing students to have bottles of water with them to help them stay hydrated and also minimizing trips to the water fountain.

- **Think outside the desk.** Flexible seating arrangements help differentiate instruction, but what happens when desks locked to chairs are all that's available? Sometimes sitting on the floor in groups with the chairs pushed back can yield results for group work.

List 5.2. Strategies for Differentiated Classroom Management

- **Understand and explain the difference between equal and fair.** Rick LaVoie (2007, p. xv) tells a story of a teacher who announces on the first day of class, "I promise I will not treat you the same at all this school year. Things won't be equal. Why? Because I know that each of you will need different things all year, the only way to be 'fair' to each of you is to treat each of you differently, and help you learn the best you can." Understanding the fundamental difference between being *fair* (giving each person what he or she needs) versus *equal* (giving each person exactly the same regardless of want or need) is fundamental for teachers *and* students in the DI classroom.

- **Establish a classroom that is cooperative.** Give students a voice in the rules and procedures. Let them know the reasoning behind why things are done as they are. For example, when assigning roles in group work, say to students, "Everyone has an important role in the success of this group work, which is why you are assigned certain roles. When you fail to perform your role, you let down yourself and the group." Then discuss this beforehand so students can self-monitor.

- **Create a list of affective expectations with the students.** Take time to solicit from the students a list of expected behaviors such as courtesy, sharing, supportive, and reliability. Post this list in the classroom and refer to it when there is a problem and, just as important, reinforce it before any problems arise.

- **Provide students classroom roles and responsibilities.** Appoint students to manage classroom clean-up, collect homework, or report on the overall experience of their classmates as a spokesperson. There are many roles students can be assigned if they are ready for them. Making these roles carry importance and prestige will develop a classroom of shared leadership. *Example:* "In one class each week a student was in charge of helping the teacher conduct routine tasks. This student wore a yellow vest all week. All students knew they would have a turn with the yellow vest, which came with other perks such as a button or a sticker when the task was completed."

- **Provide students multiple ways to express confusion or concern.** Consider having a space in class where students can write questions or give feedback. A simple easel pad mounted inside the classroom can be a great place for students to write questions or comments on the way into or out of the room. A special place for comments about classroom procedure or rules on a classroom blog or wiki can function the same way. If the process becomes a problem, talk it over with the group and ask them for their help in ameliorating it.

- **Give students insight into why the class is being conducted as it is.** Students love explanations that make sense and demonstrate that the teacher has given great thought to each of their needs. Don't assume they understand the reasons, explain them.

- **Begin class with an anchor activity.** Much classroom time is wasted while students settle in and teachers conduct routine housekeeping. Provide students with a daily anchor activity to get them focused on the lesson. Some examples are silent reading, journal entries, and special problems. Consistency with this routine will underscore

List 5.2. (continued)

the importance of the work at hand and prevent students from oversocializing at the start of class.

- **Consider how students assess personal risk.** Remember that a student's self-value and self-esteem is akin to a stash of poker chips. Kids spend these chips when they try something new. When they succeed, when they get praised, when they are recognized, when they get reassured, they get more chips. When kids get picked on, called names, punished, embarrassed, or otherwise made to feel less, they lose chips. The job of parents and educators, at its core, is to try to make sure every kid ends up with more chips at the end of the day than he or she started with (Hoffman, n.d.).
- **Reach out to the wallflowers.** There are always some students who are different and not so well liked or included naturally with their peers. This can make initial group work challenging, but it's important that these rules apply equally to everyone, at least within the walls of the classroom and one hopes within the entire school as well, including those students who may be harder to relate to.
- **Reinforce positive behaviors and compliance.** Basic behavioral science teaches that negative reinforcement, such as yelling or punishing a kid, only cuts off bad behavior temporarily but does nothing to replace the negative behavior with a positive substitute. Praising students as they try to do the right thing or do well in class encourages the positive.

    Examples: Ms. K keeps a list of kids who have handed in their work and completed their assignments on the board. Instead of singling out those who have not done their work for shame, she praises those who have, thus encouraging all students to want to be on the recognition list daily.

    Ms. L has several students with disruptive behaviors in her class and seems to spend lots of time disciplining them. By switching to recognizing the positive attempts to do what's asked of her more disruptive students than always admonishing them when they are out of line, Ms. L finds herself gradually spending more time on instruction.

- **Be consistent.** Too often teachers begin the year with a series of procedures and routines that involve students and work toward a cooperative, collaborative class, only to abandon those techniques as soon as an unexpected stress or pressure appears. The minute consistency is lost, students no longer trust the importance of the rules and procedures and are quick to stop cooperating.

Further Reading

LaVoie, R. (2007). *The motivation breakthrough: Six secrets to turning on the tuned out child.* New York: Touchstone/Simon & Schuster.

List 5.3. Why Students Misbehave

Most of the time students are uncooperative or downright misbehave because their needs are not being met in the classroom. Experience shows that most incidents of student misbehavior have to do with the teacher not paying enough attention to students' individual needs or making an attempt to understand the students. This leads to frustration or students not taking the teacher seriously, so they push the boundaries as far as they can to prove they are correct. This list gives suggestions for why students misbehave and provides suggestions for avoiding or dealing with these issues.

- **Basic needs are not being met.** Students and adults alike have relatively straight-forward motivations for their actions, as explained in detail by Maslow's Hierarchy of Needs (Figure 5.1). Once the basic needs for food, clothing, and shelter are met, students may then concentrate on more advanced needs for gregariousness, autonomy, status, inquisitiveness, aggression, power, recognition, and affiliation. Determine whether some of your students are not having their basic needs met and focus on helping them find ways to meet these needs.

- **Students are embarrassed.** One of the most powerful motivators for students is to avoid embarrassment and humiliation in front of their peers, followed by pleasing their teachers and parents. However, saving their self-esteem and feeling in control tends to be primary. When students act up in class, it's often a cover for not knowing an answer or to avoid looking foolish in front of their peers. Avoid at all costs having students look unintelligent or "less than" in front of their peers.

- **Lack of relevancy or personal connection.** There is nothing worse than busywork. When students do not perceive the work as meaningful, they don't take the work, the class, or the teacher seriously. Teachers should ask themselves if they would want to spend the day involved in the assignments they are requiring of students. Explanations for why it is relevant must be authentic or students will see through the ruse. In some cases, the very question will inspire the teacher to challenge the curriculum. Students deserve meaningful content.

- **No true connection with students.** Students know when teachers don't like them. They also know when the attempt to build the connection is false. If a teacher has gotten into a negative relationship with a student, the single best way to turn it around in a real, nonpatronizing way is to focus on the work, not the personality. Provide the student progressive challenges that are guaranteed to bring success. Praise the work for its good qualities. Slowly, the relationship will rebuild.

- **Teacher is unprepared for class.** Students feel disrespected when it is obvious the teacher has not prepared for class. Part of preparation involves returning assignments on time. When teachers give strict deadlines to students and then fail to give feedback in a timely manner, they no longer take the teachers seriously. Don't overassign work that can't be returned promptly. Prepare for class and share the plan with students to avoid seeming disengaged with their learning.

- **Students see the teacher as inauthentic.** Often teachers new to the profession identify with "heroic teachers" and try to emulate their style by using a variety of gimmicks and phrases that worked miracles in the movies. Students see through this.

List 5.3. (continued)

Students want teachers to be themselves and focus on the student, not on teacher popularity. (See Section Thirteen and the book's bonus Web material.)

- **Students know teachers do not really care about them.** Avoid discussing any student with another teacher in the presence of any other students. There is nothing worse than the student who stumbles into the faculty room to overhear the teachers mocking their students, no matter who they are. Avoid any negative talk about students among other teachers. There are better ways to bond with colleagues.

- **Home life interferes with school.** Children are not equipped to deal with the demands of school or some of the circumstances taking place in the home such as financial stress, divorce, or drug or alcohol abuse. Often acting out is a result of this, and teachers would do well to consider this and gently approach the student for more information. Consulting school professional services around any suspected issues is a next step in helping students cope with these pressures.

- **Students feel fear of teacher ridicule.** Praise and other positive rewards closely associated with positive behavior slowly teach students what they need to do to be recognized and feel good. Reinforcement needs to be consistent and frequent. Gradually students will adopt behavior that gets them the positive things they want over negative attention they don't really want or need. Praise the work, not the child. Be specific about what is being praised. For example, post on the board a list of students who have completed their work rather than a list of those who owe work. Encourage students in a positive rather than negative way.

- **Students have unclear expectations in other classrooms.** Make sure the rules and procedures in the classroom are clear and, if possible, posted in the room. Share these with other teachers and enlist their support. Never criticize another teacher with your students—doing so undermines everyone's efforts.

- **Students are lacking motivation.** Motivation is frequently called a three-legged stool. The three legs are: (a) needing to feel that the goal is worthwhile and attractive, (b) the amount of work required to reach the goal is reasonable, and (c) if the effort is put in, the goal itself is attainable. In order to be motivated, all three elements must be present. If a child seems unmotivated, try to diagnose which "leg" is missing. For example:
  - **Leg-one problem:** G is a smart eight-year-old but is having trouble learning his math facts. He thinks memorizing the facts is silly, because he assumes all adults have calculators with them all the time, and thus memorizing the facts is a waste of his time. G needs to be shown why having all these math facts memorized and automatically available are useful to him, now and in the future. Showing him how to quickly calculate prices and whether a sale on his favorite video game is a good deal may help him see some utility in having these facts at hand, despite the "academic" reason that he will need these facts at hand for all future math classes as well.
  - **Leg-two problem:** L is a bright middle school student, but never seems to write sentences longer than six or seven words and does the bare minimum of work

List 5.3. (continued)

most days. Although she knows doing well in school is important, she just doesn't seem motivated to do more than the minimum required. L probably isn't sure what she has to do to get good grades, and while she'd be thrilled to get them, she's not confident she can do all the work she thinks will be required to get there, so she doesn't try very hard. Some explanation of what L can do to improve her work, and even setting up one additional thing she can do each day or each week to get to the goal, will help the path toward the goal become more clear to L. She needs to understand that her teacher believes she's totally capable of reaching the goal, but she needs to know the work to get there is reasonable.

○ **Leg-three problem:** M wants to do well in school and, like L, seems to put in an effort but sometimes seems to stop short of his capabilities. His teacher is frustrated because M seems to perform well in class but doesn't seem to study well for tests. After talking to M, the teacher discovered that M just didn't always see the results from his efforts. He would study hard for one test, and then the questions always seemed to be different from what he studied. As a result, M gave up on studying much before a test, because his hard work never seemed to pay off. His teacher can help reengage M by helping him understand how to study and what good study skills are, how to anticipate what the teacher might ask on the test, and how to make the best use of his study time.

Further Reading

Goldstein, S., & Brooks, R. B. (2007). *Understanding and managing children's classroom behavior: Creating sustainable, resilient classrooms.* (2nd ed.). Hoboken, NJ: Wiley.

LaVoie, R. (2005). *It's so much work to be your friend: Helping the child with learning disabilities find social success.* New York: Touchstone/Simon & Schuster.

LaVoie, R. (2007). *The motivation breakthrough: Six secrets to turning on the tuned out child.* New York: Touchstone/Simon & Schuster.

List 5.4. Discipline Strategies

The word *discipline* derives from the Latin root *disciplina,* which simply means "teaching." Discipline consists of both positive action and corrective action when the positive action is not met. Too often discipline is viewed as merely the correction and doesn't take into consideration the proactive measures needed to avoid problems. This list describes a discipline strategy to help turn a child around, as well as an example of a common classroom discipline issue and a possible solution.

Social Autopsy

This is a technique designed to help students make better choices after things have gone wrong. Ask students to describe exactly what happened from their point of view and place the events on a whiteboard on a time line. Determine where decisions were made and where things started to go off track. Showing students where things started to go awry and how a different decision at that point could have led to a different outcome helps the event become instructive for the future rather than something that is forgotten and, unfortunately, repeated in the future.

Format for a Social Autopsy

- Take students step by step through a time line of events leading up to the conflict.

- Draw the events on a time line, list facts on a board or piece of paper, or both.

- Let students help identify where the conflict began. If needed, help guide them toward the point of divergence.

- Help students brainstorm solutions to the problem, and ask them what they may have done differently, as well as what they wish the other person might have done differently. Provide suggestions if needed.

- Help students reconcile with others, if necessary, and apologize, if warranted, for their part in the conflict. Ask them to remember also that "You need not attend every battle to which you are invited," that everyone has an opportunity to walk away or make another choice at some point.

  Example: Two kids are fighting in the hallway. B says that K took her scarf (or book or other) without permission, and K defends by saying she found the item lying on the floor and assumed she could have it. Taking a moment, Mrs. Q invites the girls into the classroom and helps them figure out what happened, in turn. By drawing a time line, the girls saw that B dropped her stuff while carrying what might be too much stuff toward her locker. Five minutes later, K saw the scarf, picked it up, and put it around her neck. B saw K in the cafeteria with the scarf and assumed she stole it from her.

List 5.4. (continued)

Summary: By looking at the time line and the facts, B can see that K did not intentionally take the item, and that maybe B should do what she can to be a bit more organized. K realizes that she should have asked around to see who owned the scarf, or dropped it off at the office or "lost and found" on her way to lunch instead of putting it on. Both girls agree they could have made different decisions, including B approaching K and asking her about the scarf before making an accusation. K agrees she would not have started to yell if B had just asked her about the scarf. The problem is solved, but more important, both girls learn how to approach similar problems in the future.

Further Reading

LaVoie, R. (2005). *It's so much work to be your friend: Helping the child with learning disabilities find social success.* New York: Touchstone/Simon & Schuster.

List 5.5. Strength-Based Discipline: An Individualized Approach

This list describes strength-based discipline and offers suggestions for dealing with discipline concerns in a positive manner. Strength-based discipline is a method whereby the teacher adopts the mind-set that students mean well but need guidance in how to behave correctly in any given situation. A strength-based discipline approach is intended to teach students how to make choices and learn from mistakes. It is a positive approach, based on the notion that, at the core, students are good people. This approach is inclusive. It works for all students, and by nature it is differentiated and based on the following:

- **Assumes mutual respect.** Adults model firmness by respecting themselves and the child.
- **Identifies the belief system informing the behavior.** Effective discipline recognizes the reasons students do what they do and works to change those beliefs, rather than merely attempting to change behavior.
- **Calls for students to develop effective communication and problem-solving skills.** The strengths approach to discipline is focused on getting students to do the right thing in the first place by working through behavior alternatives rather than focusing on punishment for bad behaviors that have already happened. This involves including them in conversations and problem solving.
- **Focuses on solutions instead of punishment.** When students believe they are part of the discussion and can see choices for their behavior, they will choose positive behavior rather than negative behaviors. When students act out in ways that need correction, they must understand consequences and take responsibility. This is best accomplished without threat.
- **Builds encouragement (instead of praise).** Encouragement notices effort and improvement, not just success, and builds long-term self-esteem and empowerment.

Suggestions for How to Implement a Strength-Based Discipline Approach

- **Deliver praise contingently upon student performance of desirable behaviors** or genuine accomplishment rather than indiscriminately without specific attention to genuine accomplishment.
- **Give praise specific to an action or an accomplishment** such as "Your project is well organized" rather than global and general such as "Your project is really good."
- **Express praise sincerely**, using a variety of verbal and nonverbal cues of approval rather than relying on stock phrases such as "good job" or "I like that."
- **Give encouragement for effort and progress** rather than making comparisons with other students.
- **Help students better appreciate their thinking and problem solving** throughout an activity rather than only upon completion.
- **Focus students on the process and imply future successes** rather than pointing to external factors such as luck or ease of the task.

List 5.5. (continued)

- **Encourage students to appreciate their accomplishments** and feel ownership in success rather than doing things to please the teacher or to win a competition.

- **Seek the students' input,** and offer reasonable choices about consequences for poor behavior choices.

- **Don't demand obedience without allowing for questions.** Sometimes children do not understand why or how they got in trouble. Effective behavior change will only happen when children understand what the issues are.

- **Work to discover ways to inspire children to a greater good.** Students want to do well. They need to see that caring adults recognize their efforts in all things. Often bad behavior is attention seeking. Proactive positive attention can ward off negative behavior.

- **Do not back students into corners.** For example, if you know a child has trouble controlling himself when having to sit still for a long period, help him out by talking about it beforehand and giving him options for what to do when he feels restless. An example may be giving him advance permission to stand up and walk around a little during a longer seated time.

- **Stress that students are involved in relationships of personal growth with adults.** This means that adults have a responsibility in the relationship to act as role models and to continue to grow and develop. Identify expectations for student behavior and communicate those expectations to students periodically. Develop classroom rules for both the teachers and the students to follow. For example, if students are not allowed to eat in the classroom, the teacher should not be either. If students are expected to arrive on time, so should the adults.

- **Recognize children's uniqueness,** even if the unique qualities seem bothersome. A child who asks too many questions can be seen as inquisitive. A child who talks out of turn can be seen as an eager participant. When students perform behaviors that are disruptive, it helps to validate the strength first then correct the behavior. Say, "Julie, I see you are very inquisitive, and that is a good thing, but you have to raise your hand to speak so everyone gets a fair turn." Strength-based discipline sees children first as having unique and positive attributes and then sees behaviors, not as personality traits, but as choices of action.

- **Show students lots of attention when assignments are complete;** give verbal feedback when students are on task or following directions. More attention should be given to positive than negative behavior.

- **Make sure students hear you making positive statements to others about them.** Many times, students do not believe their teachers are proud of them. If they overhear the teacher telling other teachers what a wonderful class they are, this goes a long way to building students who want to perform well.

- **Instead of using a raised voice to get a point across, purposely lower your voice when talking to a student about a negative behavior.** The student will be calmed and will pay more attention to a calm, quiet voice than a loud one. Also, it's always best to talk to a student at eye level.

List 5.6. Examples of Strength-Based Versus Deficit-Based Labels

The labels teachers attach to students influence what teachers perceive. If a student is labeled overbearing, teachers come to expect him to act in a disruptive manner. Contrarily, if the same student is labeled enthusiastic, teachers can perceive him as excited about situations, even when sometimes this strength is overblown. If teachers are to effectively differentiate instruction, they must demonstrate belief in all students. This list gives examples of deficit or negative labels and explains why or how to turn them into strength-based or positive labels.

- Depending on the label, people may perceive *the same behavior* in negative or positive ways. Because labels determine what people perceive and how they interpret the world, the label rewards some behaviors and inhibits others, even if the behavior is the same. For example, to one teacher a student can be considered rambunctious while another teacher may label the same behavior as enthusiastic.
- Teachers often unwittingly label students in negative terms that can cause inhibition rather than in positive terms that can bring out natural personality tendencies. Some labels used commonly in schools are: *gifted, remedial, ADD, overachiever, underachiever, class clown, good student, bad student*.
- Many teachers tend to focus on what needs to be "fixed" in a student, rather than on what already works. For example, labeling a student as *ADD* often prevents a teacher from perceiving that a student may be highly interested in science. The label highlights one aspect—usually the more negative—and makes it more difficult for the student to develop natural tendencies.
- Labels are always ways for teachers to understand students rather than actual qualities of a student's personality. They are not fixed qualities, they are perceptions. A student can be viewed as obstinate or as persistent.
- Becoming aware of the labels is a first step in seeing possible strengths. This is called strength-based perception rather than deficit-based perception. Strength-based perception is necessary for children to learn optimally.

Deficit-Based Label	Strength-Based Label
Class clown	Entertainer
Snoop	Inquisitive
Stubborn	Persistent
Shy	Focused
Overachiever	Achiever
Bossy	Leader
Indecisive	Deliberative
Conceited	Self-assured
Oddball	Individual
Manipulator	Strategist
Hesitant	Patient
Pushy	Eager

Questions to Ask When Perceiving Students

- Is this a child who challenges you?
- What word or phrase would you use to characterize that student (such as class clown, stubborn, or wallflower)?
- How might the characteristic you've identified be labeled in a positive way?

List 5.7. Classroom Management and Parental Communication Tips

Parents and families of students can be a substantial resource in supporting your efforts to differentiate instruction and keep classroom management under control. From ensuring students are prepared when they come to school, to helping them study, to providing outside expertise, parents are an additional resource for teachers. This list makes recommendations for good communications with parents.

- **Frequent, proactive communication works.** Make regular communication with home part of your instructional program. A classroom website or a regular e-mail to parents in the form of a classroom newsletter can help keep parents informed about upcoming projects, trips, units, and suggestions for outside learning, as well as opportunities for reinforcement of skills and the like (LaVoie, 2007).
- **Choose the best channel to get your message through.** Ask parents early on in the year how they would prefer to hear from you. Phone call? Note home? E-mail? Collect this information from students or on Back-to-School Night, and then use this as your main source of communication between home and school.
- **Vary individualized and classroom communication.** Mix bulk communication (newsletter, website) with personal, positive communication about the individual student. This communication can be formal or informal, ranging from a note to a call to e-mail or even a Facebook message. A short note expressing something positive about the student and his or her performance will go a long way to building a constructive relationship with parents, and enable you to enlist parents' support when difficulties in the classroom do arise.
- **Make suggestions or a critique that parents will hear.** Try using the "sandwich" method when critique is necessary with both students and their parents. The sandwich method places the "bad news" between two positive messages (Hoffman, n.d.). For example:

Dear Mrs. Smith,

Paul has been doing well in class and seems interested in the material. I find him to be one of the most interesting students in my class. *[positive reinforcement]* Lately, Paul seems to be having a problem handing in homework assignments on time or completing them fully. When I asked him about it, he said he was having a problem finding what he needed to get the work done at home, or he was forgetting to write down the assignment and was trying to complete the work during lunch and not finishing it. *[critique]*

I was wondering if you could help us both out by establishing a small "homework box" that keeps all the things Paul needs for work together at home—pencils, rulers, paper, etc.—so he has all the things he needs ready for him every day. *[suggestion, possible solution]* I'm also going to check and make sure he's writing down his assignment in the agenda book, and I'll make sure I post the assignments on my website, so he can check there in case I forget to check in with him at the end of the day. *[suggestions on how we can cooperate to solve the problem together]* The homework I assign is supposed to help students think a bit

List 5.7. (continued)

deeper about what we discuss in class and reinforce skills, so the work I send home is an important part of Paul's learning. I try to avoid "busy work" for kids, knowing how busy their lives are already! *[reason that the work is important, and understanding how it has an impact on home life]*

Thank you so much for your help and support. I'm sure this will help get Paul back on track with his assignments. Please let me know if I can help you in any way, or if you have any questions. I'll send you a short note in about a week, and we can update each other on Paul's progress and what seems to be working and what's not. *[positive ending and plan for future check-ins and updates]*

All the best,

Ms. Jones

- **Call parents when students are not acting in a manner that is consistent with their usual behavior.** Without prying, a simple question such as "Is there anything happening at home that may help me understand Stacy's behavior?" can help teachers find out any circumstances that might be affecting school. Questions phrased as a concern rather than a criticism will help make sure parents remain open and not defensive.

- **Become a team player.** Make sure that parents understand that the interests of school and home are aligned: student success. Once parents understand that teachers are on their side, and especially on their child's side, much resistance will disappear.

- **Don't assume the student told them.** Most parents would like more information from school, especially if things are not going well. Continuous information, more than just report cards and interim reports, keeps parents involved. As students move through school, they naturally tend to share less and less with their parents, despite questioning at home. Informing parents at the start of when children begin to struggle will go far in helping parents help their children before problems get too big and grades really begin to suffer.

- **Don't give up on the resistant parent.** Some parents and guardians have challenging personal and professional lives. Some may not be so involved or supportive of their children as teachers might hope. They may be unreasonable and argumentative. They may not be able to see problems their child is having, because it is honestly painful for them to do so. Remember that all a teacher can do is provide positive and constructive information, refer a student for additional help within the school if needed, and otherwise be an advocate for the child to the extent possible.

List 5.7. (continued)

- **Keep the overprotective parents in check.** Some parents may seek to micromanage their child's instruction. These "helicopter" parents always want their children to succeed and often try to assume their child's responsibilities. Make sure parents have a clear sense of what is expected from them, such as coaching rather than doing their child's work. By providing reasonable updates on the student's progress, these parents will feel more in control and generally back off.
- **Ask for updates and feedback.** Don't forget to ask your students' parents, from time to time, for feedback on what seems to be going well and what may not be. Knowing where parents' and students' anxiety may lie will give you invaluable information to head off problems before they start.

Further Reading

Goldstein, S., & Brooks, R. B. (2007). *Understanding and managing children's classroom behavior: Creating sustainable, resilient classrooms.* (2nd ed.). Hoboken, NJ: Wiley.

Hoffman, W. (n.d.). LD podcast conversations with Rick LaVoie. http://www.ldpodcast.com/images /ricklavoie1.mp3; http://www.ldpodcast.com/images/ricklavoie2.mp3.

LaVoie, R. (2007). *The motivation breakthrough: Six secrets to turning on the tuned out child.* New York: Touchstone/Simon & Schuster.

Section Six

Roles and Responsibilities

Differentiated instruction (DI) works best when all participants—teachers, students, parents, administrators, and staff—know their role and responsibility to support learning. One teacher using DI methods successfully often leads to students asking for similar experiences or choices in other classrooms, as they look for learning options that fit them best. This can cause some consternation on the part of those reluctant to try DI methods, but with proper supports in place, all members of the community can benefit, especially if they understand how much DI can enhance engagement and learning for the students.

List 6.1. Classroom Teacher

The classroom teacher is the one who can implement differentiated instruction (DI) with the greatest degree of consistency. Here are ten simple responsibilities of the classroom teacher when it comes to implementing DI.

- Know your students well.

- Communicate with other teachers about your students' individual learning profiles.

- Communicate with parents and caregivers about students' individual learning profiles.

- Discover ways to highlight success. Showcase student work in the room and beyond.

- Talk positively about students to other teachers. If other teachers have difficulty with a student, stand up for the student and let those teachers know the positive things about the student.

- Keep useful records. Don't keep too much information on the students—just assemble the most important pieces that give a true snapshot of each student's abilities, instructional level, and learning preferences.

- Keep learning about differentiated instruction. Attend workshops, read articles, and look for new lessons. Successful teachers keep learning.

- Try something every day. One small strategy a day will eventually add up to a noticeable, positive change.

- Discuss teaching and learning methods when the students are old enough. Metacognitive classes will keep the students focused on their own learning.

- Have fun. Teaching with new strategies should invigorate rather than exhaust. Approach these concepts with an open mind. Teachers who consistently use DI strategies experience success in their classrooms and experience relief from anxiety.

List 6.2. Students

It's important that students understand their role and responsibility in the differentiated instruction (DI) classroom. This list helps define what should be expected of students in a DI classroom environment and helps teachers make these expectations clear.

- **Students are members of a classroom community.** Unlike the standard classroom, a DI classroom will require students to work together at times with every other member of the classroom. They will be responsible not only for learning the material themselves, but also to help their fellow students learn it as well. By emphasizing to students that the classroom is like a family, with everyone needing different things but everyone also pitching in to help when needed, students will begin to understand that their success depends in part on everyone else's success as well.

- **DI students need to be respectful of others.** There is a perceived "pecking order" in every social group, and classrooms are no different. However, a good DI classroom requires that students understand that they will not be good at everything that is taught all year. Sometimes, they will know a lot already and be given advanced work to do; other times, they will need extra support and help from students who already know more than they do. Students need to be told up front that it's not expected that they will be good at everything; instead, they are expected to struggle from time to time, but they need to let others know of the struggle, so they can get the help and support they need.

- **DI students expect to make mistakes.** DI students know they are supposed to make mistakes, get things wrong but learn, experiment, and try again. At the heart of DI is making it OK for students to get things wrong in front of the teacher and their peers, without fear of punishment or ridicule. By creating a safe and respectful environment for learning, students will naturally begin to take more intellectual and academic risks than in a situation where every wrong answer comes attached with a deep dose of humiliation.

- **Differentiated instruction requires that students learn to speak up** and give teachers and classmates feedback when they don't understand something, an admission of weakness that may be difficult for many students. However, students need to know that everyone, including the teacher, has moments of "not getting it." Once this fear is known to be common and no big deal, students should gradually become more accustomed to admitting when they need help or a new way to see a task.

- **DI students know that the process is as important as the answer.** Students in DI classrooms know there's often more than one right answer to a problem and often the process is as important as a right answer. This means that students need to learn sometimes to be patient and understand that the pathway to the goal is as much a part of the learning process as the demonstration of learning in the end product, test score, project, or other assessment of learning.

- **DI students aren't tourists but participants in their own education.** This means students have to understand that their participation in class is not only so the teacher knows what they understand or do not understand, but that their

List 6.2. (continued)

participation helps their classmates learn as well. Likewise, participation with blogs, wikis, after-school activities, and so forth will help extend the student community beyond the school day.

- **DI students understand their teachers are human, too, and may make mistakes.** One of the things that students must learn is that everyone is fallible—including themselves and their instructors alike. In a classroom where everything can be fact checked on Google and new information comes out more frequently than textbook revisions, teachers will naturally start to become more mentors in learning and not just subject area experts. Likewise, students in DI classrooms will have to adapt to the fact that teachers won't be perfect, and will have to be willing to accept "I don't know, let's find the answer together" as an acceptable response, not one that signals "this teacher doesn't know what she's talking about."

- **DI students understand that the more they invest in a project, the more they will get out of it.** Research has shown that students' perception of their ability has an effect on subsequent achievement, and students in the DI classroom need to believe they have the ability to succeed (Williams & Sternberg, 2002).

- **Students need to ensure that they are asking as many questions as they are answering.** In taking responsibility for their own learning, students need to consider asking "the next question," including
  - Where can I find out more about this?
  - Are there any additional answers or ways to solve this problem?
  - Looking at all the alternative ways to solve the problem at hand, which one works best?
  - Which is the shortest?
  - Which is longest?
  - Why are they different?
  - Which gives me more useful information in the end?

- **The more students are encouraged to ask the next question, the more they will truly understand** and own the answers they seek and form the models they need to solve novel problems on their own.

- **Students need to be able to find their voice** and learn how to be heard by the teacher. Often students may run into a problem or assignment that they simply do not understand, and the frustration can cause them to say things such as "This is stupid," "This is boring." Students should learn as early as possible to try to figure out what or where their problem lies and articulate this to their teacher or peers. Saying something more such as "I'm not sure how to outline my essay" or "I don't understand why we're learning this. Can you explain to me why we're working on this assignment? What am I supposed to get out of it?" helps identify what the root cause of the problem may be and enables the student get the help he or she

List 6.2. (continued)

needs more quickly and efficiently. Broader statements such as "This is stupid" are counterproductive both for the students, who won't get the help they need, and for the teacher, who has no real way to understand what is causing the students' frustration.

- **Students need to gradually become their own advocates.** Although differentiated instruction is a mind-set that tries to help teachers connect with students, students also need to make their needs known to teachers, who are juggling the needs of multiple students simultaneously. The more students get to know their own learning style and identify the source of their frustration, the better they will be at getting the help they need.

- **Students need to exercise patience.** Sometimes the greatest obstacle to learning can be impatience with the process of learning, and not being able to understand and master everything immediately. Students can be helped by providing them context and the bigger picture about where the lesson is going and how it fits into the skills and learning they need to master over time. Adding a healthy dose of real-world significance and problems may also help students learn to be patient with their own learning and academic growth over time.

- **Students need to learn to move between class instruction and group work efficiently.** In the DI classroom, students will be expected to learn how to move from class lecture to group settings and back again efficiently to maximize their own learning. Understanding that the work done in the classroom is purposeful and valuable will help reduce the off-task time for students, but students should also be encouraged to have that sense of purpose even when the learning is more active and less closely moderated by the instructor.

- **Students in a DI classroom are responsible for learning.** We occasionally tell students that in the DI classroom, "Great power (or freedom to choose) comes with great responsibility," just like in the real world. They will be expected to take responsibility for their work (or lack thereof) much more so than in a traditional classroom, but the rewards they will get as a result will be higher as well. Making sure students understand their investment in their own learning is a fundamental part of a successful DI classroom.

List 6.3. Administrators

The success of any school that is truly committed to providing a fair and equitable learning opportunity for all its students depends on the commitment and instructional leadership of the school. Administrators play a key role in supporting students, parents, and especially teachers as they transition from traditional to more inclusive methods of curriculum delivery. This list helps clarify the role of administrators in delivering a differentiated curriculum and offers suggestions for how to support implementation.

- **Administrators are the instructional leaders in schools.** All school personnel, including the superintendent, will provide the most effective support for the differentiated methodology by becoming aware of the practices, methods, and philosophies at the core of the suggestions in this book.

- **Photocopy and distribute the glossary of *The Differentiated Instruction Book of Lists*** to all school personnel and ask that they familiarize themselves with the terms so that when teachers or parents ask questions, they are aware of the conversation.

- **Provide teachers time to plan effectively for differentiated instruction (DI).** Many teachers, especially those who have been teaching with traditional methods for a long time, will feel anxious about the planning that goes into creating new approaches and trying new lessons. Administrations that foresee this will provide adequate time for teachers to plan together.

- **Look at the typical day and decide which responsibilities can be replaced** to create the time needed to plan and implement new strategies. For some schools, this will mean replacing a regular meeting with directed planning time; for others, it may mean devoting professional development days to planning. Simply adding more onto an already busy schedule will not ensure the success of this method.

- **Be clear with teachers** that they do not have to implement everything at once. Set goals; for instance, the social studies department will try one new method a term, such as creating a project for students or setting up stations. When the goals are chunked and followed up by realistic expectations, teachers will be more willing to take the risks.

- **Be familiar with the practices teachers are attempting.** Walk around the building looking for examples of differentiated instruction. Point out successes in faculty meetings. Let teachers know the administration is both aware and supportive of the efforts in the school.

- **Provide ongoing professional development opportunities for teachers.** Set aside budget money for teachers to attend conferences, for purchasing materials such as manipulatives, and for bringing in consultants to work with teachers. Make "differentiated" an annual district or school goal.

List 6.3. (continued)

- **Communicate the importance of differentiated instruction** with parents through newsletters, articles, and other opportunities for parent communication.

- **Highlight lesson plans or projects** that have worked in faculty meetings. In each meeting expose one good example for the teachers, showing the administration is conscious of the teachers' efforts.

- **Begin discussions about how to create central databases** for storing rubrics, lesson plans, and information about students that can be useful in understanding their learning styles. Meet with technology specialists to determine the possible ways to share this information across disciplines.

- **Don't expect every teacher to get on board right away.** Work with the ones who are willing and open, and spiral out without making the reluctant feel badly about their lack of willingness.

- **Create an in-house mentoring system or a "critical friends group,"** a practice invented by the Coalition for Essential Schools. It entails groups of teachers getting together to observe student work and comparing it with the lesson plans and instructions that led to the work. Teachers observe and comment on the work, looking for ways to make the outcomes better matched to the instructions and objectives.

- **Create a resource section in the library, media center, or teachers' room on differentiated instruction.** Keep on the lookout for new articles and information about how differentiated instruction is spreading as a methodology. Encourage conversations.

- **Make it clear to teachers that this is not a fad** that will pass but a fundamental pedagogy that has been around for a very long time; it has simply recently been renamed differentiated instruction. Let teachers know that many of them have been doing the practices naturally for a long time and that there is nothing particularly new about these methods. Make it clear that the ideas in this book are considered good teaching.

- **Appoint several teacher leaders** who will present mini lessons or workshops during professional development days or faculty meetings.

- **Devote professional development days to DI.** Allow these days to include training and planning. Be clear with teachers about the rewards—the "what's in it for me?" part. Once teachers have put initial time into planning, their classroom time is freed up to facilitate the lessons, thus making less work during the actual day.

List 6.3. (continued)

- **Have teachers demonstrate differentiated lessons for colleagues** so they can see it for themselves. If no other teachers in your building are using DI techniques, there are several videos showing what DI looks like in the classroom available on the website for this book, http://www.differentiatedinstruction.co, that may be helpful to see DI in action in a real classroom.

- **Think of differentiated instruction as a long-term commitment,** not a single training program. Vary the approaches for staff development and communication about DI.

- **Get to know teachers on the same individual basis as they are expected to know their students.** Learn each teacher's strengths, interests, and goals. Take time to talk informally with teachers, showing concern for their professional and personal satisfaction.

- **Approach differentiated instruction with teachers** on both a philosophical level (why it's important) and a practical level (how it's done).

- **Allow for failure.** Any time a teacher tries something new, it may miss the mark. Let teachers know that it is OK to hit and miss on the road to new methods.

- **Hire new teachers who are trained in differentiated instruction or very open to learning about it.** Every new hire is an opportunity to strengthen the goals of differentiation in the school.

- **When interviewing new teachers, ask for sample lessons** that demonstrate ability to differentiate. When possible, observe potential hires in a practice lesson.

- **Show true support by engaging teachers** in conversations about their struggles with differentiated instruction. Enlist them to help arrive at solutions for difficulties with time, work overload, and transition from traditional methods.

- **Don't demand too much too soon.** Allow teachers to differentiate a few lessons at a time and to ease into the new planning and instructional methods.

List 6.4. Parents

Parents are a key part of the triangle of student achievement. Teachers, students, and parents all play a role in helping a student grow, learn, and mature over time. This list offers tips and pointers to help parents be a constructive participant and support structure for teachers and students in the differentiated instruction (DI) classroom.

- **Allow children to do their own work,** but support and help instruct as needed at home. We've had plenty of school projects at home that have required support, ranging from art supplies to helping a child identify and locate reliable resource materials. Although it is a temptation to "take over" from time to time, parents must allow their children to do their own project, providing only coaching from the sidelines. This coaching can include:
  - Helping the student understand why neatness and organization are important.
  - Helping the student understand basic good design with visual projects. What looks best and why? Does the placement of the items in a poster or slide presentation change the meaning or emphasis? Does the end product get the point across? Has the student met all the points on the rubric, if given?
  - Helping the student learn good study skills and to prepare for tests.
- **Practice basics when able.** The brain tends to retain things more when it gets the chance to play and transform information, so simple things like going over spelling words in the car, having a student write words on a whiteboard, answer out loud, play a quiz game for poker chips that can be traded in for TV time—whatever it is, parents can have a tremendous impact by encouraging students to learn while playing with information and putting it in as many forms as possible orally, written, and creatively.
- **Ask for help when needed.** In helping a student at home, parents have to feel that they can ask for help when they need it, too. Teachers and parents should share resources so that parents can help support students if they get stuck, for example, on homework problems in math, even if it's been years since the parent has had to do similar problems themselves.
- **Be a mindful communicator.** There's always a time when a student has a bad day (or week) due to lack of sleep, sickness, family emergency or problems, or the like. The home life of a child overflows into the school life of the student, and keeping teachers informed when a child has an event that might put them off their game helps a teacher be a bit more understanding and avoid adding stress or adding blame onto a child when he or she needs that least of all.
- **Respect teachers and the academic hierarchy.** In all aspects of schooling, the first point of contact, except in extreme circumstances, should be the teacher, not an administrator. If a parent gets a report that a teacher is behaving less than professionally, parents need to temper this with the fact that students will tend to leave out their own contributions to any confrontation or may not fully have all the details of the situation. Good problem solving starts with phrases like: "Dear Mr. X: When JJ came home from school today, he reported that _____. I was a bit concerned and curious about what happened, and I'm not entirely sure I understand

List 6.4. (continued)

the circumstances and what happened. Could you help me understand the situation better and what we can do to resolve it?"

- **Resolve problems before resorting to escalation to administration.** As easy as it is for parents to support a child's side against someone who may be treating them less than fairly, it's important to first get the other side of the story. Try to remember to get both sides of the story before looking for a higher authority to resolve the conflict.

- **Give as many compliments as possible,** both directly to the teacher and administration when appropriate. This helps gain a reputation for being someone who speaks up when things are going well as well as when they go badly, and when parents contact teachers about problems, they will be more likely to respond and to be sympathetic to concerns. (No one likes to feel attacked.)

- **Make sure students come to school prepared to succeed**—sleep and nutrition included. In addition to helping with study skills and reinforcing learning, parents also need to make sure their children come to school prepared to learn. This means not only having all the books and necessary supplies, but also that the children maintain as regular a schedule as possible.

- **Make sure students view school and learning as not only their job but also a fantastic opportunity to learn and explore.** School is not always everyone's favorite childhood experience, unfortunately. There are times parents can send a message to their children that school is something to be endured rather than relished as an exciting opportunity.

- **Encourage exploration and learning outside the classroom.** Agree to do one child-centered activity on the weekend, ranging from going to a playground, going to a local museum, going to a farmer's market, taking a walk in the park, playing games—whatever it happens to be. Over time, these experiences build the background knowledge students use in school projects. They also help build strong family and community relationships.

- **Don't be a helicopter.** For many parents, a child's success at school can seem imperative to their later success in life. However, micromanaging a child's academic life is likely to leave the child feeling incapable of managing problems and conflict independently, and leave teachers feeling defensive and less than fully cooperative. Parents should try to let their child handle situations at first, and then intervene only when necessary. If parents choose their battles wisely, they and their child will be happier in the end.

List 6.5. Support Staff

Parents and administrators should be aware that customizing learning in the classroom takes time, and teachers need a variety of supports to help them be successful, especially because classrooms have many students who need extra attention and assistance. Support staff includes counselors, speech therapists, secretaries, business managers, assistants, registrars, and cafeteria people. Everyone who comes into contact with students has a potential to influence their learning and their attitudes toward school. The school that has alignment about the importance of teaching to individuals will include support staff in delivering a differentiated curriculum. Support staff in schools are often overlooked as not being so central to teaching per se, except that everyone from administrators to librarians to classroom aides to nurses all interact with students and are critical to creating a school environment that's productive and enriching. This list gives some ideas on how support staff can help differentiated instruction (DI) permeate through every aspect of school.

- **Recognize, thank, and acknowledge the contributions support staff make, both formally and informally.** Support staff can often feel like the stepchildren of the school, not so valued or important as other members of the staff or faculty. It's important to help support staff recognize how important their job is to the efficient running of the school and to take pride in the contributions they make.

- **Treat support staff as much as possible as members of the faculty.** Invite support staff that deal directly with students, such as those providing special services or counseling, to faculty and department meetings from time to time. These staff members have important and critical knowledge of how students are progressing and where their challenges lie. Good communication with all the student's instructors is critical to help them appreciate a student's needs across subject areas as well as how to approach differentiation in the classroom itself.

- **Enlist counselors in DI.** Counselors will be supportive when they are made aware of how differentiation works and they are included in conversations regarding planning and implementation. Counselors are strong support for students who struggle.

- **Develop a list of core values about the inherent worth of each individual that stresses how people learn differently.** Share this information with bus drivers, cafeteria helpers, and those in other support roles so they understand, for example, that when they give instructions it helps to both speak and write things down or that knowing as many students by name as possible will contribute to the overall success of a school.

- **Consider adding meetings where support staff are included along with teachers to discuss student needs.** Support staff come into regular contact with students, and differentiated instruction permeates every aspect of a student's day. Support staff can serve as a resource for classroom teachers, thus encouraging collaboration.

List 6.5. (continued)

- **Alert support staff to any major changes in the lives of students so they are aware when coming into contact with the students during the day.** This will avoid misunderstandings.

- **Invite support staff to come up with a list of things they do in their jobs for students,** then ask them to come up with between one and five suggestions for ways they can customize rather than standardize their interactions with students.

- **When possible, support staff should seek to allow students to help or participate in their activities.** Asking a student to hold a door, help carry things, dump a trash can, clear a table, run a copy machine, or help set up a printer or smart board are small things that help students feel needed and part of a larger community. This connectedness is important at every level to help kids feel valuable, and this feeling helps kids stay on track academically as well.

- **Invite support staff to school events and to feel included in the greater school community.** Feeling invited and included in school special events and meetings goes a long way to recognize how support staff make meaningful contributions to the success of the school. Even part-time staff who may only be present for special services, academic testing, special education services, counseling, and the like should feel a part of the team.

Using Differentiated Instruction Techniques at Different Grade Levels

As children develop and change over time, the differentiated instruction (DI) strategies that work best will change and evolve as well. Around first grade and again in middle school, students begin to undergo developmental and neurological changes that result in large jumps in their ability to learn and comprehend more complex material. As students go through these changes, DI and personalizing learning will become even more important. In this section, the lists contain tips and strategies geared toward students at each level to help teachers choose the methods of personalizing learning that will be most effective.

List 7.1. Kindergarten

Kindergartens are one of the first "real" school experiences for children. They begin to learn about the process of formal learning, much more so than in preschool. In kindergarten, a large portion of learning is done by doing, or as part of the process itself. This list gives suggestions for general differentiated instruction in kindergarten classrooms.

- **Remember development.** Children learn when they are developmentally ready. Just because the curriculum says students should be reading by January 15 doesn't mean all students will naturally be ready. Try to avoid praising students who are ready before the others. No amount of trying will prepare them. Learn as much as possible about developmental approaches. Share these findings with parents.

- **Use a variety of learning opportunities and allow for choice.** Kindergarten classrooms are often set up for children to be taught in response to their readiness levels and interests with the uses of centers, more flexible nature, and activity-based learning. Keeping the classroom active will help keep all learners engaged.

- **Plan for all-group as well as tiered lessons.** Keep all-group activities to a time maximum of around twenty minutes. Then break off and assign smaller group activities.

- **Give informal assessments.** Cindy Middenhoff (2008), in her book *Differentiating Instruction in Kindergarten,* suggests teachers keep a notebook or clipboard near them to take notes when interacting with students to help determine their readiness levels. While each teacher can develop his or her own, something as simple as a folder with a pen and sticky notes or index cards on an O-ring can help teachers track students on the fly.

- **Teach lessons with music.** Kindergarteners are often eager to learn, and information is frequently conveyed with song. A simple good-morning song, clean-up-time song, or reading-time song, for example, will provide cues for students about transitions, as well as help them retain the information contained within.

- **Use visual cues.** Most kindergarten students will recognize signs even if they aren't reading yet. Simple signs, necklaces, badges, procedures such as "Ask three before me," or other visual cues can be used to help students "see" and cue appropriate behavior.

- **Help students learn self-management.** Young students are comforted by routine and predictability. Help children learn classroom procedures, what to do if they finish a task early, and other ways to help them learn to manage their own behavior. Offering stickers and other small rewards for good behavior work well for young children and encourage more of the same. Find a variety of ways to celebrate the contribution of each student in the class. *Example:* Julie listens well, Martin is organized, Ellen is courteous.

List 7.1. (continued)

- **Pair students with all levels of partners sometimes and homogeneously according to readiness for other activities.** Vary the groupings and avoid depending on one kind of grouping.

- **Avoid making "faster" equal to "better."** Avoid praising speed for completion of tasks. Mastery takes some students more time than others. Praise the work and achievement, not the speed at which students learn.

- **Involve parents in differentiating instruction.** Kindergarten is a great time to help parents become a partner in their children's education. Have parents share as much information about what they observe about their children as learners, as well as their interests and personality attributes that make each child unique.

Further Reading

D'Archangelo, M. (2003). On the mind of a child: A conversation with Sally Shaywitz. *Educational Leadership: The First Years of School*. ASCD. http://www.casenex.com/casenet/pages/virtualLibrary/Readings/ASCD/el200304_darcangeloASCD.pdf.

Middenhoff, C. (2008). *Differentiating instruction in kindergarten: Planning tips, assessment tools, management strategies, multi-leveled centers, and activities that reach and nurture every learner*. New York: Scholastic Teaching Resources.

List 7.2. Grades 1–5

Grades 1–5 are critical in a child's learning. Children begin to learn to read in earnest, and then between third and fourth grade, they transition from learning how to read to reading to learn. During this transition, students are starting to read to extract meaning and comprehend more complex subject matter, and this tends to cause difficulties for students with weaker language skills. This list deals with differentiating instruction in the early elementary school years, the common issues that arise with students, and how to both identify students' issues and help them succeed in the classroom.

Early Elementary

- **Focus on basic skills and identifying both struggles and competencies.** The curriculum in first and second grades tends to focus on reading instruction and basic math skills. Identifying students who are struggling with these basic skills is incredibly important to the students' later success in school. Be sure to notice the competencies in the same students so as to avoid early labeling. For every struggle, identify an area of competency.

- **Get early help to support reading.** For students struggling to "break the code" of reading, intensive instruction and emphasis on phonemic awareness will be critical. Don't delay giving or encouraging extra help and practice for students struggling with reading. Be mindful of not labeling the student.

- **Behavior issues may be learning or perception issues.** Although it will be necessary to rule out any "mechanical" issues such as sight or hearing problems, teachers should understand that a significant number of children with disruptive classroom behaviors may have speech and language disorders that have gone undetected. Experts have indicated that 96 percent of students diagnosed with a learning disability have at least one type of speech or language problem. Look for root causes before labeling a child as "bad."

- **Alter content to meet student needs.** Differentiating instruction in the early grades consists of altering content, process, products, and the learning environment based on students' readiness, interest, or learning profile. This means that for each student, teachers need to consider modifications in these areas.

Content
- Offering reading materials on multiple levels
- Putting key text materials on tape
- Using spelling and vocabulary assignments at various levels to match a student's individual needs
- Using small groups to deliver more intensive instruction to those who need it
- Presenting ideas orally and visually
- Using reading buddies, both at school and at home

Process
- Using tiered skills, with different levels of assistance, complexity, or challenge, making them available to all students as they are ready for them
- Providing centers focusing on interests and giving students the ability to explore subjects at greater depth

List 7.2. (continued)

- Developing learning contracts or personal agendas to help students complete common work and any additional or supplemental work specific to their own learning and needs
- Providing manipulatives (such as magnetic poetry for language, counters for math) to help support visual and kinesthetic learners
- Allowing flexible time to complete assignments, as is practical to complete tasks

Product

- Giving students the option of what sort of assignment needs to be completed to demonstrate knowledge and mastery of subject matter (such as a poster, diorama, play, written assignment, oral presentation, PowerPoint, wiki, webpage, or letter)
- Providing rubrics indicating what portions of the assignment must be completed and included to give students and teachers guidance as to what needs to be shown, while leaving the method of demonstration open to choice

Learning environment

- Making sure there are places where students can collaborate and work together, along with places where students can work quietly and independently
- Offering clear rubrics and guidelines as to how the work environments are to be used and what's expected of each student, including routines that enable students to transition quickly from individual to group work and back again
- Offering students a procedure for getting help from sources other than just the teacher—including other students—as well as resource material
- Being sensitive to the students who need to move around more while they learn and others who need to remain still to concentrate

Upper Elementary School

- **Frequent assessment of understanding.** While presenting a lesson, a simple "thumbs up, thumbs down" understanding check can help head off problems before they start, and indicate which students are ready to move on and which ones may need more help.
- **Consider using online quizzes and games that double as assessments,** such as those available on Quia, that both engage students and assist teachers in monitoring understanding and learning with rapid feedback. Remember, frequent assessment of understanding is not just testing—it's diagnosing issues and determining where children need more support.
- **Make assignments real.** Children learn best while doing activities and applying what they learn into other projects. Consider reinforcing math and measuring skills by assigning a poster or diorama; having students use counting and math skills while helping parents put away dishes or grocery shop; drafting letters to grandparents, politicians, and TV and movie stars and sending them. By using classroom skills in real life, students will see the importance of classroom learning in context.
- **Use concept maps to keep kids on track.** Make sure students know where the lessons are leading, have a sense of the big picture, and understand why the lessons are important.

List 7.2. (continued)

- **Teach brainstorming and how to share ideas.** Programs such as Kidspiration provide great examples of mind maps of problems that help students learn to visualize how an idea takes shape. Using group brainstorming, sharing, and then modeling the sorting and ordering of ideas will help students learn how to use this process when working in groups.
- **Use more open-ended questions.** Nonleading questions (ones that don't ask the student to guess what the teacher is thinking) are a way to give all levels of learners an opportunity to respond and get the "right answer."

Further Reading

Goldstein, S., and Brooks, R. (2007). *Understanding and managing children's classroom behavior: Creating sustainable, resilient classrooms.* (2nd ed.) Hoboken, NJ: Wiley.

Learning Disabilities Association of America. (1999). Speech and language milestone chart. LD Online. http://www.ldonline.org/article/6313.

National Institute on Deafness and Other Communication Disorders. http://www.nidcd.nih.gov/health /voice/speechandlanguage.html.

Quia Online Assessment Tool. http://www.quia.com. Retrieved January 2011.

Tomlinson, C. A. (2001). Differentiation of instruction in the elementary grades. *ERIC Digest.* Champaign, IL: ERIC Clearinghouse on Elementary and Early Childhood Education. (ERIC Document Reproduction Service No. EDO–PS–00–7). http://ceep.crc.uiuc.edu/eecearchive/digests/2000/tomlin00.pdf. Retrieved March 2011.

Language milestones in school-aged children is addressed in the book's bonus Web material.

List 7.3. Middle School

The middle school years (grades 6–8) are the most vulnerable years for students as they navigate adolescence. Most students who drop out of school end up making the decision as early as the sixth grade and then actually take action in the transition from eighth grade to high school. This is an especially important time to prevent students from falling through the cracks. The differentiated approach seeks to reach middle school–aged students on an individual basis. It can help keep students engaged and invested in their own learning. If any time is critical to employ differentiated strategies in the classroom, it is at the middle school level. This list guides differentiation in the middle school years.

- **Approach middle school students as in transition, not in high school prep.** Many teachers believe that middle school is a time to push more homework and develop more difficult and an increased amount of traditional testing to "prepare the students for the rigors of high school." These attitudes are not helpful. Students in the middle grades need to develop confidence and feel a sense of connection to school. Keep the environment positive, supportive, and less punitive as much as possible.
- **Even successful students can fail.** Students who have been successful up until middle school may experience difficulty in grades six through eight. As they go through developmental changes, physically and mentally, many students cannot rely on past strategies to get them through and they can hit a wall. All students will benefit from scaffolding techniques rather than penalties to continue to be successful as the subject areas and requirements get more difficult.
- **Social growth and maturation is important, too.** Making friends and being social are essential to middle school students as they struggle to fit in. Assignments involving group work should be prepared with social connections in mind. Teachers should be careful to group less social students with those who will encourage rather than criticize their lack of social skills.
- **Manage behavior without humiliation.** Many students will act out in front of peers at this age to receive attention. Rather than chastise these students, teachers can redirect this energy. To the student who seeks attention in inappropriate ways, say, "Joey, your strength in humor is appreciated but now I need you to pay attention and answer appropriately." In this way the student is put on alert and given guidance without being humiliated.
- **Help students find their place with group work.** In an effort to fit socially, accelerated students in the middle grades may purposely slow down their achievement so as not to stand out. When this happens, one strategy is to put achievers in working groups together to serve as role models for one another.
- **Make work meaningful.** Students in middle school are transitioning from concrete to more abstract ways of thinking. As a result, middle school students respond well to lessons that are connected to them personally. Give students choices about topics to study, such as a choice between reading a book about baseball and an adventure story.
- **Scaffold good study and academic skills.** Middle school students typically struggle with organization and staying on schedule. Providing learning contracts and

List 7.3. (continued)

chunking assignments will help them stay on track and allow monitoring for understanding.

- **Acknowledge student interest in the larger world.** Students in grades 6–8 are particularly interested in pop culture. Assignments that incorporate contemporary music and references to films and styles will spike their interest. As middle school students become more like young adults, assignments providing interest "hooks" will help them better contextualize what is being taught.

- **Work with the pack mentality.** Middle school students want to be like everyone else, making differentiating trickier at this level than at any other level. Be careful to give all students explanations for why they are being asked to do things differently. Make sure students know that everyone is treated as an individual, and be mindful of causing anyone to stand out as different.

- **Provide varied activities that allow students to investigate and explore to keep their interest.** Middle school students are active. Teachers who move from direct instruction methods to facilitating will find they are able to keep student interest.

- **Acknowledge the need for autonomy.** Students in middle school are moving from dependence into more independence. However, they cannot be expected to make this leap all at once. The level of responsibility students are able to accept will vary. When providing independent projects and assignments, also give a greater deal of structure and support. Develop levels of independence into assignments. For example, in an English class, some students may write persuasive essays while others work on introductions and conclusions.

- **Help students set and reach new goals.** Goal setting is an important part of the middle school experience. As classes move to become more student centered, balance student interest with clear goal setting. For example, allow students to choose between making a time line and performing a skit in small groups, and then challenge each individual in the group to attain an individual goal that is a stretch for them.

- **Don't keep differentiated strategies a secret.** Explain reasons for the assignments and tasks asked of students. Students feel engaged and empowered when they are spoken to like responsible individuals.

- **Don't radically change the classroom overnight.** Middle school students are in the midst of great change, and teachers who jump into the deep end of differentiated instruction will confuse themselves and their students. Start out slowly. Commit to one or two strategies a week.

- **Work across disciplines to create interdisciplinary projects.** Middle school students are ready to begin to see connections across subject areas. Build on this awareness by working with other grade-level teachers to create cooperative units. Point out the connections to students. They will appreciate the authenticity.

List 7.4. High School

High school is probably the most difficult level to get teachers to commit to differentiated instruction. For too many teachers, the notion that they have to "prepare students for college" by drilling, testing, and assigning long research papers is too embedded to evoke the need to change to accommodate students. High school, however, is a very important time to differentiate because when teens are engaged in learning, they have a better chance of discovering the unique paths to their futures. This list shows why teachers should seriously consider differentiating in the high school classroom.

- **Lack of differentiation leads to cheating.** When grades and achievement are stressed over interests and learning, students report that cheating is often the only to way get through classes they find boring or challenging.
- **Stay connected to youth culture.** Without trying too hard, teachers can make a point to know what is going on in the world of teen culture. Having general knowledge of the music they listen to, the shows they watch, and the games they play will build connection. Teachers can find out this information by casual conversations with students.
- **Consider engaging with students online.** Some teachers may also choose to engage in informal conversations with students through social networks. This can be a great way to build relationships with students, but these conversations should be kept professional and educational, not too personal. (For more guidance, see Section Fourteen: New Media Strategies that Naturally Differentiate Instruction.)
- **Make lessons meaningful and connected.** Unless coursework in high school is authentic, students see it as meaningless busywork that they complete only to get by, but not for the sake of learning.
- **Help students find a way out of difficulty.** Students who fall behind see no way of getting back on track. These are the ones who consider dropping out. Differentiation prevents students from falling too far behind because it emphasizes checking for understanding along the way, focusing on mastery, and building confidence.
- **Manage competition.** Class ranking, grade point averages, and college entrance exams deplete students' level of self-confidence. Some students may feel that unless they are the best, they have little to look forward to after high school. Ease this pressure by focusing on student interests, strengths, and learning for the sake of learning. Help students see that there are many pathways to success and many possibilities for their future.
- **Help students become self-advocates.** Students in high school are becoming grounded in a sense of who they are. They will need to be self-advocates in the future for their learning and to achieve their goals in life. They often may not realize they are in trouble, or where to go for help, or are simply afraid to ask and stand out. If a student is struggling but is not asking for help, proactively offer help or suggestions, and make sure he or she knows where to go for additional support.

List 7.4. (continued)

- **Make school more interesting than alternatives.** Keeping high school students engaged in learning is difficult at this age, as they grow bored and suspicious that school has nothing to offer them other than a pass to the next level. Use differentiated instruction methods to help students see the utility and meaning in lessons and show your interest in them and their future prospects. If students are more connected to school and the adults in their life, they are more likely to be invested in their education.

- **Assign meaningful and contextual assignments.** This is critical. When working with high school students, assign meaningful work or they will disengage. Do not assign busywork. Simply piling on large amounts of homework does not prepare students for college. Students are motivated to work long and hard on things they feel interested in and challenged by.

- **Make it applicable and connected.** High school is the perfect time to look at ways to integrate traditional subject matter. Students need to start seeing connections between school and the world beyond. When teachers make the curriculum relevant by connecting classroom learning to real-world experience, students have a better connection to the learning. The more connections teachers can make between subjects, or between lessons and real-world examples, the more enthusiasm they are likely to see from students.

Section Eight

Strategies for Differentiating Language Arts

The most important task a classroom teacher faces is the responsibility to ensure that all children are taught to read and write successfully and fluently. This responsibility is increasingly challenging as teachers encounter a wide range of student abilities. New federal mandates require that all children know how to read and comprehend "grade-level text," and states are pushing increasingly for promotion based on mastery of the appropriate level. This requirement cannot be accomplished by simply providing students with a common set of reading materials and lessons (McGill-Franzen, Zmach, Solic, & Zeig, 2006; Taylor, Peterson, Pearson, & Rodriguez, 2002). The most successful teachers use a combination of whole-group, small-group, and individualized instruction to teach reading and writing to students in the K–12 environment. Research also shows that fluency is increased when a teacher is sensitive to individual student needs; that is, the teacher differentiates instruction based on the needs of the children (Pressley et al., 2001; Taylor et al., 2002). This section offers lists that demonstrate ways that reading instruction can be differentiated. The lists are not comprehensive, but do provide examples of the most common methods that have proven successful.

List 8.1. What Exemplary Reading Teachers Do to Differentiate Reading Instruction

Numerous studies have been conducted on what makes an exemplary reading teacher. One such study, the CIERA School Change Classroom Observation Scheme (Taylor & Pearson, 2000), documented the literacy events that occurred during scheduled observations of teachers whose students demonstrated reading improvement using methods of differentiated instruction (DI). Interviews with these teachers highlighted the following characteristics needed for success as a DI reading teacher. Teachers with demonstrated reading improvement for all students do the following:

- Consistently and continually read books and articles on teaching reading.

- Remain actively involved in ongoing professional development opportunities such as workshops, lectures, and conferences.

- Collaborate with other teachers through professional organizations such as the National Council of Teachers of English and the International Reading Association.

- Participate in online forums about reading strategies.

- Form study groups with other teachers to discuss new strategies and books on teaching reading.

- Engage in informal discussion with other teachers about student successes and strategies.

- Focus on the process of reading over mastery of isolated sets of skills.

- Trust student interest as a driving factor in motivation for developing reading skills.

- Understand that there is not a one-size-fits-all reading remedy but that using a variety of approaches when integrated into an overall plan is most successful.

- Don't expect all readers to achieve the same understanding at the same time. They see the need for each student to advance to their individual "next level" no matter where they begin rather than the whole class needing to advance to the same reading level at the same time.

- Consistently diagnose each reader's level of fluency and strategize how to push all students to the next level by using individual interests.

List 8.2. Strategies to Improve Reading

Reading is a key skill to academic and work success, and students who struggle to develop these skills are at a disadvantage, compounding each year as they progress through school. Differentiating instruction starts with making sure students are able to take in material at their own appropriate level as they continue to improve at core reading skills. This list offers some strategies to help students improve at reading at every level.

- **Model fluent reading.** Read aloud to students. This is one of the most successful ways to help students understand reading. Read to them often and from a variety of genres, including poetry, prose, and nonfiction.

- **Practice by oral repetition.** Read a section from a story aloud to students while students read along on their own copy of the reading. Then have the class read the passage aloud as a group.

- **Identify a student's current reading level by using the five-finger rule.** Teach students the five-finger rule to help them select appropriate books for their reading level. If a student reads the first page or two of a book and finds more than five words they do not know, the book is probably too advanced and they should select something that instead has only two or three words they don't know, as an approximate gauge of instructional level.

- **Determine the reading level of the books assigned.** The easiest way to find the reading level of a children's book is look on the back cover. Many books include the reading level in various forms. Some books might say RL3 for reading level 3, or RL:5.9 for reading level 5.9. Less specific designations might say 007–009 for ages 7 to 9, or 0812 for ages 8 to 12. If in doubt, call the publisher.

- **Vary instructional methods.** Alternate among direct explanation, explicit modeling, invitations to participate, clarification, verification, and telling.

- **Create a literate environment.** Be sure there is an extensive variety of print materials in the classroom. This includes posting examples of student work, and allowing time for independent reading in addition to modeling reading.

- **Teach reading strategies in a whole-group setting.** Even young learners can benefit from metacognitively understanding what they are being asked to do. Model reading strategies with a big book, poster, or overhead transparency so that all students can attend to the text simultaneously. For example, using a book on how the tides work, hold the book up and ask students to identify the main point on each page. Use your assessment of students' understanding to create group assignments for the next day by identifying those students needing additional instruction and those ready to move on to material with more depth.

List 8.2. (continued)

- **Balance phonics instruction with authentic reading and writing approaches.** One size does not fit all. The National Council of Teachers of English recommends young readers learn formal phonics instruction, as well as being introduced to as many real literary texts (story books, poetry, and nonfiction) as possible so students can make the transition from knowledge of language to understanding meaning.

- **Use KWL charts,** in which students indicate what they *know,* what they *want* to know more about, and what they have *learned* about a topic. These charts are useful in helping students select appropriate reading material.

- **Try using KUDOs**—what the students need to *know, understand,* and be able to *do* after a lesson or unit—to form the backbone of your instructional strategy. Modifications to instruction will be easier if you keep this formula in mind.

- **Use audiobooks and podcasts.** Recent changes in the Americans with Disabilities Act requires that all new textbooks be available in alternative formats, including audio. If the material in the text or novel is above the student's own reading level, consider having them listen to the book rather than read it on their own. Free audiobooks and podcasts appropriate for children are also available online. (A list of online resources is available in the book's bonus Web material.)

- **Use students' preferences to help reinforce reading skills.** Use interest inventories (see List 2.3) and students' preferences to help students choose books that are engaging. Capturing students' interest is key to encouraging them to read more frequently.

- **Encourage students to expand their horizons.** With older students, genre preferences can become a safety blanket. Requiring students to make a selection from a variety of genres for independent reading will encourage them to step outside their comfort zone.

List 8.3. Tips for Differentiating Small-Group Reading Instruction

Small-group instruction is necessary to ensure that all the needs are being met of different levels of readers in the classroom. Differentiating small groups is no easy task. Each group activity must be designed according to student reading readiness, as well as interest with an eye toward pushing all students beyond their current comfort level without overchallenging them. This list provides a few examples of how to effectively differentiate reading instruction in small groups.

- **Differentiate reading groups based on** using different materials, time spent with each group, postreading assignments, and how objectives will be completed.
- **Create small groups of between four and five students** and assign each group a different task that focuses on a different reading strategy. For example, have one group focus on word recognition and vocabulary building by using a basal activity. Have another group focused on comprehension by using a worksheet that corresponds with authentic literature. Ensure that all students participate in both activities.
- **Coach from the side.** As students work in groups, provide coaching and cueing to students who need it. Walk around the groups observing who is on task and who may need help.
- **Exercise flexibility** in asking students to move from one group to another based on their needs. Let them know this may happen before class begins.
- **Acting as coach,** invite students within groups to explain what they are doing. Have the other students stop and listen while one explains.
- **Directly model** how to accomplish a task when students seem to be struggling. Sit beside the student and provide brief direct instruction before moving on.
- **Validate students** when they are performing the tasks as instructed. Be specific. For example, say, "You are understanding the main point there, Rob. Keep at it."
- **Alternate grouping between skill mastery and interest level.** Reading interest groups are as effective as skill ability in getting students to feel positive and confident about reading.
- **Plan small-group interaction to extend throughout various times during the week.** Think of the class by the week rather than each session. Plan to meet with each group for approximately twenty to thirty minutes in one week. This allows each student to receive individualized help in the area he or she needs it at least once a week.
- **Balance the genre of texts used by groups** so each student has access to several genres throughout the year. Groups can be reading a different book and accomplishing the same objectives.
- **Create whole-group questions** and write them so all students have access to them. Monitor individual group responses through journals or walk-arounds.
- **Use walk-around conversations as a means for assessment** and checking for understanding. Think of how to modify group members and objectives for the next class according to the feedback received on the walk-around.

List 8.4. Assigned Reading: Dealing with Low Interest

Students' preference cannot always rule the day in education, and we have all faced books that have been difficult to read not because they are difficult to decode or read fluently but because they have totally failed to capture our attention or interest. This chart suggests ways to make even the most deathly prose a bit more acceptable to students.

Problem	Possible Differentiated Instruction Solution
A book is above a student's readiness or instructional level	Try a book with similar material at a slightly easier reading level. Use an audio version of the same book. Have other students help read the material out loud.
The book seems to have no personal resonance for the student.	Place the book in context and why you think it is important. Does it explain a point and place in time? Are the relationships between the characters important? Helping the child see the deeper meaning or significance to the story may make it easier to understand and grasp.
The concepts in the book do not register with the student.	Try to explain the relevant concepts and contextualize the book. Have class discussions as to why the book is interesting and important. (If no one has a good idea, is there another book you can use to achieve the same end point?)
The child can't see the point or reason for the assignment.	Tell the student why you have given the assignment and what you hope she gets out of it. Is it to practice reading or analysis of text? Is it to show others what they know and how they feel about the material? Is it to share different people's viewpoint after reading the same material, and show how everyone can see the same thing in a different light?
	If you cannot come up with a good reason for why the assignment is important and meaningful, you may need to rethink the assignment.
The material is of low interest.	Is there some higher interest material that can equally substitute and reach the same curricular end points? Why is this material critical to your lesson plan?
Student complains he hates the book.	Ask the student to give you a detailed report (in writing) about what he or she hates about the book, with relevant examples. The student learns how to give you a reasoned and researched argument and to practice persuasive writing skills, and you get to hear exactly why the student dislikes the assignment.
	This also provides you with much needed diagnostic information about what the student finds difficult and how you may need to adjust the assignments accordingly.

List 8.4. (continued)

If there's not a good alternative to meet the curriculum objectives, after trying backward design or other differentiation strategies, consider looking at the possible reasons the student is "getting in his or her own way," including

- Lack of understanding
- Lack of context
- Fear of failure
- Fear of ridicule from peers
- Frustration
- Underlying learning disability or learning disorder

Notes:

List 8.5. Differentiated Writing Assignments and Strategies

Writing assignments ask students to demonstrate what they know, understand, and even feel in a different form of language than oral speech. With national assessments showing that on average only 25 percent of students write proficiently at grade level, struggling with writing is far from uncommon, and it is an area where differentiating instruction (DI) can be of significant help. Looking to the root of common problems with writing will often help guide the DI method that suits the lesson. This list discusses writing assignments and strategies to help differentiate them in the classroom.

- **Start the school year with open assignments.** Focus writing assignments at the beginning of the school year on making a point rather than saying it correctly. Have many assignments that allow students to write without being graded.

- **Use the writing process.** Research from the National Council of Teachers of English demonstrates that the single best way to improve writing and help students find their writing voice is to use the method known as *process writing*. Steps in the process are
  - Brainstorming ideas
  - Generating a first draft
  - Editing
  - Revision of draft
  - Proofreading

- **Use peer editors.** Guide students to peer review using a review guide that asks questions such as "What is the main point of the writing?" "Name two examples." "What is the conclusion?" Give students points or grades for their peer edits.

- **Keep a box with folders of worksheets** such as "combining sentences" or "creating effective conclusions" or "comma usage." At the end of a writing assignment, refer the student to the folder to complete the worksheet that refers to the student's specific writing issue. Students can thus work on the things they need to and not become bored while sitting through whole-class instruction.

- **Assign I-search papers.** Instead of a research paper, begin with an I-search paper in which students are allowed to write in the first person. Look up I-search on the Internet, or see our website, www.differentiatedinstruction.co, for ideas.

- **Give content a higher grade than mechanics.** Remember writing and editing are two different strengths. Generating and prioritizing ideas form one skill, and transcribing them in a logical format is a different skill: it requires a reflective and ongoing process of shaping and crafting the work afterwards. Getting the content and concepts down

List 8.5. (continued)

should receive more emphasis in grading and assessment than mechanics, which take more time for students to develop.

- **Use "real life" writing when possible.** Writing assignments will be more meaningful if they have a purpose and goal. The tried-and-true letters to service members, relatives, and political figures are great examples of how even young students' writing can be meaningful in some way. For older students, publishing writing in a quarterly collection or classroom newsletter, or online on a blog or wiki, will also give them a chance to display their work outside the traditional "post on a bulletin board" method, and will allow even more people to interact with their work.

- **Add sustained silent writing into the curriculum.** Many language arts classrooms devote time to sustained silent reading activities, but consider adding sustained silent writing into the mix to help students build fluency when writing for an uninterrupted period of time. See *A Non-workbook, Non-textbook Approach to Teaching Language Arts* (Charnock, 2005). Also see the list of sustained silent writing prompts and resources in this book's bonus Web material.

- **Add a classroom blog.** A blog offers students the opportunity to publish short written posts, and allows other students to comment on the posts. Blogs can be set up to allow individual, group, or whole-class posting and participation. Each post or comment gives a student another opportunity to practice writing skills.

- **Add a classroom wiki.** A wiki may be used as an opportunity for students to share their written work and even correct the work of others. Like blogs, wikis can be used for individual, group, or whole-classroom participation. By being able to track changes, teachers can monitor how a student is altering and editing documents, which is especially useful when teaching students how to revise and critique their work.

- **See Section Fourteen on the uses of Twitter and Facebook** for recommended strategies for writing and reading.

- **Write often and provide topic choice.** The more students write, the better their writing becomes. Have students write often and don't grade every piece of writing. Provide many opportunities for topic and genre selection.

- **Avoid assigning length of papers.** When students ask "How long?" reply "Long enough to make an important point." Focus on content, not length.

List 8.5. (continued)

- **Understand which aspects of writing the assignment requires.** Are you asking students to transcribe facts out of a text? To give you an opinion, predictions, or interpretation of what they've read? Or apply the knowledge in a new situation? Asking students for opinion, interpretation, or application of knowledge requires higher-order thinking skills, as opposed to repeating back facts, and may require more time for some students to complete. Allow students choice in their writing assignments.

- **Give students meaningful feedback and a to-do list.** Some students rarely review a paper once it's handed in, and some even get lost in the revision process, settling for good enough. Make critique and feedback on writing more meaningful by engaging students in questions about their topic rather than simply pointing out their errors. Create a to-do list of things to improve or work on for the current *and* future assignments.

- **Offer rubrics and examples.** It can often take students a long time to understand what a teacher considers an A or a B or even a D paper. Especially for longer assignments, providing examples of past student work helps students understand what you are looking for rather than making them guess.

- **Provide an audience.** Writing can be a solitary act, a private communication between a teacher and student, or for public consumption. Help students develop a sense of audience by varying who will read their work, and offer opportunities for students to publish their work online, as well as in print, so that it can be shared with a wider audience outside the classroom.

List 8.6. Examples of Exciting Differentiated Language Arts Assignments

This list gives examples of how differentiated instruction can work in the classroom and shares ideas of how to integrate different activities to help students engage and perform well at their level.

- **Digital story telling** is the practice of using computer-based tools to tell stories. As with traditional storytelling, most digital stories focus on a specific topic and contain a particular point of view. However, as the name implies, digital stories usually contain some mixture of computer-based images, text, recorded audio narration, video clips, and/or music. Digital stories can vary in length, but most of the stories used in education typically last between two and ten minutes. Refer to websites for more information. Search the following phrases:
  - Integrating Digital Storytelling in your classroom.
  - Digital Storytelling finds its place in the classroom.
  - Digital storytelling resources
- **The Write Site** is a multimedia language arts curriculum that makes the process of telling a story fun. Students take on the role of journalists—generating leads, gathering facts, and writing stories—using the tools and techniques of real-life journalists. The Write Site is designed for middle school students. The Write Site's instructional activities will improve students' skills while helping teachers integrate technology into their classrooms.
- **Cinderella Around the World** is an online global reading project where students from all over the world read different versions of *Cinderella* and share ideas, activities, and impressions. Lots of lesson plans and standards are met around this project. Search "Cinderella Around the World".
- **One Million Monkeys Typing** is an online collaborative writing project where students can choose stories to which they make contributions.
- **Shakespeare Group Activity.** In groups, examine the following issues and explain how they are present in any one of Shakespeare's plays. Are they important in the life of a modern teenager? One person in each group should serve as the recorder: relationship with parents, fighting with friends, true love, jealousy, low self-esteem. Have students discuss, or create a poster depicting the difference between the play and today's youth, or write and act out a play.
- **EPals Book Club** is an online book club where students can share conversation about books with others around the world. This is excellent for when students self select books and need other students to converse about them.
- **Reader's Theater** is a source of prewritten scripts that teachers can access for readers in grades 3 through 5 at Education World. Search "Reader's Theater". Scripts come with questions.

List 8.7. Tips for Differentiating Instruction for English Language Learners

English language learners (ELLs) have a special place in the literature and writing class. This list gives you suggestions for allowing nonnative speakers the opportunity to master the content as they are learning English.

- **ELLs often understand the content but are unable to express themselves confidently** in speaking or writing. Try to understand the ideas ELLs attempt to express in class. Ultimately, understanding the content is more important than saying or writing it correctly.

- **Be clear about which objectives the student is mastering.** If the objective of an essay is to persuade, give most of the credit for mastering that objective and far fewer points for usage of correct English.

- **Understand that teachers can be intimidating.** Many ELLs are culturally sensitive to authority figures such as teachers. They are taught to avoid eye contact, to only speak when spoken to, and other such cultural norms. ELLs should not be penalized for hesitant participation.

- **Help ELLs be prepared in advance.** Don't call on ELLs out of the blue to read in class or answer questions that they are not prepared to answer. This will only cause them to feel anxious. Help ELLs participate successfully by providing them the questions in advance. Alert them that they will be called on. For example, say, "Ani, I am going to call on you after Mitch. I'll ask you about Josephine's character." Or, if possible, let the ELLs know a day in advance that they will be called on.

- **Use Eva Easton's' online Authentic American Pronunciation website.** Students can use this resource independently to listen to all kinds of pronunciations. There are also lesson plans here. Do a search for Eva Easton.

- **Praise ELLs for their ability to listen and pay attention.** Many ELLs are very attentive in class, trying to get everything right.

- **Offer ELLs choices** of literature that has to do with their native background. This may help them identify with the material better and feel less isolated and different. A good reference to find multicultural books is the Multicultural Book Review homepage.

- **Don't grade papers solely on grammar and spelling.** This should be the smallest percentage of the total grade for all students. Allow ELLs to use dictionaries and translations tools when taking assessments.

- **Provide ELLs with reading guides** that list vocabulary in the reading and provide short summaries of the important points.

List 8.8. Tips for Differentiating Writing Assignments

Writing can be an ongoing process that can seem to never end, with revisions and corrections leading many students to abandon the writing process with a "good enough" attitude, but never feeling successful. In order to help students feel more successful with writing and encourage them to develop good written expression skills, teachers and students should understand the stages of the writing process well, and also the common places where even good writers can get "stuck."

This list demystifies the writing process and areas where students often get stuck. By understanding the cause and underlying challenges a student may be facing in mastering any piece of written work, teachers and students will be able to choose tools and develop strategies to make almost any writing assignment more manageable and enjoyable—at any level.

Common Areas Where Students Can Get "Hung Up" with Writing

- Problems generating ideas
- Difficulty translating these ideas into semantics, words, paragraphs, and so forth
- Difficulty with transcribing these ideas onto the page

Students can develop problems in written expression based on *one or more* of the above production points. It's important to help students identify the sources of their struggle to help them improve and develop fluency in writing and the writing process.

Students with Idea-Generation Problems Are Frequently . . .

- Dissatisfied with their own ideas, "never good enough"
- Stymied by the blank page
- Look for guidance or ask peers for ideas
- Avoid writing tasks such as journaling

Strategies for Generating Ideas

- **Use prompts or starts.** Students may get paralyzed looking at a blank page and never seem to find an idea that seems "good enough." Providing students with prompts and choices among different prompts enables students to choose an appropriate place to begin, thus avoiding writer's block.
- **Teach students brainstorming.** Help students learn to brainstorm different ideas and write them down in order to generate their own list of prompts and starts for writing. Tools and programs such as Kidspiration, Mindmaps, Evernote, and others help students develop and track their ideas, as well as save their ideas for subsequent projects.
- **Use photographs, movies, or random objects** to generate creative-writing topics.
- **Don't overemphasize the five-paragraph essay.** Focus on content and then form, not the other way around.

List 8.8. (continued)

Students with Transcription Problems Frequently . . .

- Have poor or illegible handwriting
- Have idiosyncratic letter formation
- Have idiosyncratic ways of holding writing implements
- Sit at odd angles or fidget when writing
- May have poor small motor skills across the board
- Have immature-looking drawing and art projects
- Avoid drawing and art projects
- Avoid writing whenever possible

Be aware that students with poor handwriting are subject to *reader-writer* effects:

- Readers quickly lose patience when they cannot read what has been written.
- The perceived quality of the ideas expressed is discounted when the writing is less easily read.
- When more cognitive resources are required for the actual physical act of writing, less time is spent on the critical areas of planning, monitoring, evaluating, and revising.
- When students lack fluency in their handwriting skills, their brains may move faster than their hand, causing them to lose ideas along the way, as they tend to write on a "plan as you go" basis. This has later significant impact on a student's ability to take useful notes while listening to a lecture, taking timed tests, and performing other academic skills introduced in middle and high school.
- When students struggle with the act of handwriting, they may become "minimalists," avoiding writing tasks or simply doing the minimum required. This can cause students to seem to fail to progress as expected in their writing fluency and sophistication as they progress grade to grade.

Strategies for Transcription Problems

- **Handwriting is important.** Penmanship and handwriting instruction are not always integrated into the curriculum, and poor handwriting skills plague many students throughout their schooling and beyond. Poor penmanship and poor small motor coordination may cause writing to be a physically painful and slow process for many students, causing significant problems with developing fluency.
- **Balance handwriting and keyboarding tasks with writing assignments.** Research has shown that while composition by handwriting versus keyboarding or typing uses different areas of the brain, the use of keyboards has a significant effect in improving the length and quality of text produced by struggling writers (MacArthur, Graham, & Fitzgerald, 2006, p. 250).
- **Look at the physical environment.** The days of the slanted desk are gone, but proper ergonomics—desk height, chair height, angle of the surface, and the way a child holds a writing implement—all affect the quality and quantity of students' written output. Make sure the child is physically comfortable when asked to write and is not writing at chin level.

List 8.8. (continued)

- **Teach students keyboarding skills.** Computers are a given, and all students benefit from developing good keyboarding skills as early as possible. Use common typing programs, such as Mavis Beacon or Spongebob SquarePants, and make time for students to practice their typing in classroom centers or stations to help them gradually master keyboarding skills. Don't penalize students who develop their own typing method.
- **Use speech-to-text programs.** For students who have little difficulty with oral language skills but significant written language skills, consider using programs that translate spoken word into text, like Dragon Naturally Speaking. These programs are available for almost all computer platforms, including smartphones and iPads, and may be a significant resource especially for younger students, who are still learning sufficient handwriting and keyboarding skills.

Students with Translation Problems Frequently ...

- Have handwriting issues, and their writing or typing skills cannot keep up with the speed of their ideas when writing
- Struggle with prioritizing ideas
- Struggle with organizing ideas
- Struggle with sequence
- Struggle carrying over learned grammar, parts of speech, or spelling skills into writing assignments

Translation problems benefit from strategies for transcription and idea-generation difficulties, as well as a few more specific strategies mentioned next that address the issues some students may have with working memory capacity and cognitive tempo.

Strategies for Translation Problems

- **Use outline strategies cautiously.** Students who have problems with keeping their thoughts organized and sequenced benefit from outlining their ideas in advance of writing. Although most students are comfortable composing on the fly, students with transcription problems will benefit from using outlining to order their ideas in advance of writing. Outlines can also hamper writers. Teachers who enforce rigid outline models end up compromising on the quality of student writing.
- **Use memory prompts and mnemonics.** Students who struggle with order and remembering ideas may benefit from learning to use mnemonics and other memory-oriented strategies to keep formulas, procedures, and structures in mind.
  - *Example:* When writing a persuasive essay, students can use STOP and DARE as mnemonics for the procedure they should follow. STOP: Suspend judgment, Take a side, Organize ideas, and Plan as you write; followed by DARE: Develop a topic sentence, Add supporting ideas, Reject the argument from the other side, and End with a conclusion.
  - *Elementary example:* Visualizing and Verbalizing, part of Linda Mood-Bell's language comprehension program (http://www.lindamoodbell.com), can help students see, discuss, and then write in more detail about the subject matter at hand.
- **Rule in or rule out ADHD.** Some children with sluggish cognitive tempo problems or fluctuating cognitive tempo issues may also have attention issues or ADHD.

Section Nine

Strategies for Differentiating Math

Differentiating math instruction allows students to master the course objectives according to their readiness, interests, and learning styles. Differentiation in the math curriculum is a means for teachers to adjust their lesson plans and assessments to accommodate the various levels of student ability in the classroom, thus allowing support to the student who is challenged by traditional math instruction and affording advancement opportunity for the student with an affinity toward the subject. One of the key reasons students struggle with math is that they cannot see how its application is relevant. The lists in this section provide strategies to help differentiate math instruction and assessment and provide relevancy needed for student success.

List 9.1. Using Reading and Writing to Differentiate Math Instruction

Research has proven that students are more successful at math when they apply language skills such as reading, writing, speaking, and listening to their development of mathematical concepts. The use of language, specifically through writing, has become a math standard in some states. Math teachers are often reluctant to integrate these concepts into their classrooms because they don't fully appreciate the benefits to students. This list offers general ideas for differentiating instruction in math with language skills, as well as how both reading and writing can help students better understand and master the math curriculum.

- **Use writing to help build understanding.** Communicating about mathematical ideas is a way for students to articulate, clarify, organize, and consolidate their thinking, which can build deeper understanding and build logical and mathematical reasoning.
- **Use writing to demonstrate fluency and mastery of concepts.** When students write about math, it's easier to see how they are thinking about the steps in problems and where they may have misunderstandings.
- **Encourage students to discuss the problems they are working on.** Discussion in math class helps students explore and think about mathematical ideas, thus increasing their level of comfort and fluency with math. Sometimes students are able to talk their way through problems and more easily recognize where they are missing a step or a connection.
- **Expose students to reading and writing about numbers and numerical literacy.** There are numerous articles and resources available highlighting the importance of being numerically literate, and how the misunderstanding of numerical concepts can skew public opinion and debate. Consider making some of these books, or sections from them, part of a math journaling project.
- **Have students read about real-life applications of numbers.** The BBC has a series of free podcasts, called *More or Less*, discussing the numbers in the news, how to make sense of the statistics, and how to determine whether they are reliable. These entertaining shows help highlight the importance of math, and are a great example for students on how to think critically about math. Use podcasts and other media to help students better understand math, as well as report on what they have learned from these real-life-based resources.
- **Use journaling as a means of reflection.** Journaling about math provides opportunities for reflection on how students problem solve. Teachers can assess student attitudes about math from their writings about thoughts and feelings on classes, assignments, projects, and assessments. These attitudes are important in creating projects and assessments.
- **Use journals to explore real-life applications of math.** Math journals encourage the process of discovery as students learn to create their own math problems. It also allows them to think and explore real-world problems.

Example: Mr. L has each of his middle school students keep a math journal. Once a week, he gives them a news article about a math concept, and asks them to "find the

List 9.1. (continued)

math" and comment on what they think about what the math means. In the fall, this often involves articles about the electoral college system and how representatives are calculated; other times in the year it may deal with finance, business issues, or statistics. Over time, students have begun to bring articles to his attention, and are beginning to look at the facts and figures presented with a more critical eye than earlier in the year.

- **Assign journals as a way to reach students via different learning styles.** Journals support differentiated instruction by focusing on multiple intelligences. School activities often work on linguistics or logical reasoning but math journals are a successful merger of both. Looking beyond a problem alone allows students to more fully integrate math as a language itself, and helps those students who otherwise feel less confident about their math skills.

- **Use journals to scaffold instruction.** Multistep problems involve following a logical sequence. Journaling acts as a scaffold in the steps to a solution and helps teachers identify where in the process students need additional support.

- **Go beyond the symbol.** Using written language, math instruction can become more concrete for verbal learners. This can be achieved via math jokes, such as "A Piece of Pi: 3.14159." "There are only 10 kinds of people, those who understand binary and those who don't." "Classification of mathematical problems as linear and nonlinear is like classification of the Universe as bananas and non-bananas." "Math is like love; a simple idea, but it can get complicated." If you can incorporate things like humor into math, students will start to have a deeper appreciation for it as just another language form, and have less fear.

Further Reading

Math with a Laugh Series. Educator Faye Nisonoff Ruopp partners with comedian Paula Poundstone to come up with fun and funny math problems to help engage kids in math. Books include *The Sticky Problem of Parallelogram Pancakes,* geared toward fourth and fifth graders; *Venn Can We Be Friends,* for sixth and seventh graders; and *You Can't Keep a Good Slope Down,* for eighth and ninth graders. http://www.heinemann.com/products/E00931.aspx. Retrieved January 2011.

List 9.2. Five Specific Ways to Integrate Writing in the Math Curriculum

Using journals in math class can foster learning in many ways. Students who use journals for math are actively engaged in their own learning and have the opportunity to clarify and reflect upon their thinking.

Five Types of Math Journals

1. **Problem explanation** is a type of journal that students use to reflect on and explain their thinking about the steps they followed in a problem-solving process to determine where their thinking fell apart or where they had a breakthrough or an "Aha" moment.

   For example, "I divided 375 by 17 and didn't know if I should go backward to think about the 15 or forward to think about 21 as either being the number to use. I am familiar with those numbers, but not 37 or 17." This example gives the student an opportunity to think more about the problem he got wrong and give the teacher insight into the student's questions. It can serve as a basis for reteaching. Here are some questions to ask as prompts for this kind of journal:

   - How many times did you try to solve the problem?
   - How did you finally solve it?
   - Could you have found the answer by doing something different? What? What method did you use to solve this problem and why? Was this hard or easy?

   Use problem explanation journals after formative assessments and at the end of lessons when the work seemed especially difficult for students. They can also be effective halfway through projects to check for understanding. Have students

   - Review problems and identify where they were not certain about the next steps. Encourage them to express what they were thinking, as in the example above.
   - Share examples with students so they know how to journal.
   - There is no right or wrong way to journal. The goal is to open dialogue for further understanding about how learners think.

2. **Creative association** is a type of journal that is used for students to begin making associations with the real world and their study of math. Entries in this type of journal are made when students have thoughts or make observations in the world that strike them as mathematical. For example, a student carries the notebook with him and sees a building that is especially interesting because it has multiple triangles on the roof. The student then makes note of this in the journal. Or another example, a cashier struggles to provide correct change and the student takes a note of this. These notes can be kept as voice notes as an application on a cell phone or on tape, or written on cell phone notes or a traditional notebook. These notebook observations can be shared with the class once a week so students inspire one another to see the world as a place where math concepts live. Develop lessons and projects from these observations.

List 9.2. (continued)

3. **Feeling journals** are a type of journal in which students reflect on their feelings and thoughts as they relate to math problems, assignments, lessons, units, and assessments. These types of journals can be used to help teachers understand and help students, as well as providing students an outlet for frustration that may serve to help alleviate this experience. A benefit of math journals is the ability for the teacher to highlight, review, or spot-check a concept briefly.

   Here are some questions you can ask your students as prompts for the feeling journal and use to help with specific, difficult problems:

   - I knew I was right when_____.
   - Where else could you use this type of problem solving?
   - What would happen if you missed a step? Why?
   - What other strategies could you use to solve this problem?
   - Write steps for somebody else who will be solving this problem.
   - Were you frustrated with this problem? Why or why not?

   In general about math:

   - What do you like about math?
   - What don't you like about math?
   - Is math your favorite subject? Why or why not?
   - The best math exercise I ever did was _____ because _____.

4. **Daily topic journaling** is a type of journal that is used at the start of class as an anticipatory set to get students' attention connected to the subject matter. In general, the teacher writes a prompt that students respond to for a short, focusing time. Some examples of prompts are

   - Count the number of rectangles in the room. Why do you think rectangles are used more than circles and triangles?
   - Is zero a number? Do you think it should be? Why? Why not?
   - How many total candles have been on your birthday cakes to date? Why do you think candles are part of the cake tradition?
   - Why do you think some kids like math and others don't?

5. **Question and answer journal** is a type of journal used as a communication tool between the student and the teacher or other experts (such as peers or parents) who may have the ability to help with the answer. As students work independently or in groups, any time they have a question they write it in their question journal. Students can use flags or place the journal out on the desk when there are questions waiting to be answered. The questions are to be about steps in a process, reasons for a process, or to check an answer the student is uncertain about, but not to ask for answers that are solutions to problems.

List 9.2. (continued)

Tips for Student Journals

- Sometimes it is best to let students choose their own journal style, one that allows them to express themselves, thus causing them to connect with math on a personal level.
- Encourage students to both write about and draw about math problems. Drawing can help explain as much as writing.
- Provide feedback on student writing as this will encourage them to take the task seriously.
- Take time to explain to students why they are writing in math. This will help guide their attitudes and build a relationship with the teacher.
- Students need lots of practice writing their ideas. Have the journaling process become routine both in and out of class.
- Older students may be assisted by peer feedback to validate their writing and to see how their ideas affect others.
- Don't worry about the mechanics of the writing unless it's part of a final report or project. Also, length is less important than consistency.
- Keep track of your writing prompts for recycling and sharing with other teachers. One teacher kept a packet of over 175 possible math journal questions. As the year progressed she found that many math journal questions flowed naturally from the math lesson, reading story, or everyday events, so the packet grew.
- Journaling math problems can help teachers differentiate content, process, and product according to a student's readiness and interests. It takes only a moment to alter a question to align to a student's interests.

List 9.3. Group Work as a Way to Differentiate the Math Class

According to the National Council of Teachers of Mathematics (NCTM, 1991), learning environments should be created that promote active learning and teaching; classroom discourse; and individual, small-group, and whole-group learning. Group work is an important dimension of mathematics learning. This list gives teachers ideas and strategies on how to incorporate group work effectively into the math classroom at any level.

- **Assign group learning to help students move between concrete and abstract.** Group learning activities can be designed to help students start to bring abstract mathematical concepts into a more concrete, real-world context. This can involve everything from manipulatives to projects finding math in everyday life.
- **Use group work to scaffold instruction for students with math disabilities or struggles.** Students with math disabilities can benefit from peer interactions to learn mathematics skills and concepts. When activities depend on everyone's contribution, all students are forced to work together to arrive at the final product or solution. This encourages students who struggle in math to become more invested in their own learning as well.
- **Structure group work to be interactive.** Working independently side-by-side is not effective group work. Students will receive the benefits of group work when each member of the group is responsible for a portion of the work and there is a shared outcome.
- **Form groups with a variety of students.** In effective groups, each member's strengths have authentic importance to the ultimate success of the group's activity. A strong group creates a situation in which individual learning styles, skills, and talents are valued, and students learn from each other in the areas where they are not so expert.
- **Model effective group work.** In order for groups to be effective, make sure the expectations for group work are clear, and give examples of how you expect students to interact through modeling an interaction before breaking into groups. This will help students understand what is expected.
- **Create group projects that allow for multiple solutions.** In groups where there are several possible outcomes to the task or more than one solution to the problem, the exchange of alternative ideas and viewpoints enhances that growth and stimulates broader thinking. Although many students are initially uncomfortable with less defined answers in math, helping them realize there are many options is important and encourages risk taking and deeper thinking about math concepts.

Further Reading

Andrini, B. (1991). *Cooperative learning and mathematics.* San Juan Capistrano, CA: Resources for Teachers.

Pedrotty Rivera, D. (1996). *Teaching students with learning and behavior problems.* Boston: Allyn & Bacon.

Willis, D. (2006). *Research-based strategies to ignite student learning: Insights from a neurologist and classroom teacher.* Alexandria, VA: ASCD.

List 9.4. Ways to Integrate Group Work in the Math Curriculum

Productive groups in the classroom don't happen spontaneously. It is not effective to simply place students together with a shared assignment. Although students may choose friends for private study groups, it is a different matter to accommodate group members in a classroom and complete a project where they follow instructions, work through packets, and complete daily goals. When preparing for successful group work, the teacher is often at a loss about how students can work together in what has traditionally been taught as an independent experience that is highly direct-instruction and teacher-centered. This list suggests three ways for teachers to begin thinking about putting students to work with one another.

1. **Paired problem solving.** Allow students to work in pairs to solve problems. This works best with multistep problems. In pairs, students can
   - Work together to solve story problems or even create them.
   - Combine sequencing and patterning exercises such as analyzing the game of tic-tac-toe to determine which opening move wins most often.
   - Solve puzzles or write multiplication stories.
   - Create graphs together. Modeling on paper helps students bridge from concrete manipulatives to abstract thought. Doing this in pairs helps them discuss and cooperate and therefore work toward a common solution.
   - Work backward. Have students choose or start with a solution and then create the problem that supports it.
   - Create a mystery. Place simple problems that preview concepts needed for the lesson in a container and have students read and construct a story about what they mean.
   - Make a glossary of math vocabulary, including such words as *algebra*, *geometry*, *probability*, *mass*, *mean*, *hypotenuse*, *Pythagorean Theorem*, *variables*, and *volume*. Then have students define all the words. See how many different mathematical words students can collect, define, and learn.
2. **Group testing.** Most math classes operate under the premise that all students need to take tests individually. The reality is that rarely in life are we called upon to solve life's problems alone. Group testing is an effective way to get students to work together to learn math. Ideas for group testing include
   - Create different tests for different groups depending on their ability level.
   - Break students into small groups of three to four. Assign each group a different type of math problem. Have each group write five problems of that type. Compile the problems into a class math test or have groups exchange papers and solve the problems.
   - Allow students to solve complex problems, using the book as a guide. Allow them to search for the answers given the steps in the book. This may seem counterintuitive, but imagine a pilot in a cockpit not being able to refer to a manual for help with a problem.

List 9.4. (continued)

3. **Math projects.** When students in groups are given specific projects to work on, they can find pleasure in working collaboratively, and these kinds of lessons tend to be much more interesting and fun for students. Here are some ideas, and there are thousands more on the Internet.

   ○ **Fraction mosaic**—Create a mosaic using exactly 100 pieces. These may be seeds, different-colored squares of construction paper, and so forth. Then write the fractions and maybe percentages of each seed or color on the back to evaluate mathematically.

   ○ **The million-dollar project**—Have students "spend" one million dollars on things in catalogs. This teaches subtraction, addition, and decimals.

   ○ **School surveys**—Students come up with five questions to ask twenty-five people about what changes they wish to see in their school. They graph their results.

   ○ **Geometry project**—Students find twenty geometric figures in the "real world" from magazines, newspapers, or from photographs they have taken. Arrange the photos according to shapes.

   ○ **Newspaper scavenger hunt**—Students find items such as decimals, fractions, percents, ordinal numbers, and so forth in the newspaper, cut them out, and make an original design of all of their findings.

List 9.5. Math Manipulatives

Manipulatives are hands-on objects that make the abstract ideas of mathematics concrete. They are scaffolding tools. For example, you can talk about dividing a circle into a group of triangles and draw it on the board for students to observe passively, or you can give students an object, such as a paper pizza, and have them slice it into as many triangles as possible. Allowing students to hold, move, and interact with the concrete substance is a proven way to get them to understand math. This list offers further rationale for using manipulatives and provides examples of manipulatives and their uses.

The use of math manipulatives is not a fad. States including Texas, North Carolina, Tennessee, and California are now mandating the use of manipulatives in their state math requirements. Texas has actually altered the state law to include language requiring appropriate manipulatives to be used when new concepts are introduced (Peavler, DeValcourt, Montalto, & Hopkins, 1987). The mandate states that students are to be actively involved in structured activities that develop understanding and the ability to apply skills.

Concrete manipulatives. There are static as well as virtual manipulatives. Concrete manipulatives can include items such as

- Buckets of pattern blocks
- Trays of tiles and cubes
- Collections of geoboards
- Tangrams
- Counters
- Spinners
- Coins and money
- Food and measuring tools

They can be anything that makes a concrete representation of the abstract idea.

Virtual manipulatives can be found on the Web. Virtual manipulative sites differ from those sites where the act of pointing and clicking results in the computer's providing an answer in visual or symbolic form. The key is for students to be able to construct meaning on their own by using the mouse to control physical actions of objects by sliding, flipping, turning, and rotating them. Currently, most virtual manipulatives are modeled after concrete manipulatives such as base-10 blocks, coins, pattern blocks, tangrams, spinners, rulers, fraction bars, algebra tiles, geoboards, and geometric plane and solid figures, and are usually in the form of Java or Flash applets. Examples of virtual manipulatives include

- The Great Balancing Act: explore the mean and median
- Parabola games: explore parabola properties, transformations, and their use
- Leap Frog: explore number patterns
- Fire, Fire!: explore trigonometric ratios
- Transformations: an introduction to transformational symmetries

List 9.5. (continued)

Some Common Questions and Answers About Using Manipulatives

Question: How do I fit them into my instruction?

Answer: Use them whenever you are explaining an abstract concept that has a concrete representation. For example, fractions are measurements, and all geometry theories can be made visual. Some math series are specifically designed for use with manipulatives. One such series is the Chicago Math Series, which comes complete with instructions and accompanying tools.

Question: How often should I use them?

Answer: As often as you can to illustrate points. They are not useful for students who have already grasped concepts, so teachers need to pre-assess. However, when introducing new content, they can stand beside the verbal explanation. Periods of use should not extend beyond fifteen to twenty minutes and are often much shorter, being just long enough for students to grasp the concepts.

Question: How do I make sure students see them as learning tools, not toys?

Answer: Talk with students about why manipulatives help them learn math. These discussions are essential for first-time users and useful refreshers to refocus from time to time. Discuss the similarities and differences between using manipulatives in class and playing with toys or games. With toys or games, children can make up their own rules. With manipulatives, they are given specific problems and activities. However, make it clear that they're free to make discoveries and explore new ideas.

Question: How can I communicate their value to parents?

Answer: Parents will respect any tool that inspires their children's interest and success in math. When you use manipulatives and students are inspired, it may be helpful to send e-mails to parents describing what you did in class and what successes you observed. Then encourage parents to ask their children about the lesson.

Question: Are they useful for upper-grade students, too?

Answer: Absolutely. This is especially true with algebra, which is often lost on students who are not naturally abstract thinkers. There is a manipulative tool called "algebra tiles" that helps students understand polynomials and other Algebra I concepts. These can be found online in places such as Amazon.com.

Some Practical Tips for Using Concrete Manipulatives

- **Allow adequate time.** Time for free exploration is worth the investment. Free exploration time allows students to satisfy their curiosity so they don't become distracted from the assigned tasks.

List 9.5. (continued)

- **Make a glossary.** Make a manipulative glossary for students that have corresponding uses on it. For example, a box of coins may be labeled as uses for counting, decimal recognition, and subtraction.
- **Make manipulatives easily accessible.** Store materials in a readily available place with clear labeling for easy access. A clear system makes the materials more accessible. Some teachers designate and label space on bookshelves. Others use zip-top plastic bags and portion materials into quantities useful for pairs or groups. Still others place a supply of each material at students' tables so they're always within reach.

Further Reading

Clements, D. H. (1999). Concrete manipulatives, concrete ideas. *Contemporary Issues in Early Childhood,* *1*(1), 45–60. http://www.gse.buffalo.edu/org/buildingblocks/Newsletters/Concrete_Yelland.htm.

Moyer-Packenham, P. S., Salkind, G., & Bolyard, J. J. (2008). Virtual manipulatives used by K–8 teachers for mathematics instruction: Considering mathematical, cognitive, and pedagogical fidelity. *Contemporary Issues in Technology and Teacher Education, 8*(3), 202–218. http://www.editlib.org/index .cfm?fuseaction=Reader.ViewFullText&paper_id=26057.

National Council of Teachers of Mathematics. (2000). *Principles and standards for school mathematics.* Reston, VA: Author. http://standards.nctm.org.

List 9.6. Project-Based Learning Ideas and the Math Class

Projects for math class are a lively and engaging strategy that take a bit of planning upfront, but can be used repeatedly. It is often easiest to try some of the already designed projects before trying to create original ideas. This list provides suggestions for already created projects and a few tips for starting students with them. The websites where they are located can be found by searching for the name of the organizations listed below.

Prepare Packets for Student Success

When starting a new project, it is ideal to present students with a project packet. The packet will guide them through the project and keep them focused on a day-to-day basis if the project spans multiple days. Here are some elements to include in the packet:

- **An overview:** an introduction that outlines the project. It should be written in an exciting and illustrative way telling students what they are going to do and why it is important. The intention is to orient students and capture their interest.
- **The outcome:** this part describes the end product of the activity.
- **The process:** a step-by-step outline for completing the project. The outline should include a time line with deadlines for steps and checkpoints along the way. When engaged in long-term projects, there should be accountability for parts toward completion along the way so students get an understanding of pacing.
- **The resources:** websites and other resources students will use to complete the task.
- **The evaluation:** how the activity will be measured. Preferably, there will be a project rubric or a checklist for evaluation.
- **The reflection:** sums up the activity and encourages students to reflect on its process on a daily basis as well as the end result. The student writes this.

Eleven Places to Find Successful Math Projects

1. **CAMS (California Academy of Math and Science) Inventors Inc.** Economics teacher Greg Fisher recommends that the best way to teach financial literacy is to help students actually create their own business. The California Academy of Math and Science has developed guidelines for successful investor projects, broken down into five sections:
   - Questions on investments, and an individual investment portfolio
   - Entrepreneurship time (developing a business plan to market a product)
   - Time to invest (stock market research, selection, and tracking)
   - The convention (a business convention where students display their business plan and product, with marketing and advertising)
   - Wrapping up the project (debriefing)

List 9.6. (continued)

2. **CIESE—the Center for Innovation in Engineering and Science Education—** sponsors and designs projects for elementary, middle, and high school students with real-time data available from online sources and global collaboration with peers and experts. Each project includes a description as well as links to the relevant National Science Standards and NCTM math standards. All projects focus on science and mathematics, but have many interdisciplinary aspects as well, including social studies, language arts, art, and foreign languages.

3. **Data Library** from the Math Forum contains lists of ongoing data-sharing projects as well as downloadable Excel spreadsheets along with other sources of data on the Web.

4. **eLanguages** "is a global online community of teachers sharing ideas and working together with their students on curriculum relevant projects." Students can join an existing project or start their own. eLanguages is flexible and can support activities in all subject areas across grade levels.

5. **GLOBE** trains teachers to help students improve their achievement in science and math, and in the use of computer and network technology. The website states that the program is a "worldwide hands-on, primary and secondary school-based science and education program. GLOBE's vision promotes and supports students, teachers and scientists to collaborate on inquiry-based investigations of the environment and the Earth system working in close partnership with NASA, NOAA and NSF in study and research about the dynamics of Earth's environment."

6. *Hands-on Math Projects,* volume 2, by Carolyn S. Carter with Sara Cohen, Marian Keyes, Patricia S. Kusimo, and Crystal Lunsford, contains two chapters devoted to "Projects That Help Middle-School-Age Youth Discover the Science and Mathematics in Everyday Life." Available online as a free PDF.

7. **The Mathematics of Quilting** exposes learners to plane geometry, symmetry, and tessellations. In Making Art through Mathematics, learners explore Cartesian coordinates, 2-D and 3-D geometry, measurement, symmetry, and volume. There are many websites available exploring math quilts and the construction process.

8. **IEARN** "enables young people to use the Internet and other new technologies to engage in collaborative educational projects that both enhance learning and make a difference in the world." Math projects, for example, include Mathematics and Agriculture (ages 10 and up), Connecting Math to Our Lives (all ages), and Mathematics Virtual Learning Circle (all ages).

9. **Making Mathematics** includes open-ended research projects suitable for grades 7–12, supported by grants from the National Science Foundation. Math projects, available online and can be freely reproduced, are rated from 1 (no algebra) to 4 (advanced algebra and beyond). Projects contain the problem statement, prerequisites, warm-up problems, hints, resources, teacher notes, extension problems, and results. Additional resources include a teacher handbook with advice and activities for teaching research skills, a mentor handbook, and mathematics

List 9.6. (continued)

tools with important supporting content regarding proof, number theory, Pascal's triangle, geometry of complex numbers, iteration, and numbers and infinity.

10. **MathMovesU** is an initiative from Raytheon Company to make math more interesting for middle school students. Middle school students can enter a "virtual world" of math and engage with games, polls, flash cards, word problems, and factoids all centered on their passions: music, sports, and fashion. Students earn points for bragging rights and can enter sweepstakes to win prizes. The MathMovesUniversity section of the site features a glossary of math terms and a large number of hands-on worksheets for students looking for additional help and support. They have additional resources that offer scholarships and grants for your school.

11. **Project Exchange** is a place for teachers to share project-based high school curriculum: visual and performing arts, mathematics, science, language arts, social studies, digital design, and world language.

Source: Deubel, P. (2010). *Math projects.* Retrieved September 19, 2010, from http://www.ct4me.net/math _projects.htm. Adapted with permission from Computing Technology for Math Excellence.

Further Reading

Deubel, P. Math projects. Computing Technology for Math Excellence. http://www.ct4me.net/math _projects.htm. Retrieved September 2010.

See the book's bonus Web material for additional links and resources.

WEB

List 9.7. Beyond Traditional Quizzes and Tests: Differentiated Assessments in Math

Many students fail to learn math simply because the testing methods in schools are not designed for all types of learners. This list provides information about how to differentiate math assessments.

Why Differentiate Assessments?

- Students are able to display knowledge in many different ways.
- Students who are not skilled test-takers will be able to succeed in showing their abilities and therefore build self-esteem.
- Differentiated assessments do not interrupt class time as do traditional tests, but instead are measurements of incremental growth.
- Differentiated instruction assessments give ongoing information on the strengths and weaknesses of each student, providing the teacher the opportunity to work within those.

There are several types of popular alternative assessments.

Portfolios: Types of Math Portfolios

- Showcase—a folder where students place the problems and work of which they are most proud.
- Teacher-student portfolio—an interactive tool where students place work and teachers comment on it.
- Open-ended questions—an ongoing dialogue between teacher and student regarding specific math questions.
- Videotapes of student work
- Mathematical autobiography—a student's life history with math. This can be an ongoing journal with examples of problems.
- Draft, revised, and final versions of student work on a complex mathematical problem.

Math Rubrics

- Math rubrics can be used for projects and complex problems. Teachers should share the rubrics with the students when presenting and explain the problem. Unique in their scales, here are three examples of math rubrics.

List 9.7. (continued)

Sample One

Scale I: Understanding the Problem	Scale II: Planning a Solution	Scale III: Getting an Answer
−2 Complete understanding of the problem	−2 Plan could have led to a correct solution if implemented properly	−2 Correct answer and correct label for the answer
−1 Part of the problem misunderstood or misinterpreted	−1 Partially correct plan based on part of the problem being interpreted correctly	−1 Copying error; computational error; partial answer for a problem with multiple answers
−0 Complete misunderstanding of the problem	−0 No attempt, or totally inappropriate plan	−0 No answer, or wrong answer based on an inappropriate plan

Sample Two: Simple Version for Problems

Points

6. Exemplary response.
5. Competent response.
4. Minor flaws but satisfactory.
3. Serious flaws but nearly satisfactory.
2. Begins but fails to complete problem.
1. No attempt.

Sample Three

Level 1.	Level 2.	Level 3.
No evidence of a strategy or procedure, or uses a strategy that does not help solve the problem.	The solution is not complete, indicating that parts of the problem are not understood.	Uses a strategy that leads to a solution of the problem.
No evidence of mathematical reasoning.	The solution addresses some, but not all of the mathematical components presented in the task.	Uses effective mathematical reasoning.
There were so many errors in mathematical procedures that the problem could not be resolved.	Some evidence of mathematical reasoning.	All parts are correct and a correct answer is achieved.
There is no explanation of the solution, the explanation cannot be understood, or it is unrelated to the problem.	Some parts may be correct, but a correct answer is not achieved.	The solution shows that the student has a broad understanding of the problem and the major concepts necessary for its solution.

List 9.7. (continued)

Why Rubrics Are Effective

- Each student is judged on the same criteria, making them fair and equitable.
- The teacher develops them before instruction begins, so lessons target specific knowledge and skills needed.
- Directs students' attention to important concepts.
- Can be used for self- and peer evaluation.
- In math, points are given for procedure, not just solutions.
- Teachers must employ backward design, understanding the outcomes before the assignment is given.
- There are many online rubric-building tools to make creating math rubrics simple. See "Further Reading" for a listing of the best websites for this important resource.
- The teacher, or person who is observing, writes down his or her observations of the student, providing a record of student growth, strengths, and needs.

Anecdotal Records

Another way to assess student work in the math class is through anecdotal records rather than number scoring. Anecdotal records are written reports describing milestones about a student's positive, cognitive development. They provide a snapshot of a student's development over time. When using these records, keep the following in mind:

- Keep the focus on achievement rather than problems.
- Be specific about what performance accomplishments and problems are observed rather than focusing on student interpersonal behavior.
- Focus on using verbs rather than adjectives to describe learning. For example: "Susan is multiplying numbers with ease when the numbers are even and often struggles with odd numbers that have carry-over," rather than "Susan is good at multiplication."

Math Project Presentations

Math projects offer a break from the textbook-to-test mode and allow students to demonstrate mastery and interact with classmates using a combination of oral presentations and rubrics for their assessment. These presentations will help verbal learners as well as students who struggle with traditional test taking. Here is an example of a math project:

Goal: To illustrate understanding of percentages and interest rates.

Tasks: Students choose a career and research an average starting salary for such a career. Next students come up with a price range for their home mortgage given the salary and determine what they can afford. They shop online for homes in the area in which they believe they wish to live. Once they find a home in their price range, they determine the annual amount of mortgage, what they will put as a down payment, and what the amortized interest rate will be over time on a thirty-year mortgage.

List 9.7. (continued)

Further Reading

Math Project Journal's *Ultimate Math Lessons* book contains over one hundred high school algebra, geometry, and advanced algebra projects. http://www.mathprojects.com/ProjectBook/Default.aspx.

The National Council of Teachers of Mathematics Illuminations website provides ideas for math curriculum projects for grades K–12. http://illuminations.nctm.org.

Rubric Bank. http://intranet.cps.k12.il.us/Assessments/Ideas_and_Rubrics/Rubric_Bank/rubric_bank.html.

Rubric Resources. http://www.aea5.k12.ia.us/pd/assessment/rubrics.htm.

Notes:

List 9.8. Math Anxiety and Differentiated Instruction

Math anxiety is a quite common occurrence that stems from students' lack of confidence. More often than not, this kind of performance anxiety results from having to do math one way when the learner requires different modes of instruction to learn. Many students with math anxiety have an overreliance on procedures in math as opposed to actually understanding the math. When one tries to memorize procedures, rules, and routines without much understanding, the math is quickly forgotten and panic soon sets in.

The following tips will help students understand how to overcome math anxiety.

Debunk the Following Myths with Students

- **You're born with a math gene: either you get it or you don't.** Everyone has the ability to learn math if it is presented in a way they can understand it. Unfortunately, many math classes are taught as solving formulas that require memorization rather than being taught the underlying framework for why math is important.
- **Math is for males; females never get math!** Whether girls can do math, science, and engineering is an outmoded question these days. Some women do better than some men in those fields. One of the world's brightest scientists was a woman. Think Marie Curie, who was a Nobel Prize–winning physicist.
- **It's hopeless, and much too hard for average people.** Math is something everyday people do every day. They balance checkbooks, read and analyze sports statistics, measure and use fractions in cooking. When given practical applications, anyone can learn math.
- **If the logical side of your brain isn't your strength, you'll never do well in math.** Math can be learned in many ways. Reading and writing approaches to solving math problems have been in classroom use for many years. The idea that one side of the brain is stronger than the other is no longer a valid concept.
- **There's only one right way to do math.** Many people arrive at solutions using differing processes. When teachers provide students the opportunities to wrestle with math concepts on their own, they are sometimes able to come up with correct answers using their own processes.

Provide Students the Following Kinds of Instructional Options

- Let them work in groups or pairs to solve problems.
- Incorporate physical movement into math drills.
- Use brainstorming to understand the underlying concepts.
- Focus on the whys of math as much as the hows.
- Demonstrate concepts using manipulatives until students achieve mastery.
- Let them work in a group to design a math game.
- Have them read about math and why it's important.
- Have open-book tests.
- Apply math to real life.
- Teach students rhythms to come up with common math drills.
- Let them write multiplication stories.

List 9.8. (continued)

- Let them use hand-held devices such as calculators to complete functions.
- Use graphic organizers to understand concepts.
- Check for understanding before moving on.
- Recommend math-related films such as *Rain Man, Goodwill Hunting, A Serious Man, Flatland,* and *Shrek the Third.*
- Focus on mastery, not speed.
- Describe the world with numbers.
- Introduce patterns, card games, and poetry.
- Use sports statistics.
- Have students write out in paragraph form what they do not understand.
- Set out clear goals for each class.
- Review old concepts before beginning new ones.
- Help students monitor progress by keeping a progress chart.
- Don't assign a lot of busy work or too many problems as homework.
- Bring parents into the conversation when the student demonstrates math anxiety.

Section Ten

Strategies for Differentiating Science

Science is based on questions and inquiry, and it is a natural environment for differentiating instruction. In this section, the lists are designed to help teachers frame lessons to encourage excitement and engagement in science, while assuring every student can perform at his or her level. Technology can also be infused into the science classroom to encourage students to interact, explore, and discuss science, especially as it affects their daily lives. This brings new avenues for students to extend learning beyond the classroom and for making science a way of thinking about problems, rather than just an isolated part of the curriculum.

List 10.1. General Differentiated Strategies for Science

Science, at the heart of it, is all about experimentation and finding out the unknown through sequential testing and experience. A large part of differentiating instruction is about providing students hands-on experience, whether as individuals, groups, or project-based learning, which is a normal and natural part of science instruction. This list offers strategies for differentiating science instruction at different levels and suggests ideas to help teachers make science exciting for students.

All Levels

- **Help students get excited about science.** Someone invented almost every object in the classroom, whether it's a whiteboard, a book (think printing press), ink, light bulbs—you name it. Each invention or advance that made each "thing" in the classroom possible involved the scientific process of experimenting, trying out different ideas, and eventually settling or discovering the one that worked. What's not to love about science?

- **Help students see science in everyday things.** Seeing science in action in things we take for granted can help students have a greater appreciation for the inquiry process and engage them in the subject matter at hand. Science is full of great stories of people struggling with ideas, trying to make the world a better or more predictable place, or simply trying to solve problems. Sharing these stories can help students see their own potential as they solve their own problems every day.

- **Encourage students to watch interesting science-based shows in their free time.** There are numerous shows on TV and the Internet for all ages that help bring science to life. Shows such as *MythBusters* are excellent at showing the scientific method at work as the hosts explore common myths on a variety of topics and test their veracity. Encouraging students to take a look at some of the more engaging science-friendly shows in their down time will help reinforce that science is fun, as well as demonstrating core scientific concepts such as hypothesis formation and testing.

- **Integrate multimedia assignments into the curriculum.** Consider integrating fun multimedia assignments into your curriculum, such as having students listen to podcasts such as "Lab Out Loud," produced by two science teachers for the National Science Teachers Association (NSTA). Over one hundred shows have been produced on wide-ranging subjects, all free and available for educational use. This can be a great alternative or adjunct to text reading assignments.

List 10.1. (continued)

- **Record or podcast the science classroom.** Consider recording and podcasting your own classroom lectures, study notes, mnemonics, or other classroom-specific information that students can access from home. One science teacher we know has a series of podcasts of her favorite lessons and study songs she keeps on her classroom website, available to students whenever they need them and as study tools, while also creating an archive and library of her work she can reuse each year as needed.

- **Use podcasts and videos as class preparation, especially for labs.** Consider recording short "prep" videos of lab projects for students to view, at home, prior to a lab day. By seeing the experiment in advance, the students will have a better idea of what to do, so they will be able to spend more time focusing on the data collection, observation, and interactions during the lab, rather than focusing only on procedure.

List 10.2. Inquiry-Based Instruction and Science

The National Science Education Standards emphasize inquiry-based instruction, which helps students and teachers alike to create more situations in which students solve problems within a thematic framework. Inquiry is a key part of differentiating instruction and personalizing learning, as students begin to experiment and make meaning of the world and how it operates. This list discusses inquiry-based instruction in the science classroom, and how to help students become engaged in the inquiry process.

- **Inquiry is fundamentally a student-centered approach to teaching and learning.** By giving students opportunities to solve problems, develop and exercise critical-thinking skills, learn to transfer concepts to new problems and situations, and test their ideas and presumptions, science naturally offers the opportunity to help students become critical thinkers and problem solvers in a way that may not be so apparent in a language arts or social studies classroom.
- **Inquiry gives students a framework for testing ideas.** Beyond hands-on learning and experiments, inquiry instruction requires that students engage in the scientific process by coming up with suppositions, and then asking questions, testing theories, and revising their theories and assumptions based on integration of results. This framework can be used across the curriculum, and science teachers are critical to helping students make this intuitive leap.

Types of Inquiry

Type of Inquiry	Description	Examples
Structured	Teacher provides problems to students to investigate and explore with hands-on activities, along with procedures and materials. Students are responsible to determine the outcome.	Classic laboratory activities and structured labs with materials, procedures, and questions to be answered are provided.
Guided	Teacher provides a problem or a question along with materials. Students develop the process and determine the outcome.	Students are given an egg and supplies and are asked to create a system that would allow the egg to be dropped from a ladder without breaking.
Open	Students determine all aspects: problem, investigation, procedure, and outcome.	Students take a field trip to a local wetland. Working in small groups, students identify a problem to research and conduct their investigation based on their observations at the site. Questions might include what the effects of flooding are on surrounding areas, or the possible impact of vegetation on water flow, etc.

List 10.2. (continued)

- **Celebrate curiosity and questioning of assumptions**. Inquiry and problem solving creates an atmosphere of curiosity in the classroom, engaging students at every level. By adopting a "Miss Frizzle—Magic School Bus" approach to science (Get messy! Make mistakes!) students learn that asking questions is as important as finding answers; that uncertainty is normal, as is making mistakes; and that asking questions, trying to find answers, and testing our assumptions is the key to learning.

- **Provide real-world opportunities**. Create projects that let students work with their environment, or try to solve local problems. When students make real-world connections to academic topics, learning comes alive. For example, students at the Science Leadership Academy in Philadelphia developed a flow versus batch process for producing bio-diesel. They then connected with a community in South America to test the process, which is now being used to help provide a portion of the energy needs for the community. Not all projects will be this big, but it demonstrates that students, even from inner-city schools, can have meaningful effects on their communities.

- **Use labs as often as possible.** Science classrooms at all levels lend themselves to labs, hands-on experiences, and more.

- **Stress collaboration**. Almost every scientific breakthrough is the result of collaboration. Help students understand that collaboration is key to the way science works in the "real world" as well.

- **Use science fairs to differentiate.** Science fairs typically involve single-student long-term projects and investigations, demonstrating core science principles, often in the context of everyday life. Some students will come up with their own projects, but other students may require prompts or ideas to choose a worthwhile project. When assigning or supporting science fair projects, help students select and plan projects that are investigative and seek to answer a question, and help them avoid the "how to" or "observation-only" projects that are not question/inquiry based.

List 10.3. Multimedia Projects, Science, and Differentiated Instruction

Science is naturally an academic subject that lends itself to multimedia and hands-on learning. This list provides ideas on how multimedia can be usefully incorporated into the science classroom to help students better understand and appreciate complex subject matter.

- **Ask students to demonstrate learning through multimedia.** Long-term projects with rubrics can provide opportunities for students to produce their own multimedia projects and learn to demonstrate their understanding by incorporating text, audio, and visuals beyond a mere poster or in-class report.

  Example: Ms. J has an annual project called the "Cell-a-bration" as the culmination of a unit on cell structure. For two to three weeks in advance, students work in small groups to find analogies in the real world to parts of the cell, and then produce presentations, webpages on a wiki, PowerPoints, models, posters, and more (at their group's choice) showing how a mitochondria might be similar to a refrigerator or how a nucleus may be like a databank, and so forth. The Cell-a-bration allows students to demonstrate and share their knowledge of parts of the cell and their functions with others, while the means of presentation are left up to student choice and collaboration. Rubrics provide the basic grading criteria, but more important, students are constantly engaged and pushed to make connections between their "book knowledge" and the real world.

- **Focus students on using the tools to best demonstrate the goal.** For example, video is best used when both seeing and hearing is important, but other times, audio alone or pictures in a slide show may be enough. Help students choose the tools available that will help enhance their project and not distract from it.

  Example: Ms. F's fifth-grade science class does an annual unit on force and basic physics. As part of the group project, students design and construct over time a bridge out of toothpicks and glue. Each component of the bridge has an associated cost assigned, and each group has the same "budget." Each team member has a responsibility for the project, either as designer, builder, construction manager, or accountant. At the end of the construction, the bridges from each group are tested for their strength. Students videotape the bridge stress testing, and later review the tape to see what aspects of their bridge failed, and why, and what alternative choices could have improved performance.

List 10.4. Practical Advice for the Laboratory

Labs can be some of the most exciting aspects of science education and can make many complex subjects more "real" for students. However, making sure a lab goes well and students get results, often in a limited period, can be challenging. This list offers some tips and tricks to help make those lab sessions go better for all students.

- **Keep the big picture in mind.** Make sure students understand the purpose and big picture of the lab, and what they should expect. This will help them self-correct or ask for help during the lab if things go off-track.
- **Preview the lab.** It's always a good idea to walk students through a lab experiment before they do it themselves. Although a few minutes of preview is helpful, consider making a short video or audio for students to watch or listen to in advance of the lab, so they know what to expect and what to do. This also gives you an opportunity to begin a "lab video library" that students can refer to in subsequent years, which may also be shared with other teachers and students as needed.
- **Labs are like kitchens and require preparation.** A typical lab can be a lot like cooking a recipe. There are specific directions, and we are promised to have predictable results if we follow the directions closely. Teachers need to make sure all students, like good cooks, understand they should read all of the directions first, line up all equipment, and be prepared before starting the experiment rather than try to do the lab without advanced preparation.
- **Have all tools at hand.** Make sure students have laid out the steps needed in the lab, and if working in groups, have assigned each participant a duty. This will help each student take ownership for their portion of the experiment.
- **Emphasize the importance of data collection.** Make sure students have their data-recording sheets ready in advance of the lab or have their charts, observation templates, and so forth set up in advance. Consider providing data sheets or templates in advance for students, especially for the first few labs. This helps students understand what data they should be looking for and walks them through the lab process before requiring them to be independent with their lab and data preparation.
- **Be prepared = More meaningful experience.** For even the most basic labs, students will make the best use of time and get the most out of the lab if they are prepared. Ensure that students understand that by getting everything set in advance, they will actually have the time to focus on what's happening and spend less time worrying about what comes next.
- **Help students stay on track.** Many students, especially those in elementary or middle school, do not yet have a good natural sense of pacing and timing. Make sure students have a sense of timing for the lab, and make reminders during the course of the lab about where they should be in the process. This will help prevent many of the inevitable time crunches that make completing labs in one class period a challenge and that can even pose a hazard in more advanced classwork.

List 10.4. (continued)

- **Accept lab failures as valid answers.** Although many labs can be rather predictable like recipes, and variations are not encouraged, it's important to also teach students that real life is not always so predictable. Encouraging students to look at mistakes as learning opportunities rather than as "getting the wrong answer" or "messing up" is important. If a student's experiment has turned out badly, encourage him or her to write up the lab and the reasons for its failure rather than just repeat the lab.

- **Differentiate demonstrations versus experiments.** Don't forget to emphasize that "real science" is based on setting up experiments when you do not know the answer in advance. Although some labs typically are set up to demonstrate well-known principles, make sure students also understand the nature of experimental and discovery science, and try some labs where the exact result may not be known in advance.

- **Help students, even at the youngest levels, understand experimental design.** Consider encouraging students to ask and answer open-ended questions like the following:
  - What are we doing?
  - Why?
  - What are we trying to learn?
  - How do you think we can find this out?
  - What would you do to test your idea?
  - How would you change this lab to make it better?
  - What questions do you still have after the experiment?
  - What would be the next experiment you would do to find the answers to your questions?

List 10.5. Technology, Differentiated Instruction, and Science Class

Technology is incredibly helpful at almost all levels in science class. Not only is technology an inherent part of science and experimentation itself, but technology allows us to access resources that would otherwise be unavailable. This list discusses incorporating technology into the science classroom and how it may be most helpful in developing an inquiry-based science curriculum.

- **Data collection.** Almost every lab in science requires collection and analysis of observations and data. Teachers can help students begin to master spreadsheet tools, data analysis, and graphing by using tools as simple as Microsoft Excel, Numbers on the Mac, or Google Spreadsheets. Data collection can be done in writing or on the computer, iPods, or other devices, depending on availability.

- **Presentations.** Instead of another poster or report, consider requiring students to demonstrate their knowledge and findings in a Keynote or PowerPoint presentation, and maybe even narrate the same as a podcast.

  Example: Students studying plant structure were required to make an analogy of the different parts of a plant to some other object of their choosing—such as a computer, house, or school. The students were required to gather pictures of each of the analogous parts of the object and put together a slideshow, using the pictures and the reasons for the similarity together. They were required to create a podcast talking about the similarities to narrate the slideshow they had created.

- **Research projects.** In addition to classroom work and experimentation, students are frequently asked to do research projects in science. As discussed in other sections, projects in science can be constructed to report back findings, as well as incorporate multimedia components into the final result.

- **Virtual dissections.** Many examples of virtual dissections are available online and can work as substitutes when necessary for actual dissection and to help elucidate the inner workings of organ systems.

- **Group projects.** Students can use and navigate many online resources as part of any research project, as well as use online tools for completing the assignment. Students can be encouraged to use a wiki to communicate with each other, pool resources, and link to other relevant resources on the Web.

- **Virtual field trips.** The Internet allows science teachers to bring resources directly into the classroom, allowing students to take a virtual field trip to a volcano, for example (http://volcano.oregonstate.edu/fieldtrips). Preexisting virtual field trips online vary in quality, ranging from videos to PowerPoint presentations.

- **Visualizations of complex concepts.** One of the best integrations of technology and resources in the classroom is the ability to bring conceptual things, such as cell structure, to life with some of the videos available on the Web. BioVisions, part of Harvard University, has some amazing video animations of the inner life of a cell that can help students at all levels understand and anchor complex cellular interactions by "seeing" them come to life through animation (http://multimedia.mcb.harvard.edu).

List 10.5. (continued)

Tips for Integrating Technology into Science Class

- **When using technology in the science classroom, make sure it helps achieve the curriculum end goal.** For example, integrating spreadsheets into a lab requiring data collection makes more sense than trying to use a spreadsheet for creating lists alone.

- **Use technology to help enhance learning.** Some concepts in science are best when demonstrated. Using online video to help show these concepts in action will help students understand concepts by creating real-world anchors. For example, a lesson in chemistry on exothermic reactions may be interesting, but when accompanied by video of explosions, it becomes much more exciting and attention grabbing.

- **Use technology to help students collaborate.** Wikis, classroom blogs, and websites work best when they provide opportunities for students to interact, collaborate, and extend their learning in the classroom. Sites such as Quia allow teachers to even create their own curriculum and unit-based video games, which act as assessment and study tools for students. For example, you can pose a question on the classroom blog, asking students to make predictions that evening for homework, about the outcome of a planned in-class experiment. The following day, the students get an opportunity to test and see whose predictions were most accurate.

- **Encourage students to explore and ask questions.** If students have questions, encourage them, when applicable, to write to a scientist or expert and ask them the question directly. Many times, experts from the field may even be willing to speak to your classroom via Skype or other video-conferencing program, and let all your students ask them questions, bringing the scientists, as well as the science itself, alive.

- **Go to the expert.** Videos from many of the leading scientists in their field are available online. For example, James Watson, the co-discoverer of the structure of DNA, has a wonderful presentation available, talking about how he and Francis Crick made the discovery and what it now means to the research he does today.

- **Help students create their own experiments.** *Wired Science,* from PBS, has several examples of student-created videos demonstrating science topics. Encourage your students to create their own videos and create a classroom home-grown video library.

- **Use technology to make science exciting.** Never forget that science is all about exploring and making sense of the world. When teachers can help students prove things to themselves, they will own that learning more than they ever would if told about it alone.

Section Eleven

Strategies for Differentiating Social Studies

Social studies is an ideal subject area for differentiating instruction because the content lends itself to active engagement. The options for projects, group work, and authentic civically focused work offers learners a way to transcend the traditional memorization of facts, which are impossible to commit to long-term memory without deeper application. The lists in this section offer ideas and examples of how teachers are introducing differentiation into their classrooms.

List 11.1. Gallery Walks

Gallery walks in the social studies classroom are a way for students to become actively involved in gathering, organizing, and sharing information. This method puts the teacher in the role of classroom facilitator rather than that of information dispenser. Gallery walks also get students out of their chairs and actively involve them in synthesizing important concepts in consensus building, writing, and public speaking.

Gallery walks consist of groups of students collecting information on a given topic and presenting the information on a chart or poster. After all the groups have assembled their posters, they put them up around the room in various stations. After the posters are up, students walk either individually or in groups around the room as though walking through an art gallery or a museum. They take notes, make observations, and compile the information from the charts into one synthesized whole.

To Prepare Students for Gallery Walks

- **Choose a topic to present.** Refer to curriculum standards to find a topic that has a great deal of information. The example used here will be from an eighth-grade social studies class on a unit about the Vietnam War.
- **Create questions.** Come up with a list of compelling questions for the groups to answer. Be sure some of the questions call for higher-order thinking.

  For example, assign a group of more advanced students the following question: "Come up with three opposing viewpoints as to whether or not the United States accomplished anything worthwhile in Vietnam. As a group, decide which you agree or disagree with and why." A question for less advanced students is: "Present ten reasons that the United States went to war with Vietnam."

- **Gather resources needed to answer the questions.** This may involve bookmarking places on the computer, gathering tapes and books, or arranging a trip to the library.
- **Create a student packet.** The packet should include
  - Overall introduction to the gallery walk
  - Description of the activity with time lines
  - Questions for creating the poster, as well as questions for viewing the gallery
  - Rubric for success (see example in this list)
  - Names of group members and assigned roles
- **Divide the class into groups.** Each group will create a different poster, chart, or "station" based on a question that relates to an important class concept. Sometimes gallery walks work well when students are divided into ability groups for the poster making. This allows teachers to assign questions along Bloom's Taxonomy (see List 3.3), allowing the students who are ready to tackle synthesis and evaluation to not get bogged down while students working on comprehension work to reinforce concepts.
- **Provide sufficient time for gathering information and responding.** Some gallery walks are used as a simple fifteen-minute icebreaker, but the most benefit can be gleaned from a week-long project involving graded oral and written reports.

List 11.1. (continued)

- **Initiate the gallery walk.** Student teams rotate to provide bulleted answers to questions posted on charts arranged around the classroom. In the student packet, the teacher will have included a list of questions each group should ask of every poster they observe. Some typical questions may be, "What is the most important information on the poster? What did you already know before viewing the poster? What are any questions the poster raises for your group?" After five minutes at a chart or "station" the team rotates to the next question.
- **Group debrief.** Once the group has visited all the posters, students return to their seats and work to prepare an overall presentation of the entire gallery. Each group will have the opportunity to give the presentation to the large group.

Advantages of a Gallery Walk

- In addition to addressing a variety of cognitive skills involving analysis, evaluation, and synthesis, gallery walks promote cooperation, listening skills, and team building.
- Gallery walks work best with open-ended questions—that is, when a problem, concept, issue, or debate can be analyzed from several different perspectives.

Student Evaluation

The following rubric can be used as a self-assessment tool, or for older students it can be used to evaluate one another in groups. A specific rubric for your gallery walk curriculum objectives like the one shown here is also beneficial as the groups present their findings to the class.

Student Rubric for Evaluating Group Work

Criteria	Distinguished	Proficient	Basic	Unacceptable
Workload	Did a full share of the work or more; knows what needs to be done and does it; volunteers to help others.	Did an equal share of the work; does work when asked; works hard most of the time.	Did almost as much work as others; seldom asks for help.	Did less work than others; doesn't get caught up after absence; doesn't ask for help.
Getting organized	Took the initiative proposing meeting time and getting group organized.	Worked agreeably with partner(s) concerning times and places to meet.	Could be coaxed into meeting with other partner(s).	Did not meet partner(s) at agreed times and places.

(Continued)

List 11.1. (continued)

Student Rubric for Evaluating Group Work (*continued*)

Criteria	Distinguished	Proficient	Basic	Unacceptable
Participation in discussions	Provided many good ideas for the unit development; inspires others; clearly communicated desires, ideas, personal needs, and feelings.	Participated in discussions; shared feelings and thoughts.	Listened mainly; on some occasions made suggestions.	Seemed bored with conversations about the unit; rarely spoke up, and ideas were off the mark.
Meeting deadlines	Completed assigned work ahead of time.	Completed assigned work on time.	Needed some reminding, work was late but it didn't affect grade.	Needed much reminding, work was late and it did affect quality or grade.
Showing up for meetings	Showed up for meetings punctually, sometimes ahead of time.	Showed up for meetings on time.	Showed up late but it wasn't a big problem for completing work.	No-show or extremely late. Feeble or no excuse offered.
Providing feedback	Habitually provided dignified, clear, and respectful feedback.	Gave feedback that did not offend.	Provided some feedback; sometimes hurt feelings of others with feedback or made irrelevant comments.	Was openly rude when giving feedback.
Receiving feedback	Graciously accepted feedback.	Accepted feedback.	Reluctantly accepted feedback.	Refused to listen to feedback.

Sources: Frandsen, B. (2004). Participation rubric for group development. http://www.stedwards.edu/cte/resources/grub.htm. September 2010. Parr, J. (2003). Group discussion rubric. http://www.mashell.com/~parr5/techno/group.html. September 2010.

An individual postassessment after the gallery walk will show teachers who grasped the concepts and at what level. Although these projects take time, the information gleaned from them will last longer and result in better skills for the future than simply covering a lot of content at a superficial-memory level that students will forget as soon as the test is over.

List 11.2. Time Lines

Time lines are a form of graphic organizer that helps students develop historical perspective, understanding, and feeling for the passage of time. One of the greatest challenges for students of all grades and levels is to be able to "feel" time, since they have had so few years of life themselves. Historical perspective is an additional challenge because students are typically self-focused and have a difficult time seeing how something that happened in the distant past relates to their current lives. This list provides ideas about different uses for time lines and how to make them an effective classroom tool. In general, time lines help students who are visual, sequential, or have challenges in these areas.

- Time lines can be used at the beginning of each unit in a history class to show where the unit lies in relationship to others.
- To be effective in teaching, time lines need to have graphics and references that appeal to the age group using it.
- Time lines can be interactive. Teachers can give students questions to make inferences or add information to them. For example, if a time line is recent, students can interview parents and grandparents for information to add to the time line.
- Time lines can be relational. For example, topic-specific time lines regarding inventions can be integrated with time lines regarding political and economic history to help students gain perspectives on different changes happening simultaneously in different parts of the world.
- Teachers may construct a poster-type time line for the periods covered throughout the year to be placed around the upper perimeter of the classroom. It could be kept in place during the entire course and referred to with each unit.
- Time lines can be used for almost any unit of time, such as the history of an invention, political history, or the history of women's rights.
- When using time lines, be sensitive to cultural diversity and try to include information pertinent to all the students' backgrounds.
- Students can create time lines by drawing pictures that correspond to important dates on the time line. This way, they interact with the information rather than simply taking it in.
- Many textbooks have time lines in them or the teacher resources for the books include them. These can be used creatively by asking students to compare and contrast various time lines and offer suggestions for missing information.
- Give students half-filled-in time lines to complete as they read about a certain period or event.
- Time lines can be large scale and painted in hallways or on playgrounds to depict important events in the history of the school.
- Time lines can be used to teach young children history. Begin by having students complete time lines of their own lives. This will give them a visual understanding of important events.
- Use a time line as an assessment tool. Present students with a list of events and ask them to create a time line that places the events in order of occurrence. This can help them understand cause and effect. For example, when studying the Civil War, the battles would come before Reconstruction.

List 11.3. Political Cartoons

There are many uses for political cartoons in the social studies classroom. Political cartoons are historic artifacts as well as ways for students to understand editorial views. They are especially helpful for visual learners and engaging for students who like art or have a strong sense of humor.

- Editorial cartoons cover a lot of high-level concepts: metaphor, simile, hyperbole, satire, irony—things that are harder to convey in text alone.
- Editorial cartoons can help develop students who are much more sophisticated into interpreters of current events. Political cartoons invite students to have a viewpoint on current and historical events.
- Have students gather a collection of historic political cartoons and then try to find current ones that provide the same sentiment. This will help students make links from the past to the present. They can compare and contrast these.
- Have students create their own portfolios of editorial cartoons collected from a variety of sources. As an extension activity, challenge students to design their own editorial cartoons that counter the sentiments of the cartoons in their portfolios.
- Use cartoons to discuss current events. Assign a cartoon of the day and rotate responsibility for bringing it to class among the students. The students who present the cartoon begin discussion about it. Ask: What does it represent?
- Use archived cartoons to understand political sentiments throughout history. Use cartoons in student unit packets to add interest and engage visual learners.
- Have students choose a political cartoonist to research and choose their favorite cartoons, explain the style, and describe the political views of the cartoon.
- Use cartoons to inspire discussion; have a debate about the viewpoints in the cartoon.
- Begin a discussion about freedom of speech, whether or not cartoons are fair and kind, and why they have survived in our society. Challenge students to think about when cartoons may not be an acceptable expression of free speech.
- Invite students to make up their own cartoons or give them cartoons without words and have them write an appropriate caption.

Further Reading

Cartoon-of-the-week editorial. http://www.globecartoon.com.
Editorial cartoons. A resource page featuring links to several syndicated editorial cartoonists. http://unitedfeatures.com/?title=C:Editorial%20Cartoons.
Politically correct cartoons. http://www.conservativecartoons.com/index.php.

Digital Cartoon Creation Tools

GoAnimate. http://goanimate.com.
ToonDoo. http://www.toondoo.com.
XtraNormal. Online tool to create your own animated movies. http://www.xtranormal.com.

List 11.4. Authentic Civic Projects

One of the reasons students find school boring is that they are unable to see how it connects to their lives outside of school. Social studies classes are a way for all students to see, no matter what their learning styles, how they fit into a democratic society. Authentic civic projects are those in which students research real-life community issues and participate actively in the community. This list gives examples of such projects.

- **Blog to blog.** Choose a common issue in a community, such as school taxes or whether or not a historic building should be saved. Any issue that has two sides or points of view will serve well for a blogging project in which students blog on different sides of the issue. Invite bloggers to publish the blogs on the Internet and open them up for comments. Have students make comments on each other's blogs and invite other classes and family and friends to make comments as well. This project gives students' voices and opinions on real issues an authentic audience.
- **Local politics, local communities.** Have students identify local issues that are coming up before the city council. Invite students to attend a city council meeting and listen to opinions on issues as a pre-activity. Once they choose the issues they wish to work on, have them research how decisions at the local level are made and how these decisions affect local residents and the students in the district.

Examples of Authentic Civic Projects

Local government city garden. Students wanted to turn an old lot into a community garden. They had to develop a scaled drawing of what this garden would look like and create rules for who would use it. Then they had to find out the steps and processes for getting the local authorities to grant permission to take over the lot. This led to meeting with city officials, Realtors, environmentalists, and law enforcement officials to discuss their plans and discover what information they needed. As a long-term project, this led to the students obtaining the property and setting up and taking care of the garden.

Steps Involved in This Project

- Identify a public issue.
- Determine who the stakeholders are.
- Research how to handle trash removal and crosswalks.
- Develop a process for political action campaigns.
- Set goals, cite ordinances, and raise public awareness.
- Carry out the project.
- Enlist greater community.
- Keep updates.

Understanding how the local government works. Students study world governments but rarely do they understand how the world around them works. This project introduces students to their local governments and helps them see the processes behind everyday things they take for granted. This is a unit that helps students understand government and taxation.

List 11.4. (continued)

Steps Involved in This Project

1. Have students brainstorm questions about all the things that happen in the communities where they live. For example, local businesses operating, garbage collection, streets being paved, mail delivery, schools, concerts coming to town.
2. Form two or three questions around each item on the list. Examples of good questions: Who pays for these things? What happens when one person wants something like a new cell phone tower and others don't? Discuss these questions and have students choose the one they find most interesting.
3. Divide students into teams to discover the following about what they chose:
   - Who makes the decisions for this?
   - Who pays for it?
   - Where does the money come from?
   - How are changes made?
   - What was the last big decision made in this category in your local community?
   - What were the issues surrounding it?
4. Provide students with a time line as well as resources about where to find information about local government such as webpages, phone numbers, Chamber of Commerce, Town Hall, the mayor's office. Create a supplementary reading station that has books and articles about how local government is run, taxation, and the process for electing officials.
5. Once the students are in teams and the projects have begun, the teacher acts as a facilitator. Students may need a lot of help with forming and refining their questions, making a plan for finding information, and finding out how to contact people outside the school.
6. Have students make presentations about their findings.

For younger students, this project can be scaled back to their developmental level. The teacher can scaffold much of the information that older students may be able to get themselves. Some topics for younger students may be discovering how the school runs, or how a grocery store gets the food on the shelves.

General Points for Authentic Civic Projects

- Authentic projects are good for all kinds of learners in the classroom because every student study can relate to them. The project is complex enough to have everyone involved at their own level while participating in the group.
- Teachers acting as facilitators with these projects can monitor student progress and intervene when necessary.
- Authentic projects take a great deal of planning and work but once the planning is complete, the teacher is free to work during class alongside the students.

List 11.4. (continued)

- When preparing authentic civic projects, think about communication skills. When students seem disengaged from their group, have them learn how to communicate via the telephone or in writing to a public official. Present a short lesson on how to write a respectful and appropriate e-mail.
- Engaged students retain their knowledge. Civic projects will help them understand history, politics, and government throughout the world.

Teachers can use the following rubric to help guide them after the brainstorming and topic-selection steps. This rubric is a self-assessment tool for the teacher to understand where the students are before taking the next steps.

Rubric for Authentic Civic Project

1. Lower-order thinking only	1...2...3...4...5	Higher-order thinking is central
2. Depth of knowledge: Knowledge is shallow	1...2...3...4...5	Knowledge is deep
3. Connectedness to the world beyond the classroom: No connection	1...2...3...4...5	Connected
4. Substantive conversation: No substantive conversation	1...2...3...4...5	High-level substantive conversation
5. Available resource support for student achievement: Negative support	1...2...3...4...5	Positive support

List 11.5. Multimedia Presentations

Differentiated classrooms are student centered. Today's student presentations are enhanced by technology, but often content suffers when the focus is on the tools of the presentation rather than the content. This list describes the various tools used in multimedia presentations, the potential pitfalls associated with each, and some tips to avoid them.

Word-Processing Software

- **Benefits:** Makes student work legible and editing easier. Encourages revision and makes collaboration easier.
- **Pitfalls:** Students focus on styles of fonts, size of letters, and margins to make a document seem longer. Students may be tempted to use "cut and paste" rather than rely on own composition skills when citing sources and doing research.
- **Solutions:** Rather than simply telling students which font and font size to use, provide them with questions their writing must address, including:
  - Students write at least five arguments for an issue you are studying. Have some students prepare at least five arguments for the other side. Using the printed argument lists, stage a debate.
  - Tell students how many facts must be included in the writing, and how to use proper sourcing to avoid accidental plagiarism.
  - Ask students to explain why or how after each statement, requiring them to add their own interpretation to any information presented.
  - When writing an essay, teach students to write a conclusion that is a new statement rather than repeating the question.
  - Ask students to submit outlines of longer projects and source lists prior to composing the essay or paper.

Spreadsheet and Database Software

- **Benefits:** Spreadsheets and database software are extremely useful tools for students to know how to use well. It is in every student's interest to understand how to use these programs, as well as when they are most helpful. Spreadsheets and database programs such as Microsoft Excel, Google Document Spreadsheets, or Apple's Numbers are great for organizing and displaying data. Graphing components help students create tables and graphs to show relationships between data points and statistical information.
- **Pitfalls:** Many teachers do not know how to use these tools and therefore cannot teach students. Often teachers rely on a short-staffed tech department to teach all the students, leaving many without the skills. Because teachers don't know how to use these tools, they shy away from incorporating them into their classrooms even when the tech department has taught the students the skills.
- **Solutions:** Many of today's students are tech savvy and have the ability to figure programs out without much trouble. Some programs come with excellent tutorials, thus making their use less complex and obtaining meaningful results easier than ever before.

List 11.5. (continued)

- ○ Teachers who capitalize on their students' knowledge will gain a valuable class resource. Poll students and see whether anyone knows how to use databases and spreadsheets and, if not, discover students who are willing to learn. Invite students to have their parents who are users of these tools to teach them. Have students teach the classes while the teacher learns alongside them.

- ○ Teachers are often uncomfortable admitting what they don't know. Students respond to a teacher's lack of knowledge in counterintuitive ways. Many students respect teachers for showing students they have an openness to learn new things. By learning alongside students, teachers model love of learning and the need for lifelong learning. This approach places an emphasis on learning as a process.

Spreadsheet and Database Activities for Social Studies

- ▪ Create a spreadsheet or database comparing information such as literacy rate, mortality rate, and per capita income. Create and answer questions about the information gathered.
- ▪ Students use a database program to chronologically order the states as they entered the Union.
- ▪ Using a spreadsheet program, have students compare the major industries of various states. Have them create a bar graph of the data and then write a summary report of their findings.

Desktop Publishing and Graphic, Paint, and Draw Software

- ▪ **Benefits:** Desktop publishing software allows students to easily integrate texts and graphics to produce sophisticated end products. Having students produce flyers, brochures, advertisements, reports, and more (the options are seemingly endless) can lead to engaging assignments and projects that allow students to demonstrate their understanding in a more multimedia format.
- ▪ **Pitfall:** Similar to those for word-processing or database software. Students can easily get caught up in the minutiae of altering fonts or picture sizes and lose sight of the main purpose of the project.
- ▪ **Solution:** Make sure students understand the purpose of the assignment. For example, after studying about the electoral process, have students create posters and flyers for their favorite candidate or feature themselves as if they were running for office. This project can be engaging while teaching students the importance of "making the case" for a candidate and his or her ideas through this multimedia format. Keeping students focused on making the flyer persuasive will be important rather than allowing them to focus too much on the font size and style.
- ▪ **Pitfall:** Students do not believe they are artistic and their design quality suffers. Teachers do not think attention to design is a skill that everyone should know about and they accept subpar work based on the belief that the presentation is not important to success in the project.
- ▪ **Solution:** Team up with the art teacher to develop projects using graphic or draw software. If your school does not have time for this kind of teaming, find someone in

List 11.5. (continued)

the community who can come in and help students learn the basic design principles needed to make presentations sparkle.

Some General Ideas for Using This Software or Art in Your Class

- Students create posters advertising jobs for women to work in factories. Discuss the history of women taking over men's jobs in the factories.
- Students design a poster supporting or opposing an event in history. Have students debate the issues.
- Students create a newspaper from the period they are studying.
- Students create a graphic depiction of a story from history.

Multimedia Software Such as PowerPoint, Keynote, HyperStudio, and Web Tools

- **Benefits:** Students can use these tools to make a presentation that uses text, pictures, video, and audio interactively to help emphasize points and create a dynamic oral presentation. Encourages students to think outside the box and use a wider variety of resources to help illustrate their point of view. Websites and wikis allow the publication and sharing of presentation through the Web to a wider audience.
- **Pitfalls:** Using these tools takes a significant amount of time even when students understand how to use them. The biggest pitfall with their use in classrooms is that content can suffer. The bells and whistles may take over and the requisite knowledge may not be demonstrated.
- **Solutions:**
  - Use rubrics when giving these assignments.
  - Coach students not to rely on the presentations to give all the information.
  - For PowerPoints or other slide presentations, students place too much information in their slides. Make sure they understand that slides are not their note cards but should be used to illustrate their talk. (This is a common mistake adults make as well.)
  - Be sure the task matches the tool. Too often teachers assign significant projects for insignificant tasks. PowerPoint presentations should not be used to present lower-order thinking. When presentations fall short and seem as though not enough effort or thinking went into them, it is often because the learning was not presented as a higher-order skill. These tools are not helpful for knowledge application or comprehension tasks. Rather, they take students' thinking to a new level.

Projects That May Benefit from the Use of Multimedia Software

- Create a multimedia or video presentation on current events and issues.
- Students research and report on one of the many ways people traveled during a historical period (e.g., wagons, canal boats, stagecoaches, trains). Gather these together to make one stack as a class report.
- Divide the class to research the importance of invention throughout periods in history. Use wartime study as an opportunity to view the role of invention and women rather than simply studying the battles and government leaders.

List 11.6. Research Methods

Too many of today's students and recent college graduates understand research only as looking something up. With the proliferation of the Internet, teaching scholarly research methods takes on new importance. There is a plethora of information on the Internet. It is all too much for students. Teachers have a responsibility to teach students appropriate use of this information. Because every student will have different ways of sifting and sorting through information, it is important that research methods allow for differentiation to the students' strengths. This list provides practical tips for teaching research in the age of new media.

- **Allow students to refine and adjust topics after they begin working.** The better students feel about the topic, the greater the chances for real learning.
- **Teach elementary students to research by asking them questions** and then pointing them to specific online pages to find the answers. Use bookmarks and social bookmarking as scaffolding tools.
- **Help students narrow down their focus and their topics** before they begin to research. And once they have identified something, have them do preliminary research prior to committing to it.
- **Use and introduce students to primary source documents.** Primary source documents are the original document rather than someone's commentary on a document. Examples are "The Declaration of Independence," the speeches of Martin Luther King Jr., and archived letters from Civil War soldiers.
- **When asking students to do research,** instead of prescribing the number of sources, ask them to discover a variety of types of sources, as in a reference, a primary source document, and a speech.
- **Distinguish among books, articles, and primary sources.** Be sure to explain the difference between scholarly and popular articles. Popular articles are found in newspapers and magazines. These may be appropriate for some research, but students should also be introduced to scholarly articles.

Sample Checklist for Determining Whether Online Material Is Scholarly

- Experts or scholars in the field write the article.
- The author's name is included.
- The audience for the article is people who seek expert and scholarly information.
- It includes specific and cited research.
- It contains a bibliography
- The date of publication is included.
- People making quotes are specifically named rather than saying, "One woman thought . . ."
- The language is scholarly or has some technical words.

List 11.6. (continued)

Different types of research materials are important for a full breadth of research and to engage all learners. Allow research of

- Photographs
- DVDs
- Videos
- Online databases
- Books
- Magazines
- Articles
- Interviews
- Anecdotal evidence
- Primary source documents
- Documentary films

For each type of source provide students with the proper way to cite its use. In addition, teachers can provide students with a short question-and-answer sheet to fill out on each resource they review to determine whether it is the one they wish to use or not. Some questions for these include

- What question in your topic does this research answer or address?
- How is this resource better than other ones?
- Will this resource strengthen your paper or presentation? How? Why?

List 11.7. Class Discussion

Every social studies teacher includes discussion in his or her teaching repertoire. But too often discussion is merely a teacher-centered process in which the student is not engaged in higher-order thinking. There are several discussion models that can help make this strategy more effective, especially as a way to model thinking and critical problem solving. Students, depending on their learning profiles, will enjoy and feel successful at one kind of discussion activity over another, so to assure success for all, teachers are encouraged to try more than one.

Educators for Social Responsibility (ESR) Model

This describes a process for dialogue. The steps are

1. Present positions.
2. Each group asks questions, then restates the other group's position as accurately as possible.
3. Each group presents a list of the agreements between the two positions.
4. Each group presents the questions that both can explore to resolve some of their differences.

Debate

A debate is a discussion in which participants articulate, justify, and clarify their positions on an issue. In this informal debate plan, rebuttals attempt to refute statements made by the opposing side. Students love to debate topics in class. The difference between an effective debate and an ineffective one comes down to planning. For effective debates, consider the following:

Before the Debate

- **Select the topic:** The topic for a debate evolves from what you are teaching. Provide students with a few questions to debate and let them choose which carries the most interest.
- **Take a stand:** Every debate has two sides, the affirmative side and the negative side. The affirmative side, "pro," supports a proposition. The opposing or negative side, "con," opposes the proposition. The teacher can divide the class into pros and cons, or students may choose their own stance. A good ongoing exercise is to ask students to prepare debates for a side that they do not in reality agree with. Students can participate in one-on-one debates or group debates. In a group debate, students take turns making statements and giving rebuttals.
- **Research:** Provide enough time for research and demand the research be significant. Fact gathering should support the student's point of view. Three to five resources are recommended. Give students a structured framework to guide their research. Provide students a template for taking notes and encourage students to understand the model before beginning research.

List 11.7. (continued)

The Debate

- Be clear who the debate monitor or moderator is. Teachers can have students take on this role if the teacher fully explains what is involved. A student moderator should be able to speak clearly and keep everyone on task in a respectful manner. The moderator formally introduces the debate topic and recognizes students to speak, alternating between pro and con.
- Opening and closing statements
  - Students may volunteer to make opening and closing statements, or the teacher may appoint students.
  - Setting the tone for the debate, the students should have a prepared speech (one to three minutes).
  - The debate begins with an opening statement from the pro side, followed by a statement from the con side.
  - Opening statements should include each side's opinion with a brief overview of the supporting evidence.
  - The debate ends with closing statements from both sides.
  - Again the pro side speaks first, followed by the con side.
  - The planned closing statements (one to three minutes) should restate the opinions with strong supporting evidence.

Socratic Seminars

This is a discussion style developed by Socrates (c. 470–399 B.C.). He engaged his students in intellectual discussion by responding to questions with questions, instead of answers. This method is still used regularly in law schools and other graduate-level coursework to encourage deeper thinking, and it should be encouraged at all levels to inspire students to think for themselves rather than being told what to think.

In this method

- Students dissect a text, problem, or an event in order to better understand it.
- They ask questions and probe each other's answers from different perspectives. This method works well to understand complex issues.
- Students are given roles to help them be productive in the seminar. Some students are speakers, some are listeners.
- Participants in the seminar are expected to listen carefully without interrupting. They must make direct eye contact with others and must use each other's names. This device allows teachers to give a voice to all students and to let talkative students develop their listening skills.
- Roles can rotate within a seminar or from seminar to seminar. The goal is for students to become proficient in a variety of roles.

List 11.7. (continued)

Decision Making

An interesting way to engage learners in class discussion is through decision-making models. This method can be done as a large group or broken down into small groups once the students are familiar with the method.

- Chose a topic that involves a decision. This works best when the decision involves an action that needs to be taken. For example, should a school begin recycling or not? How can the U.S. prevent future massive flooding along the Mississippi River? The focus of this model is a step beyond debate. Students are not arguing over whether something is right or wrong; instead they are determining what will happen if they take action on something. This can be done with real-life examples or with examples in which students take on fictitious roles.
- Divide a posterboard, a blackboard, or a whiteboard in half. On one side write what happens if the class decides to take action. On the other side write what happens if the class doesn't take action.
- Have the class come up with a rating system or a points system. Score the two sides. Make it clear that once the decision is made, the entire class must go along with it. Discuss each point in its entirety.
- Make the decision. Vote to consensus based on the pros and cons.
- Create a strategy or plan of action.

Problem Solving

Similar to the decision-making model, students are responsible for coming up with a solution to a problem. Again this can be done in either small groups or as a whole class.

- The first step is to present the students with a problem to be solved. For example, the North Koreans are about to invade South Korea. What is the course of action that the United States should take? This is a complex problem that will involve much discussion.
- Once the problem is described, students can be assigned certain roles in the discussion. Or the entire class can use DeBono's Thinking Hats method to solve the problem. In this method, everyone in the group brainstorms solutions during one period, followed by another time in which everyone plays devil's advocate. Together the class works toward a new solution to the problems.

These class discussion devices are all intended to bring students into a more lively discussion that involves higher-order thinking; they can be scaled up or scaled down depending on student ages.

Section Twelve

Strategies for Differentiating the Arts

While some teachers may assume that differentiating instruction is most suitable to core subjects, it's equally important for all classes, including the arts classroom. In order to be true twenty-first-century learners, students need to be able to express their ideas using multimedia formats, so the arts are actually important core skill areas for all students. All students need opportunities to tap into their creativity—especially those who assume they are "not good at art"—making it critical for art educators to differentiate instruction for all students in their classrooms.

List 12.1. Group Work in the Arts

Group work in the arts can be rewarding for students but also can cause concerns about making sure each creative voice is heard in the final project. A quick look at the recent *Work of Art* television show (www.bravotv.com/workofart) demonstrates how difficult it can be for artists to work together at times. However, collaboration often brings out the best in artists and challenges their presupposed ideas by providing meaningful critique and guidance. This list provides some tips for designing group projects for the art classroom that will be challenging and successful for students of all abilities in a differentiated instruction environment.

- **Identify the goal or learning outcome.** As with any group project, first identify the learning outcome or goal and then base the project to best meet the goal.
- **Identify the steps toward the goal.** Each member of the group should have an opportunity to participate in the project in the period given.
- **Create checkpoints to keep group work on task.** As with any group environment, structure is important to keep people on task and working toward a common goal. Smaller subassignments will help keep students focused on larger, more imaginative projects.
- **Offer projects as design; projects to solve problems.** Projects involving designing something to fix a particular problem (real or imaginary), rather than projects based solely on aesthetic outcomes work well for group projects and allow projects to be more easily segmented among group members.

Examples of "Design Your Dream _____" Prompts

Invent a Dream Machine

- All great inventions and designs start with solving a problem someone has. What's your biggest daily problem? Getting homework done? Household chores? Having enough time with friends? Can't remember that great idea you had yesterday?
- Brainstorm with your group and think of the kind of problems you all share. Then think of possible solutions: real, imaginary, and fantasy. Do you want a Homework Machine? What would it look like? What different functions and features would it have? How would you make sure it worked not only for you, but for other people as well? Could you design it and then design an advertisement for it to help sell it on TV? Do you want to film an infomercial for your final invention?
- For this project, your group needs to settle on one problem to solve and then, using materials provided, design a machine to solve your problem. (Bonus points are given if you include "how it works" in the design.) Over the course of this project, you'll be asked to
  - Have a drawing, like a schematic, of all the different parts of the machine
  - Build a prototype based on the schematic of your imaginary machine
  - Write a description of the machine, what it does, and how it solves the problem
  - Design an advertisement for your machine
  - Shoot a short video advertisement for your project

List 12.1. (continued)

- At the end, all members in the group should be able to identify what part of the project they contributed to, where their idea is in the final project, and how they helped make the dream machine come to life.

Design Your Own Clubhouse

- Kids have always liked to feel like they could have their own house, club, or place to get together with friends and do what they want, without parents or other adults telling them what they can and can't do. For this project, we want you to design your own dream club and a clubhouse for you to meet. The club can be for anything you want: a hobby, something you love to do, a school subject—you name it. After you decide what your club is focused on, your group will deign the clubhouse to provide a place for you to all get together and do that activity.
    - **Activity or theme considerations:** Is it a video games club? A baking cookies club? Dancing? Sports? A watching sitcoms club? What would be the perfect environment for your club?
    - **Location considerations:** Where would it be located? As a tree house? In a city? In a forest? On a farm? On a boat?
    - **Equipment and design features:** Then think of the stuff you would want there, real, imaginary, without thought of costs or anything else. What would your clubhouse look like? What do you need to do your activity or reason to get together? Comfy couches and big screen TVs? Computers? Snacks? Phones? What different functions and features would it have? How would you make sure it worked not only for you, but for other people as well?
    - **Getting members:** Could you design the club and clubhouse and then design an advertisement for it to help recruit other members? Are there any rules or special clothes, hats, outfits, or pins people need to wear to identify each other as club members? What's your secret handshake?
    - **Details (what's required):** For this project, your group needs to settle on one club theme and then, using materials provided, design a clubhouse for your club. Over the course of this project, you'll be asked to
        - Have a drawing, like a schematic, of the clubhouse and its location. Why is the clubhouse located at that spot? How do members get in and out of it? Is it a secret club or a public one?
        - Next you'll build an architect's model of your clubhouse from the drawing or plan.
        - Then write a description of the club, any rules for membership, and how you join.

List 12.1. (continued)

- Design an advertisement to help attract new members to the club, and what you'll have so members of the club can recognize each other (membership cards, pins, etc.).
  - And finally, shoot a short video or record a podcast advertisement for your club.
- At the end, everyone in the group should be able to identify what part of the project they contributed to, where their idea is in the final project, and how they helped make the perfect club come to life.

Points of Differentiation in Group Work

- This sort of prompt incorporates multiple parts into a project that encourages student collaboration, exercises imagination and design skills in different mediums, along with opportunities to express and advocate for their vision, and helps others see its importance, utility, and beauty.
- Instruction is differentiated by allowing students' choice between projects, materials, and aspects of the project that speak to their own vision and voice.
- Teachers help guide students and groups along the process in class and by providing check points and due dates for each subset of goals.
- Teachers can create a wiki, blog, or other online website to host student multimedia projects and share them with other students and families.

List 12.2. Ways to Help All Students Feel Successful in Art

Some students will seem to come by the arts naturally, and others will not. The goal of art instruction, at least in part, should be to allow each student to explore self-expression and communication in mediums beyond written language. This list explores ways to differentiate art instruction and help all students appreciate this form of self-expression.

- **Identify those needing additional guidance.** Students' production of work may have to do with their experience and facility with the materials, as well as with their ability to generate ideas. A simple "before we begin" questionnaire, especially for larger projects, can help you get a sense of which students may need more support during the session.

- **Getting unstuck.** As with writing, many students may get "stuck" when asked to create a piece of artwork on demand. Guiding students through the idea generation stage of a project and how to formulate a plan before beginning will help the students produce a better piece, as well as teach them about project planning and management, which can be abstracted to other core curriculum experiences.

- **Feeling accepted and confident.** Students who seem shy, resistant, or unconfident often feel their ideas are not "good enough" or lack confidence in their own idea generation. Keeping a list of questions, prompts, or other "stock" ideas may help these students get over their fear of the blank page and find a starting point from which they can then make the project their own.

- **Make projects meaningful and relevant.** Consider assigning projects that are personally relevant and perhaps relate to other curriculum-based materials. By choosing projects that engage the student with subject matter they already know, have a connection with, or otherwise have a motivation to learn, you are more apt to gain a child's interest and motivation for the project at hand.

- **Managing materials and demonstrating concepts.** Some students may not be well versed in creating art, or they may have motor, visual, spatial, or other problems that make it difficult for them to make their ideas come to life using typical art supplies. Consider offering alternative ways for these students to demonstrate their understanding of core concepts, such as finding examples of use of color, symmetry, perspective, or good design through pictures from magazines, online, and so forth.

- **Encourage and nurture student expression.** Encouragement and assistance from instructors is incredibly important for students struggling to express themselves artistically. Students' inner critics can get in the way of their production, and the self-evaluation may keep students from freely experimenting for fear they will "get it wrong" or "make a mistake." Making the art room a place of freedom, acceptance, and expression should be a core goal.

- **Make art relevant and the end point clear.** Make sure you understand and communicate the "big idea" behind the curriculum goals. If you are trying to teach symmetry, for example, bring in examples from math, science, or other classrooms to help make the material relevant to students.

List 12.2. (continued)

- **Reveal the art found in everyday objects.** Art and design are incredibly important in many of the things we use every day, from chairs to computers to dishes to glasses to even how websites are laid out. Help students understand the relationship of art and design, and how it can improve usability and functionality.

- **Encourage attempts and make "failures" meaningful.** Art class may be one of the few aspects of a student's education where there is not always a "right" answer, and students who are talented in other classes may feel less confident in the art room, where matters are often more open-ended. Make sure students feel they can experiment a bit, try new things that may make them uncomfortable, and even find "failures"—broken pottery, poor color choice, and so on—can be opportunities to learn a grow.

- **Connect art to academics.** Show students how color, design, layout, and other concepts from art class are relevant to academic projects such as posters, slides, website design, and user interface. As students see the applicability of art to the rest of their subjects, they are less likely to be dismissive or lose interest in the process.

- **Connect art to business.** Recent business books such as *The Back of the Napkin* by Roam (2008) and *Business Model Generation* by Osterwalder and Pigneur (2010) show how important art and drawings can be in fleshing out ideas and communicating ideas effectively to others. Helping students see how even rudimentary drawings can aid communication will help bring the importance of even basic art home to everyone.

- **Show creativity at work.** Have students watch popular TV shows, such as *Project Runway, Work of Art, Top Chef, Iron Chef America*, or the like. These shows feature "challenges," in which each person starts with the same "assignment" but is allowed to use any of the materials on hand, or specific materials supplied, to come up with their own solution to the assignment or problem posed. Watching others start from the same place but come up with such radically different end points may help show students that there are many answers to one question, and that their ideas and thoughts are likely to be as good as or better than someone else's.

List 12.3. Technology, Differentiated Instruction, and Visual Arts

Integrating technology in the visual arts can be broken down into three general areas or "buckets":

1. Using resources available online to help teach and instruct on points ranging from how-to to elements of good design
2. Using technology to create art and work on projects
3. Using technology to keep records of ideas, inspirations, and completed works and share those with others.

This list discusses how to use and integrate technology into the classroom for each of these three areas.

1. **Videos of artists and designers discussing process.** There are a plethora of resources online to help teach students at almost any level about elements of good design. Many videos and websites talk about the importance of design in everything from websites themselves to everyday objects. Here are a few that are both entertaining and instructive:
   - **Seth Godin: This Is Broken.** Seth Godin, a well-known marketing guru and blogger, talks about the website This Is Broken, discussing what "broken" means, and the reasons that many things may be broken, often on purpose, and ways to fix them. He offers great insight into both using your head when doing something, as well as how the end product of your work can be received. (http://www.ted.com/talks/seth_godin_this_is_Broken_1.html)
   - **Yves Behar on Designing Objects That Tell Stories.** This great presentation features a designer who has created some amazing, well-known products and discusses the creative process and design. (http://www.ted.com/talks/yves_behar _on_designing_objects_that_tell_stories.html)
   - **RSA Animates.** The RSA (Royal Society for the Encouragement of Arts, Manufactures, and Commerce) has produced a series of animation and drawing videos to go along with some compelling talks from people such as Sir Ken Robinson or Daniel Pink. The animation series demonstrates how the art and drawings help elucidate the points made by the speaker and brings the discussion to life more vividly. (http://www.thersa.org)
2. **Technology to create art**
   - Digital painting is coming to the forefront and is being used as an element for both online and offline graphic design. A wide range of programs, from Adobe to Corel to others, can be used to teach students how to "paint" without actual canvas and brush. Free Web-based programs such as Queeky are also available. (http://www.Queeky.com/app)
   - Digital tools such as Photoshop can be used to combine and alter images to create entirely new works of art.

List 12.3. (continued)

○ When using digital tools in an art class, especially if it involves a "remix" or "mash-up," it's important to also spend some time teaching students about issues such as basic copyright infringement, when alteration of existing images is appropriate (or inappropriate), and when it does not constitute fair use.

○ Encourage students to use and create their own images, go on photo walks, or use material on photo websites such as Flickr (with appropriate creative commons licensing) in their art work and projects. Learning how to use art and pictures to represent ideas and illustrate their oral presentations will help teach students effective presentation creation skills that are critical for effective communication of complex ideas.

3. **Using technology to record ideas, inspirations, and completed works and to share work with others.**

○ Encourage students to record their ideas for projects and collect inspirations that can be aided by technology. Wikis, blogs, applications such as "Evernote", and social bookmarking tools are great ways to save and store inspirations for later use.

○ Technology can easily be used to take pictures of or record works of art, and share the same out to the world through a website such as Flickr or Picassa. Websites such as Etsy even allow artists to market and sell their works of art to others, if they so choose.

○ Websites are great for allowing students to show their families and friends their work, both the finished project and works in progress. Many communities exist on the Web to allow students to share their work, largely based on type of work.

○ The use of technology in the arts classroom should be done with thought toward recording work for later use and portfolio building, as well as sharing with others for joy and perhaps for critique as well.

List 12.4. Technology, Differentiated Instruction, and Performing Arts

Technology can assist students in not only recording and preserving practice, performance, and the like, but can also help them learn to self-reflect, self-edit, and learn how to improve the performance. Technology is often now becoming part of a performing artist's repertoire, with musicians recording multiple tracks that they can sync during live performances, as well as multimedia art performances, like those of the Blue Man Group, which uses everything from pantomime to video to music and percussion to create its shows. This list offers some ideas on how to integrate technology into the performing arts in a meaningful way for students.

- **Technology can teach children how to express themselves through yet another medium.** For example, in the performing arts, we want students to begin to appreciate how music (and its execution) augments a performance.
  - It can change the mood and atmosphere.
  - It can signal performers and audiences.
  - It can build anticipation.
  - It can set a theme and illustrate points.
- **As students start to experiment in multimedia presentation,** understanding how they can express their own feelings and passion in their music or performance is an important element in making a regular piece or assignment special and elevated to that next level.
- **Helping students see great performances through online video** enables them to begin to dissect the elements of what makes a great performance and how they can adapt those factors into their own work. For example:
  - Audience engagement
  - Fluidity
  - Projection
  - Carriage
- **Ability to change roles may best be taught by seeing others, and then trying similar things in class.** Helping students understand how the disparate elements combine to make a good versus great performance may illustrate or critique in a more meaningful way.
- **Using simple recording techniques** and posting them to a class wiki or website will help students compare and contrast their own performances, as well as open up performances for family and friends to appreciate.
- **Common open source software,** such as Audacity (available for PC and Mac platforms), allows simple multitrack recording and editing of sound, thus letting students experiment with creating their own soundtracks, or experiment with how sound, background noises, and the like create a realistic setting and cue imagination.
- **Encourage students to go on sound tours of their home and school environment.** Closing their eyes and picking out sounds in the background, or picking out instruments in a piece of music, contributes to students' development of important critical listening skills in the performing arts and across the curriculum.

Section Thirteen

Strategies for Physical Education and Health

The differentiated instructional model in the physical education and health class encourages the teacher to respond to the needs of all learners, with consideration of their existing readiness and interest levels.

List 13.1. Tips on Using Differentiated Instruction in Physical Education

Physical education is no longer only about sports and physical activity. With unprecedented numbers of youth suffering from depression, obesity, attention disorders, and inactivity, the introduction of health into the K–12 curriculum offers opportunities for teachers of physical education to customize the classroom per the individual needs of the students. This list provides tips and rationale for the strong integration of health and physical education as a way to differentiate for students.

- **Use the three approaches to differentiation.** There are three main approaches to differentiation that can be used in physical education and health classes. These are differentiation by task, differentiation by outcome, and differentiation by support (Harrison, 1997).

  ○ **Differentiation by task** involves having students perform tasks according to their interests and abilities. For example, a teacher may set up four different stations for practicing hand–eye coordination and let students choose which station to attend. The two key words when differentiating by task are *readiness* and *interest*.

  ○ **Differentiating by outcome:** Students are grouped according to the outcome the teacher believes they are ready to master. Some students may be asked to run a mile, whereas others may be timed running a 600-yard dash. Personal best is a value that factors into a strong differentiated physical education class.

  ○ **Differentiation by support:** Different students require varying levels of support as they work toward mastery. A differentiated classroom will set up units of study that offer various types of support depending on the student's needs. Examples of these supports are direct one-on-one instruction, written or videotaped instructions and demonstrations, individual self-paced work, and coaching.

- **Combine PE and health.** Combining physical education with health studies offers a natural way to allow students with different learning styles opportunities for success. Health class provides students with opportunities to write or give presentations about topics such as healthy eating, heart rate, and metabolism or good exercise habits.

- **Emphasize process over product.** Differentiated physical education classes must stress process over product for everyone to be successful. When product is stressed, the class focuses on competition and success is measured on a curve against winning. When process is stressed over product, style becomes more important than drilling. To help students develop style, teachers should respond to how individuals approach the objectives and communicate individually with students. For example, when a student is kicking a ball the teacher may say, "You put a lot of back kick into that—watch the angle. It makes the ball fly higher."

List 13.1. (continued)

- **Help students maintain records and compete against themselves rather than each other.** As part of physical education, helping students record and set goals to push themselves a little bit at a time will help them see their progress and help with motivation. Students who may be struggling with physical fitness need to see that they can still make progress and succeed, rather than being trapped in comparisons between themselves with other, more fit or able students. This method also helps high-achieving students set more personally relevant goals for progress rather than being used by other students as markers of their ability and achievement.

- **Integrate lessons with other parts of the curriculum.** Physical education and health curriculums are perfect places for integration of writing and mathematics for students who tend to excel in those domains. Statistics, facts, and graphs are useful tools for presentations; reports and studies about health are also ways to involve all kinds of learners in the physical education class.

- **Be patient: some things are developmental.** Recognize that physical ability is developmental. Selecting the most suitable grouping options for learning enables students to maintain maximum attention and developmentally appropriate involvement and enhances student productivity and comprehension.

List 13.2. Strategies for Differentiating Skill Training

This list covers different strategies teachers can employ while students learn new skills. Just as with traditional academic subjects, students require a mixture of practice, encouragement, and risk taking in order to master new skills, and this list provides additional ideas and resources for implementation of differentiated instruction strategies in physical education.

- **One skill at a time.** Students learn by mastering simple concepts before moving on to more difficult ones. With this in mind, remember that Bloom's Taxonomy (see List 3.3) works in the physical education class by starting with knowledge. Full explanations with examples will help students move from one skill to the next.
- **Specific feedback.** Rather than telling students they did a "good job," be as specific as possible about what they are doing right or need to do differently. For example: "You are holding the bat too high up, try moving your hands down to the base for greater force of gravity" gives a student relevant feedback and rationale for why small tweaks may make a large difference in performance.
- **Stations.** An effective way to differentiate the physical education class is with the use of stations. In the gymnasium set up a variety of activities in different locations. Each station involves a different activity, requiring various amounts of effort. Task cards at the station identify how the exercise should be performed and also identify three levels of intensity (high, medium, and low) at which the students may work. The teacher will demonstrate how to use each station before students rotate through them. Examples of elementary stations:
  - **Make the basket.** Students toss beanbags into a wastebasket. This is good for hand–eye coordination, balance, and aim. Move the basket closer or farther away for different-level students.
  - **Cone dribble.** Set up a series of cones and give each student a ball and a small sack to sling over his or her shoulder. Have students weave in and out dribbling the ball. After each cone, have something for students to pick up without losing control of the ball. Use different-size objects and spread the cones out at different lengths for varying ability levels.
  - **Heart rate count.** Using a jump rope and a stopwatch, have students count their heart rates for one minute. Then jump rope as fast as they can for 30 seconds. At the end, count the heart rate again.
- **Say it in many different ways.** If students do not understand your coaching, vary your descriptions. Give students a few examples, "It's like riding a bicycle." "Think of kicking your legs like in a swimming pool." What one student catches onto, another student may need a different example or description to put the sequence of a movement together.
- **Solicit student feedback.** Teachers can never ask too many questions about a student's experience. When students struggle, ask them to be specific about where they are experiencing frustration. Likewise, when a student suddenly gets it, ask what clicked for the understanding to take place. Incorporate his or her response into your examples for other students.

List 13.2. (continued)

- **Be alert to peer pressure and put-downs.** The physical education class can be a place where students tease or bully one another in ways that are not always obvious. Teachers should be aware of remarks students make to one another, as well as nonverbal communication such as eye rolling or sighing when someone doesn't get it right. Talk to students about mutual support. Don't allow any breach of respect.

- **Coordinate learning profile with teachers.** Classroom teachers have a great deal of information about learners that can be valuable to the physical education teacher. Is a student shy in class? Does she enjoy reading and individual work? These insights can help physical education teachers prepare differentiated lessons and understand their students.

- **Let young kids play.** Young children do not always have to be involved in fully structured time. Allowing for active time during which students are allowed to make up the rules, run around, and play is very important to developing their interest in movement and teaming. Put out a lot of objects and let students freely choose what to use and how to play with it.

- **Rhythm activities.** Developing coordination and understanding rhythm is not only good for physical activities; studies show that when students practice moving to and listening to various rhythms, it increases brain activity. Rhythm activities in the physical education class, therefore, can enhance learning across the curriculum.

- **Explain to students.** When introducing students to new activities or objectives, take the time to explain to them both why they are learning and how differentiation is being introduced. Let students know that their individual learning styles matter.

- **Use music.** Many students respond to music. It motivates, soothes, and helps connect them to their interests. When using stations or taking time to practice or play, use music as a background. Let the students choose the music sometimes for enhanced interest.

- **Employ visualization techniques.** Visualization helps students become determined, calm, and ready for action. Teach students to visualize the activities and objectives before they begin them. Visualization also works well when getting students to imagine themselves as strong and healthy. There are visualization tapes that can assist with this technique if the teacher feels uncomfortable.

- **Provide pictures with written instructions.** Physical education teachers traditionally rely on verbal instructions to games and activities. Not all children can understand through verbal instruction alone. When possible, provide written instructions for students to refer to as they listen along with the teacher. Diagrams and pictures also help students who are visual learners understand.

- **Talk to parents.** Many parents are very competitive and want their children to succeed in sports to fulfill their own desires to relive their competitive days. This is especially difficult when the student is not so interested as the parent. Teachers can talk to parents and explain how important it is for them to focus on process and discover true interests before pushing students to succeed in athletics.

- **Balance competition with collaboration.** Competition is great for students who enjoy healthy competition. However, not all children are energized by competition. When physical education and health classes emphasize both collaboration and competition, more students find activities they will develop into lifelong health habits.

List 13.3. How to Encourage Everyone's Participation

Getting everyone to readily participate is the physical education (PE) teacher's challenge. This list offers tips on ways to engage all learners in the differentiated physical education class.

- **Stress mastery over competition.** Not all students are competitive, but many think that physical education is all about competition. Stress how mastery of curricular goals is key to physical education. Share the curriculum with students when they are old enough to understand objectives. This will help them see what is expected of them.
- **Explain the benefits of being physically active.** Stress how activity will give students more energy and how more energy will allow them to move better, which will lead to feeling better about themselves. Take time to discuss these ideas with students using a discussion format. Provide questions and facts and allow for discussion.
- **Emphasize the value of teamwork.** Give students examples of why it matters to show up for the other members of the team. Stress how every role on a team matters.
- **Use interest inventories** (see List 2.3) to figure out what students feel most comfortable doing. Here are some sample questions to ask:
  - What is the first memory you have of a sport or contest?
  - Are there any games your family plays?
  - Do kids in your neighborhood play outdoor games? What kind?
  - Would you rather play with a ball or a rope?
  - Which do you do best? Run, jump, hop, skip, swim?
- **Expose students to a variety of activities.** Make sure all the activities are not competitive. Maximize resources by looking for books and articles on games and noncompetitive activities.
- **Provide varying opportunities for success.** For example, if students are learning to climb a rope, have different levels of reward rather than just the getting to the top. If students are learning to throw a basketball into a hoop, give some students the goal of getting ten baskets, while others may be rewarded for getting one. Be sure to make it clear you believe that all goal attainment is equally valuable.
- **Share fact sheets with students on the value of activity.** For example, discuss how many students participate in different sports around the world, or provide facts about how much energy a game of volleyball expends.
- **Balance teamwork with individual activities.** Some students prefer to be active on an individual level while others prefer to be on teams and still others like to participate in a group. Provide students options and explain the difference between a team and a group.
- **Group students with similar athletic or physical activity interests** together to participate. For example, every weekend a group of students go on a bicycle ride together.

List 13.3. (continued)

- **Keep track of students' progress.** Allow students to see success over time in a variety of areas, such as how far they jump, how long they can run, how many games of tennis they play. Make sure these are not compared with other students but instead are used to demonstrate individual progress in any area of concentration.
- **Know students' names.** Be sure to call students by their names.
- **Give students nicknames.** When students get a positive nickname, they feel a special part of a group. If the teacher cannot think of a good name for everyone, invite students to come up with their own nicknames. Emphasize positive names.
- **Be clear about locker-room rules.** Students often do not want to participate in PE because of the teasing and concern around body image that takes place in locker rooms. Some schools force students to take showers and this traumatizes some students into fearing physical education. Be sure to have clear boundaries for students about how to treat one another with respect in the locker room.
- **Be a role model for respect.** Teachers should never let students hear them passing judgment on other students. The days of "tough coaching through humiliation" are long gone.
- **Model the activities expected** of students even if they are difficult. There is no better role modeling than for students to see teachers struggle alongside them to gain mastery. Try to find some activities where you are not an expert and model improvement and perseverance.
- **Talk to individuals.** Sometimes physical education teachers take on the role of coach and talk to the class as though to a team. Students need to be recognized and validated as individuals in order to buy into the class.
- **Emphasize fun, laughter, and enjoyment.** Many students consider physical activity as work and sweat. Inject the class with laughter and fun.
- **Have students bring music.** Invite students to bring in their own music to physical education class. Allow them to work through a series of physical stations listening to the students' music of the day.
- **Invite guest speakers.** Invite guest speakers into class to talk about staying healthy—such as someone who recovered or overcame a health issue, a professional athlete or coach, or a local sportscaster.
- **Balance examples of achievements of women and men athletes.** Highlight the athletic successes of women as well as men. Women's soccer has played an important role in getting girls involved in athletics. Highlighting or featuring stories of female success will inspire girls to get involved in health and wellness.
- **Balance sports, games, and understanding wellness.** Help students see that physical education encompasses far more than competition. Be sure that each student sees how he or she has an individual stake in staying healthy.
- **Be sensitive to cultural differences regarding sports and health.** A good way to assess how students from different cultures respond to athletics is to ask simple questions with a survey. For example: "What is your family's favorite sport? Why?

List 13.3. (continued)

What kinds of foods does your family enjoy? Are there any differences or rules your family has about boys and girls participating in sports?" Have students discuss the role of athletics and physical activity in their families and keep an eye out for differences that may be cultural. Try to be sensitive to differences.

- **Differentiate for the student with special needs.** In the physical education class this means having less focus on time limits, providing both oral and written instructions for games and activities, allowing students to work with partners, and coaching students without disabilities on how to work with students who have them. Use assistive materials. For example, with softball, use Velcro balls and mitts or larger bats and a batting tee. If any individual is in wheelchair, allow the student to push a ball off a ramp with the bat or any other way that will work for him or her.

- **Connect students to their memories.** Invite students to explain any neighborhood or childhood games they may have played that they enjoy. Find a way to integrate these into the curriculum.
  - Invite students to form groups and invent games and make up the rules.
  - Have students choose sports or health heroes to write reports and give presentations about. This will help the bookish student feel comfortable in class.
  - For students interested in animals, be sure to let them know the various animal-related activities, such as playing polo or swimming with dolphins.

- **Balance teams.** Modify the activity to create a level playing field when dividing teams so there are fewer students who are obviously "better" than others. For example, have skilled students use their nondominant side when participating. Let the student understand what it is like to be a beginner again.

- **Avoid too much competition.** Try to incorporate activities that do not promote winners and losers. Formulate curriculum that has all students working toward the same goal or outcome. Group cooperation games work well for this. Programs such as Project Adventure also work well.

List 13.4. Ideas for Coaches

Although they are not part of the regular school day, coaches are often the most influential teachers students encounter. Here are some tips for coaches that will allow them to reach every player on the team.

- **Build individual relationships.** Coaches sometimes have a tendency to talk to the whole team rather than seeing young people as individuals with individuals' strengths and challenges. Get to know the team members as individuals. When they feel known, they are able to perform better.
- **Focus on participation.** Winning is nice, but a focus on participation will encourage team members to keep trying and keep coming back if the winning streak is off.
- **Encourage buddies.** Everyone on a team should feel there is someone who is watching out for their experience. Buddies can be responsible for cheering and encouraging the specific performance of this player. If the team member does not play, the buddy can let her know she was important to be present and ask how she liked the game.
- **Celebrate teamwork over victory.** Even when a team loses, there is a cause for celebration. Have a team party when you stop for pizza on the way home just because the team performed well together.
- **Point out everyone's assets.** Discover one unique thing that each member of a team brings to the group and point these out so everyone is aware of the other's assets.
- **Stress interpersonal connection over praise.** When coaches notice the character qualities of team members and point them out, they are encouraging positive connections. For example, let players know their patience is appreciated; thank players for sharing their time and energy in support of the team. Build relationships based on these interpersonal connections; they will go much further than praise for a winning job.
- **Redefine the term *winner*.** Let players know that winners are people who show up consistently, try their hardest, support their teams, keep a sense of humor. When these qualities are associated with and are more important than actually winning a game, team members benefit and grow from participation.
- **Practice listening.** Coaches think their jobs are to talk. Many team members just want to be heard about their experiences. Ask players why they like to be on the team, what their favorite part of practice is, and whether there are things they think they could contribute to the team other than the obvious.
- **Emphasize respect and fun.** Create traditions for the team that are simply for the fun of it. Examples may be developing a team cheer or song, holding practice some day in funny costumes or something out of the ordinary such as pajamas. Do the unexpected. Have fun!
- **Communicate with classroom teachers.** Teachers have a great deal of insight into team members. If you notice a team member feeling down or losing interest, check in with the classroom teacher to discover whether there is any information you are missing that may help the teammate. It could be that the student has struggled in a class, had trouble with a friend, or had problems at home.

List 13.4. (continued)

- **Don't show favorites.** It's difficult for coaches not to like the top athletes the best. However, when coaches treat everyone as the star of the team, players are more likely to improve and feel comfortable showing up for practice and games.

- **Partner with parents.** Get to know the players' families. Parents have a great deal of insight into students and can be a source of information to help coaches better understand team members. Exchange e-mails and provide a team list for easy communication with parents.

- **Discover important adjunct roles.** Many times nonathletes want to participate in meaningful ways with teams. How these adjunct roles are treated will determine whether or not they will catch students' interest. Team managers, schedule coordinators, and team communications are all areas that can enhance the team and individual players' experiences if a coach gives some thought to making them roles of utmost importance. To do so, make it clear to the players why they need the support of these roles. Coach team members to show expressions of gratitude for all participants. In team pep talks, highlight the roles and accomplishments of the adjunct members.

- **Talk with the team about losing.** If the team is on a losing streak, don't get stuck in a negative spiral. Talk to the team about losing. Point out the various benefits of continued play, continued support, and positive attitude. Don't sidestep the issue of losing. Meet it head on and ask teammates to discuss their personal feelings about losing.

- **Point out the value of showing up.** Young people who learn to be consistent and responsible to a team are learning valuable life lessons that will shape their character for adulthood. Coaches will keep everyone engaged when they point out all the important reasons that each member should keep showing up, no matter if the team is winning or losing.

- **Let players be teachers.** Allow expert players to model plays and moves for their teammates. This will allow for the expert to improve and stretch as well as give the other team members the opportunity to identify with student leaders.

List 13.5. Physical Education and the Unhealthy Student

Many students are unhealthy due to having poor eating habits, being inactive, and being overweight or underweight. This list offers suggestions for how to work with these students without ostracizing them or causing them embarrassment.

- **Adolescents do not think like adults.** When instructing and creating lesson plans, try to think like an adolescent and predict possible reactions. Remember, unlike adults, young people

  ○ Are more willing to take health risks.
  ○ Have great peer pressure around what to eat and how to spend free time.
  ○ Do not have a sense of aging and therefore believe they are going to live forever, thus having an attitude that they can begin to think about health issues "later on."
  ○ Follow examples set by influential adults. This presents a problem when influential adults are involved in unhealthy habits.
  ○ Have a great fear about their body image and will do anything to conceal their fear.

- **Set an example.** Be a good role model of overall wellness. Point out personal habits such as running every other day or not smoking.

- **Emphasize a child's strengths.** Find out what energizes students and try to encourage them to stick to doing these activities. If it's something they enjoy, they are much more likely to do it.

- **Foster a positive atmosphere** that feels safe, inviting, free of sarcasm, insults, and harassment, and be a consistent source of comfort and encouragement. Be sure to listen to how students talk to one another and immediately discourage any insulting behavior or derogatory remarks.

- **Encourage activity at home.** Brainstorm activities with students that they can do at home. For example, watch their favorite television program and do sit-ups during the commercials.

- **Focus on behaviors, not outcomes.** Help them control behaviors and focus on *how to* change, not the results of changing. Introduce progress charts. Show students how long it takes to gain new muscle, lose weight, or run a mile.

- **Face the facts.** Denial is dangerous. Parents and teachers need to acknowledge when a student seems to be losing weight, gaining weight, or is overweight.

List 13.5. (continued)

- **Develop a social support network.** Find a social niche where an overweight child is with others who share the same positive attitudes toward physical activity and health or at least support the child's needs and intentions.

- **Avoid the spotlight.** Overweight children should not be placed in situations in which their physical performance is on display for all to see and critique. It is better to offer physical activity settings in which the overweight child can blend in and work at his or her own pace and level.

- **Develop a schoolwide program.** Incorporate a variety of all-school activities such as
  - Encourage a family fitness day.
  - Have students do a cafeteria audit, pointing out all food that is healthy and why.
  - Have the principal or another school leader walk or run with students on a regular schedule such as once a week.
  - Initiate a fitness challenge among students and faculty.

Section Fourteen

New Media Strategies that Naturally Differentiate Instruction

New media applications on the Internet offer teachers an exciting opportunity to differentiate instruction using the Internet. By their nature, new social communication platforms provide differentiated opportunities because students work at their own pace, use their individual voices, and, for the most part, interact with authentic audiences. Social media is far more than simply a pest that needs constant monitoring.

Today's most skilled teachers are finding ways to effectively use online platforms to engage all their students. When using these tools, students experience high levels of interest, engagement, and fascination in the learning process. New media tools are the tools today's students not only feel comfortable with, but they are the tools today's students will use in the future in their work and social lives.

The lists in this section are by no means exhaustive. Every day new platforms, applications, and uses crop up. These lists are meant to give a flavor of some of the more well-known new media platforms and to offer ideas for what to do with these tools in the classroom, as well as some general information for teachers who are not so familiar with their uses.

List 14.1. How Online Tools Can Help Organize and Differentiate Instruction

Digital Tool or Technique	Advantages	Differentiation Implications
Classroom website	Posts all assignments Makes handouts available as digital downloads Provides supplemental material Offers rubrics for projects or assignments Provides links to Homework Helpers Lists classroom rules, expectations Provides syllabus or other guide as to instructional goals for the marking period, semester, and year	Allows students to access assignments from home even if they are absent Allows students to reprint any forgotten worksheets, forms, etc., from home Provides students (and parents) with guidance and reinforcement of classroom expectations Allows teachers to provide remote homework assistance and support for students needing additional help Allows teachers to post additional enrichment material for those students interested in exploring lessons further
Classroom blog	Allows teachers to start and continue discussions started in classroom outside class Allows teachers to seek student input and commentary on news articles, topics related to classroom material, and/or post supplemental material to enhance understanding	Provides students with additional opportunities to practice written communication, as well as peer-to-peer interaction Offers opportunities to enhance critical-thinking skills and participate in authentic discussions
Classroom wiki	Similar to classroom website; allows central destination for all information related to classroom Wiki, like blog, can have permissions set to allow students to add material as appropriate to classroom wiki	Wikis can be configured so every student has his or her own page to consolidate work output Great tool for collaborative working and project-based work Great tool for constructing student portfolios; and helping students, teachers, and others view student work

List 14.2. Ways to Use Facebook in the Classroom

Facebook is not only a social connector, but it can also be used by teachers and students as a learning tool. Facebook can be used for creating class projects, teaching social skills, mentoring opportunities, or enhancing communication. These are all differentiation techniques because they are based on student interest, allowing students to work at their own pace and according to their readiness. Here are some ideas to get teachers thinking about ways to engage all students using this social network.

- **Keep your professional and your personal Facebook accounts separate.** Create a separate account just for your classes. This keeps your Facebook relationship at school on a professional level. Don't "friend" students on your personal account.
- **Control who finds your classes.** You can control who finds you in Facebook via the search privacy settings. You can select whether or not you want people to see your picture or if they can add you as a friend. Go to "**Settings** > **Privacy** > **Search**" to access.
- **Have students create a student page in addition to their personal page.** This allows you to access them as students and avoids having access to their personal information. Ask students to create a *Limited Profile with Controlled Settings*, friend you, and add you to the Limited Profile List. Students should not show you Photos, Videos, Status Updates, Friends, Posts, or Notes. Mini-feed and Photo Albums should be turned off.
- **Create groups.** Groups allow you to manage basic information, memberships, photos, videos, links, officers, and a wall. Name the group something fun. Use the "officer" position as a reward for students with exemplary behavior.
- **Have parents sign a classroom use waiver.** List the ways you will use Facebook in the classroom; state the rules and expectations. Have parents sign off ahead of time.
- **Redefine the term "friend."** Many teachers are disturbed by the idea of making friends with their students. Make it clear to the class that you are using the term "friend" as used by Facebook rather than as the usual use.
- **Be consistent.** Keep posting messages, use as many Facebook apps and resources as possible, and update status reports so your students know this is a viable tool. If it is not used consistently, students will lose interest and the community you create will fade.
- **Follow current events using the news feed.** Most news channels have Facebook pages. Students can join these groups and follow news feeds about topics relevant to what is being studied.
- **Practice foreign language.** Facebook pages are written by students all over the world. Find a teacher in a foreign country who is willing to set up a pen-pal system by using Facebook. Have students write about preselected topics.
- **Use the Facebook Poll app to get student feedback** about classes and topics. The poll application can be found under http://www.facebook.com/apps/application.php?id=20678178440. Spend some time conversing with others on this page about how to use this in your classroom.

List 14.2. (continued)

- **Keep current with the political issues** of the day locally and nationally. Most politicians have Facebook pages. Students can join these pages and analyze issues and compare and contrast candidates and their views.
- **Become an activist.** Learn about and participate in the discussions around a cause. Students have great interest in causes. Have each student choose a cause and join the page as the first step in making a plan for how to become an activist.
- **Find mentors.** As a career-building tool, students can seek advice and counsel from professionals already in the field. For example, if a student is interested in becoming an environmentalist, he can do a Facebook search for groups and research people in the groups. Next, the student can compile a list of questions and send messages to individuals in the field asking for their insight.
- **Communicate with students.** Teachers can create a Facebook page for the class and post homework assignments, answer questions via the chat function, or encourage students who are going to be absent to message in ahead of time.
- **Post class notes.** Using the note function, teachers can post their notes so students can refer back to them and avoid carrying around unnecessary papers. All students can stay organized about the important class information this way.
- **Share interesting information.** For example, if a class is studying the economic system in another country, students can post links to research and upload photographs and videos on the topic to the page.
- **Hold brainstorming session.** Students can add their thoughts to the class any time they occur, thus allowing for more opportunities for brainstorming with each other. This is useful for generating topics or sharing ideas.
- **Share examples.** Share examples of "exemplary work" through photos or posts.

List 14.3. Ways to Use Twitter in the Classroom

Twitter is another one of the more popular social networks, allowing for short, 140-character messages to be posted. Twitter is popular in part because of the many applications available for Twitter on mobile phones and desktops, allowing access on the go. Postings can even be "synced" so they can post simultaneously to other social networks like Facebook. When students are engaged in social media in the classroom, it makes their learning feel more relevant and engages students through mediums where they are already spending large amounts of free time. Social networks such as Twitter work to differentiate by allowing all students to participate and feel engaged on an individual level, and allow their voice to be heard and valued. This list provides suggestions for how to use Twitter in the classroom.

- **Use as a mini–search engine for research.** Any topic can be searched by words. For example, search the term "War in Afghanistan" and students will come up with an aggregated list of people with tweets about the war. Teach students to sift through these tweets for the ones that will provide good information. (There are also many ongoing conversations on educational topics—search for #edchat or differentiated instruction to find them.)
- **Gather real-time data.** Suppose there is an event happening such as an earthquake or a hurricane. Students can gather real-world, immediate data by searching for it on Twitter. Often information on news events will show up from individuals involved in the event and be propagated around Twitter before detailed information is available through traditional news sources. (News outlets frequently use Twitter to help identify breaking stories.)
- **Determine what is going on in the world in real time.** Use twitterfall.com and type in a buzzword such as global warming or South Korea, and watch the buzz of the day come pouring in. Ask students to evaluate these data against a criteria sheet for determining good information.
- **Practice application of language arts terms.** Write poetry. Have students use Twitter to write short lines using metaphors, similes, and other literary devices.
- **Compose a class "tweet story."** Have students advance the story on the same story account.
- **Compile viewpoints on a topic.** Create a page around a central question or topic and have students contribute to gathering viewpoints. For example, perhaps there is a controversial Supreme Court case that students can comment on. The Twitter page allows for an aggregated place for viewpoints and links to articles to back the viewpoints.
- **Use as a parental communication tool.** Provide updates such as "reading projects due tomorrow." Or "school lets out at five tomorrow." Even local governments are using Twitter to help let people know of road closures and emergency situations and using information gathered to allocate resources during snowstorms and other events, identifying areas of greatest need.

List 14.3. (continued)

- **Use to gather immediate feedback about class trips.** Have students tweet impressions in real time when on extended trips.
- **Use Twitter poll to gather data,** create graphs, and learn about public opinion polls. It can also be used for parent feedback: ask parents a question and have them respond via the poll.
- **Explore characterization in literature.** Have students assume the role of a character and tweet as that character would think or how that character might see the world.
- **Practice vocabulary.** Post a word and have students tweet when they hear it and note how they hear it being used. Or add synonyms and antonyms to the weekly word.
- **Communicate with experts or mentors.** Follow professionals in the field and ask questions or make comments on their work.
- **Follow live events and conferences.** Often live events will have a "hashtag" or # followed by a code, which will aggregate messages by that subject. This can help students follow commentary at live press conferences, the G8 summit, the Olympics, and other events.
- **Monitor students' frustrations and questions.** Invite students to post questions when working on projects. Answer the questions when convenient.

List 14.4. Using Ning in the Classroom

Ning has historically been a site where anyone can set up his or her own mini–social network. Although it has recently gone to paid options for the majority of users, Ning still offers free "mini" networks for educators through a "scholarship" from Pearson Education. The free network option for educators is limited to 150 people.

Advantages and Disadvantages

- Ning allows the combination of blogs, forums, groups, chat, and setting up RSS (Really Simple Syndication) feeds and notifications for all members. Think of it as a more private version of Facebook, with a select membership of your choosing.

- Ning allows e-mail to be sent to members within the network.

- You can opt to receive an e-mail to your traditional e-mail address when there are updates or events announced to the network through an RSS feed.

- Ning allows every member of the group to have his or her own blog within the group, and to have his or her own membership page.

- Ning allows you to create that walled garden, or members-only club type of social network, eliminating much of the distractions and "spam" that might otherwise crop up in Facebook or other public social networks.

- Ning is often a good choice when creating a school-based, district-based, or classroom-based social network, where concerns might exist otherwise about the participation of children in more public-based social networking sites.

- Classroom 2.0 (http://classroom20.com), a fantastic social network made up of educators, is based on a Ning framework and provides a good example of how a subject-specific social network can become a great resource.

- Like any social network, a Ning site is only as good or vibrant as the participants. Until there is a critical mass of interested parties, the network may seem dull or not worth the time of the participants.

- There has to be a good or compelling mission to the social network, and someone should be tasked to manage it, providing input and a reason to keep people engaged; otherwise, it would tend to die off for lack of attention.

List 14.4. (continued)

Examples of Ways to Use Ning in the Classroom

- **Debate project.** Use for an exploration and discussion of issues and candidates surrounding the presidential election—a wonderful opportunity for students to connect with other students around the country in a private online social network to share information and ideas related to the presidential election.
- **Advanced project space.** Set up a Ning space for a small number of students working on an advanced topic. It's a great way for them to share ideas, resources, and links, and the tagging means that they build a really accessible and searchable resource. There are some lively debates and discussions going on there, and the students have made it into an inviting, rewarding social space by sharing photos, videos, and music.
- **Collaborate with other students in different parts of the country** working on the same project, unit, or lesson. Begin conversations with these students sharing ideas, questions, and work.
- **Use Ning as a parent communication forum.** This can be used to post volunteer activities and information about extracurricular activities and school events.

List 14.5. Blogging in the Classroom

- Blogging encourages kids to write and respond to each other's writing both inside and outside the classroom.
- Blogging provides a way for the students to discuss topics and explore ideas in depth.
- Blogging allows others to read and comment on a student's writing.
- Comments can be moderated by the teacher to prevent any inappropriate or overly harsh critique.
- Blogs allow the addition of multimedia resources, podcasts, video, pictures, and more as supplements to the written content, thus allowing additional modes of expression for students and projects.
- Blogs allow "linking" to other online resources, making research, support, and bibliographies for writing more interactive.
- Reading blogs can help students learn more about media literacy and the credibility and reliability of source material.
- Blogs are a great way to allow students at all levels to interact outside the classroom itself, and students are often more likely to respond honestly without the same social pressure often present inside the classroom.
- Blogs allow students to work and respond to questions at their own level, allowing an easy way for teachers to encourage writing while differentiating instruction simultaneously.
- Blogging is becoming a part of everyday life for many, both as content creators and content consumers.
- As blogs continue to be adopted by companies and individuals as a channel of expression, blogging is a skill and technological tool that all twenty-first-century learners should know how to use.

Advantages of Blogs in the Classroom

- Blog posts are dated, so you know exactly when the student completed and submitted the work.
- There's no paper involved, so the work cannot be lost or forgotten, by you or the student.
- Blog posts encourage writing and help students extend their learning by thinking more deeply about classroom material.
- Blogs encourage commentary between students, who quickly learn to be respectful of each other's work.
- Blogs can be used to break down larger projects into smaller, manageable pieces over time.
- Blogs can aggregate resources for students and teachers to share.
- Blogs can incorporate multimedia (video, audio, pictures, slideshows, etc.) into assignments, allowing students to demonstrate more in-depth knowledge rather than recall-based testing.
- Blogs can serve as portfolio work that can help educators assess a student's progress over time, identify any subject matter weaknesses, and even track year-to-year progress.

List 14.5. (continued)

Suggestions for Integrating Blogs into Instruction

This list includes tips for getting students to blog, as well as how blogging can be integrated into existing curriculum and lesson plans. Many of the suggestions are geared toward helping students make connections between the classroom and "real life," thus placing learning into context, a keystone of differentiating instruction.

Blogs for Students. Student blogging is a great way to get students of all skill levels to extend their written expression skills. Blog posts (in the wild) tend to have a less structured format than the typical in-class five-paragraph essay, and this allows students to express their views in a public forum while allowing others to comment on their work.

How Blogs Can Be Integrated into Existing Lessons and Curriculum

1. **Require students to post once a week to their blog** on any topic, or by choosing a topic from a list provided by the teacher. Specify the length of the post, and whether you require any points to be supported. This provides an additional opportunity for students to practice writing while providing an additional method of assessment of student progress.

Social studies examples

- "Once a week, you will be required to write a blog post of at least three paragraphs on a news story of interest to you. You will have to place a link to the story itself on the post and discuss why the story caught your attention, why it's important, and what it means to you. If you can't seem to find a story, you may pick one from those listed on the classroom blog or from one of the following news sites (Time.com, New York Times.com, etc.)" (Helps teachers learn students' interests while helping them learn critique, media literacy, and relating news to self.)
- "Once a week, you will be required to read the classroom blog and respond to the article posted in a comment of at least three sentences, indicating how the article related to what we studied this week in class." (Helps students make connection between news and current lessons.)

Language arts examples

- "Once a week, you are required to write one blog post of at least two paragraphs, talking about your outside reading book. The first post this month should discuss the general plot of the book. Your second post should discuss your favorite character. Your third post should discuss three important events in the book. The fourth should be your review of the book, including links to any other reviews online, the author's website, if any, and your recommendation (on a scale of 1 to 10) on what you thought about the book."
- "Write a five-verse poem based on one of the prompts given on the classroom website/blog. This assignment will need to be published on your classroom blog by Friday at 6 P.M. to receive credit."

List 14.5. (continued)

Science examples

○ "Once a week, you will be required to write a two- to four-paragraph blog post on 'science in the news,' based on any article found on one of the following websites (*New York Times* Science, Health, or Technology sections; *Wired Magazine; Science Magazine; Popular Science; Discover Magazine;* etc.). Link to the article and discuss why it's important and what it means to you."

○ "Last week we discussed clouds and the water cycle. Extreme weather conditions, such as hurricanes, can disrupt the normal water cycle. Thinking about what we learned about the water cycle and what happens during and after hurricanes (for more, read these news articles [links provided]), write a minimum of three paragraphs on how hurricanes could disrupt the water cycle and how it might come back into balance."

Math example

○ Students are periodically required to find a news article relating to math concepts currently being studied in class. For example, when studying percentages or probabilities, articles talking about the rise or fall of test scores in schools and what those numbers really mean might be relevant. Advertisements discussing "25 percent off regular prices" or "additional discounts" can be used to help students figure out whether a sale or deal is really beneficial or not.

2. **Require students to comment or reply on at least one other student's blog post per week.** This encourages reading and interacting with each other's written work. Since you and all students will be able to read the comments, it will encourage them to be constructive in their criticism rather than unduly harsh. Comments may also be moderated if necessary.

3. **Ask students to post to their blog once or twice a week as a journaling exercise.** Free-form writing helps encourage creativity. Posts may also provide additional insight into student interests, helping teachers and other students form better relationships over time.

   ○ Individual blogs can be a way for students to create a portfolio of their writing over time. As well as answering questions and prompts assigned in class, the blog, by its sequential nature, will begin to demonstrate a student's growth and learning over time.

   ○ Consider requiring students to answer a question periodically on their blog that requires them to go beyond the material at hand. Prompts and questions relating the material to the real world or personal experience will help the students make connections to the subject matter, and will require them to apply what they learn to new situations, thus enhancing their understanding of the material.

Subject-specific examples

○ **Social studies.** "This week, we read about how the American colonists resented England's imposing taxes on imported goods without representation, leading up to the famous Boston Tea Party. There is a new political movement called the Tea Party in America that doesn't like the Federal government's imposing any

List 14.5. (continued)

additional taxes. How is this similar and different from the original Tea Party in Boston Harbor?"

○ **Science.** "We are studying how over thousands of years, the Earth's plates move, and that these disruptions can lead to earthquakes, volcanic eruptions, and other events. In the past few years, there have been several large earthquakes and eruptions that have affected people across the globe. Pick one of the events you think has been caused by movement of continental plates, and write about how you think damage might have been minimized on the surface, and what kind of things the local people should think about in protecting themselves from future events. Assume the people living there will have to rebuild rather than simply abandon their current homes."

○ **English**

  ▪ "We've read several novels this year, and each one represents a different author's perspective on the world. Some authors love describing the surroundings in great detail, while others concentrate more on the characters, their emotions, and their development throughout the story. If you were going to write a story, which approach would you take and why? How do you think setting or surroundings affect you? Does your home or school become another character in your life? Why or why not?"

  ▪ "We've been talking about persuasive writing in class. One purpose of persuasive writing is to get people's attention. Take a peek at the news headlines on news.google.com. Which headlines grab your attention to read more? Pick three headlines and write a paragraph about why each one caught your attention and whether the news articles delivered on the promise of the headline. Did the headline match the content? Why or why not?"

  ▪ *Bonus:* "Which headlines did you skip over? Why? Was it the subject matter or the headline itself that made you decide to skip the article? Can you rewrite the headline to make it more attention grabbing?"

○ **Math.** "Sometimes math can seem unrelated to day-to-day life. But studies have shown that adults with weak basic math skills end up having a lot of stress later on in their jobs because almost every job requires some basic level of math. From the list of professions below, pick two and describe how that job might require you to use math. Alternatively, ask your parents or another adult how they need to use math in their job, or simply at home, and tell us about how math is important to them on a daily basis."

○ **Foreign language(s)**

  ▪ "One of the goals of learning a foreign language is to develop a sense of fluency in the language. This means that instead of constantly translating between your native language and the new language, you can begin to think and speak in the new language without needing to pause to find each new word. When we all learned to read, we started out by reading each word by itself and eventually built up to reading full sentences, gaining meaning out of the order of the words, as well as out of each individual word itself. How does fluency in reading relate to fluency in speaking a language? Is reading the language we're studying easier for you, or is speaking it easier? How does this compare with learning how to read or speak your native language?"

List 14.6. Wikis in the Classroom

Wikis have become popular in education because they are lightweight Web-based sites that work well for collaborative projects. This list will help familiarize you with wikis and their use in the differentiated instruction classroom.

The most famous wiki is, of course, Wikipedia. Wikipedia, the crowd-sourced encyclopedia, is kept more current than print-based texts, while taking advantage of the diverse knowledge on almost any subject available, often without much editorial screening for "importance." Regular wikis function much like Wikipedia, allowing a number of users to change and update the content independently. Unlike a blog that has a more rigid time line and sequence associated with posts, wikis are more like webpages that can be updated and changed, be open to the public or password protected, and generally function more like an interactive document.

Examples of Wikis in Subject-Specific Lessons

- **Science.** For this year's biology class, Mr. Z has assigned a group project to the class. Small groups of four students (of mixed ability) are assigned or choose a topic based on the units covered in the marking period. Over the course of the eight-week marking period, the group is supposed to do research on the subject matter, report and share that information with each other, and by the end of the marking period produce a poster, PowerPoint presentation, and written report about the topic. Grades will be based not only on the final presentation, but also on participation in the process, as shown by edits made to the wiki.
  - Group A has been assigned to work on Mendel and the basic discovery of genetic inheritance. A wiki for the group has been created, and each student knows he or she is responsible for a portion of the work.
  - Mary is great at organizing, so she sets up a schedule of what needs to be done and the due dates on one page of the wiki.
  - Joe likes doing research, so he puts his name by several of the research-oriented tasks, and reports back on the wiki not only with a summary of what he's learned, but also with links to references and books, making it easy to incorporate that information into the bibliography for the project.
  - Juan is creative and has a good eye, so he is going to concentrate on providing the visual aids, graphs, charts, and other visuals for the poster and slide show.
  - Jean and Mei both participate by helping with the research, drafting the written text for the project as the research comes in, asking questions and making suggestions for what should be done next, and helping manage the project to conclusion.

  Advantages of a wiki-based project approach:
  - The wiki is online, enabling all students to access it from their homes or libraries.
  - Online access means the group can work together even if they are unable to be in the same place at the same time.
  - All students can contribute to the end product, and each person's contributions can be tracked.

List 14.6. (continued)

- The group can work on one final version of the project at a time, rather than e-mailing and potentially confusing many versions and changes as it travels between group members.
- Each student knows what the others contributed, and what their individual responsibility is. This makes the students more responsible to each other, as well as allowing Mr. Z to track the group's progress over time and make sure no one person is falling behind or not contributing.
- Each student can play to his or her strengths and help teach the others about his or her own portion of the project. Students also have an opportunity to help and mentor each other during the process.

- **Social studies.** Ms. F is a middle school social studies teacher who created a wiki for her class, and uses the same wiki each year as her "base of operations." The wiki acts like a classroom website, and allows Ms. F to post links to many resources that help her students and their parents be aware of what is going on and what is expected in the classroom. It also saves Ms. F time by eliminating many calls and e-mails, because the answers to most every question is already posted online. She has links on the wiki to her Schoolnotes.com site, where she keeps the calendar and due date for all assignments, and to the Quia page, where students and parents can look at their online assessments, links to online study resources, videos, podcasts, educational games Ms. F has created through Quia, and more. There's even a link to the online version of the textbook they use in class, so kids can never forget to bring their book to school.

Advantages of a wiki-based approach:
- The wiki is easy to use, and because it serves as the information hub for the class, reduces the number of excuses about forgotten assignments, agenda, books, and the like, and the amount of time spent fielding calls from students has dropped dramatically.
- Ms. F feels that she has more time to integrate all the "deep diving" material for students who are really interested in a particular topic, by simply linking to great outside resources on her wiki. She has more time to think of creative projects, as well as help students keep on track for those assignments by having the time lines prominently displayed online.
- The wiki is very easy to update, and much of the material can be reused each year, just by tweaking and adding new and exciting things as they become available.
- The wiki becomes a giant online textbook and resource over time for her class. Her students and parents are thrilled, because the wiki makes things easy and there's never any conflict at home about what's due and what's not—it's all online.

List 14.6. (continued)

- Parents and students can monitor test scores, helping keep parents informed and students on track.
- Ms. F uses the wiki as the main management tool that lets her post assignments for students at all levels, as well as track their progress as students answer questions and comment on the class blog (linked to the wiki).
- As students become more comfortable with interacting online, Ms. F has even been able to hold "open office hours" online via Skype or Ustream, where she lets students know she is available at a certain time a few days a week to answer questions, talk about school and assignments, and more. This virtual office hours policy has helped her coach students who need help outside of class, and even helped students who were absent catch up with material they've missed, further helping students to maximize their learning and avoid common pitfalls.

Further Reading

Sites Offering Free Wikis

PB Wiki. http://my.pbworks.com.

Wetpaint. http://www.wetpaint.com. Wet Paint hosts many wikis and has a great list of wikis used in education that show what other educators are doing with wikis in the field. http://wikisineducation.wetpaint.com.

Wikispaces. http://www.wikispaces.com. Educational Wikis also has a great site with links to wikis currently being used in classrooms around the country. http://educationalwikis.wikispaces.com.

List 14.7. Cultivating a Positive Digital Footprint

The Internet has created enormous opportunities to share information. This information is indexed, and can even be found through the Internet Archive: Wayback Machine long after the website itself is no longer active. (See the book's bonus Web material for links.) As a result, what teachers or students post online can be found through search in perpetuity, making it necessary that everyone become aware of how to cultivate a positive digital footprint. This list offers some advice on helping students and teachers make appropriate choices about what information to post online.

- **Much of Facebook's content is indexed** and can be found in a Google or other search engine's search results, so consider everything posted on Facebook as public, searchable, and "on the record."

- **Facebook has very specific privacy settings**, and students as well as teachers should be careful when filling out this information. Facebook uses the data posted about a user to serve up targeted ads in the margins, so you may want to think twice about providing too much personal information in your Facebook profile. For example, for security purposes, it is recommended users do not use real or full birth date in profiles to avoid any problems with personal information becoming public.

- **Encourage students to think about their own profiles objectively.** Given that colleges and employers frequently look for information about individuals online, students should be advised to take a look at their social network profiles to see what it says about them and whether they would want to hire themselves for a job based on the information included online. Note as well that it is not illegal to consider this information in hiring.

- **Ask students to think before posting.** Postings admitting to poor judgments, bad behavior, and more has led to trouble and even arrests for some individuals who have chosen to post about antics, later found by authorities. Taking a moment to run a post past a "What would my grandmother say if she read this" or similar filter will help students develop a sense of appropriateness with online conversations.

- **There have been several cases of people and teachers being fired for posting "inappropriate" content on social networks**, ranging from pictures of themselves with alcoholic drinks in their hand to using expletives in posts. One teacher at a parochial school was fired for participating in a poll that indicated he did not believe in God. Although the law as to what information posted voluntarily on a social network can form the basis for job or school disciplinary action is unsettled, it is wise to keep personal and public social network profiles appropriate and G rated.

List 14.7. (continued)

- **There have been incidents in which students have used social networks and text messaging to engage in cyber bullying or have posted inappropriate comments about their teachers.** As a result, if teachers discover inappropriate content about themselves posted on a social networking site, approach an administrator about school policy regarding such incidents before taking it up with the student or his or her family members directly, online or offline, in any way.

- **Encourage students to set up Google alerts for their own name.** Google has a feature called Google Alerts that will notify a user by e-mail when a keyword, such as a name, is indexed by the search engine. By keeping an "ego alert" file for their name, students will be notified if a news item, blog post, or other item about them appears online, and will be able to know where and when they appear online.

- **A great set of videos regarding online activities** has been produced featuring James Lipton, called *Give It A Ponder* (http://www.giveitaponder.com). They show young people about to make decisions about texting and their consequences, asking them to think first before hitting *Send*. Mixing humor with the message through these videos can help teach students that an ounce of prevention is better than a pound of cure.

List 14.8. Administrative Considerations When Using New Media in the Classroom

Although the incorporation of new media into the classroom is becoming widespread, it poses inherent challenges for administrators and information technology (IT) departments. Balancing the need to access a wide scope of available resources across the Internet, yet ensuring the security and appropriateness of the sites, can be difficult. The IT department and administration may often feel they are having an arms race between allowing open access to information and ensuring that inappropriate content remains outside the school walls, let alone trying to ensure that faculty and students stay on task and aren't distracted by the constant barrage of social information online. This list discusses the considerations often faced by administration and IT departments with allowing new media tools to be incorporated into classrooms, and potential solutions to the challenges faced.

- **Ideally, the instructional and technical considerations** of implementing online tools and computers into instruction should be driven by instructional goals and pedagogy first.

- **As with any aspect of differentiated instruction, student learning needs to be the primary focus.** For example, if teachers want to use a blog or wiki to encourage extending classroom discussions beyond the classroom, encourage writing, critical thinking, and the like, there are often numerous technical solutions available, both within and outside "firewalls," to accomplish these goals.

- **Once the instructional goals are clear,** IT departments should be able to implement low- to no-cost solutions that offer appropriate levels of security as required.

- **Ideally, there should be no separation between instruction and technology,** as unique or separate concerns of technology should always be used in support of instruction, but be looking ahead to make sure the infrastructure is prepared for growing technological needs over time.

- **Teachers and administrators should regularly meet and involve the technology departments** of the school and district in all meetings regarding professional development, instruction, and planning. By keeping technology as an integral part of the instructional process, IT will be able to evolve alongside instructional needs and work more in concert with pedagogic goals.

- **Despite the best plans and implementation, there will always be some poor behavior** or inadequate execution from students, teachers, and IT departments alike. Administrators and IT departments must look at the process of integrating technology into the classroom as an ongoing, evolving process, where mistakes will be made but rapid course corrections will work toward keeping things on track.

List 14.8. (continued)

- **Many IT departments work hard to restrict and protect their infrastructure,** constructing firewalls to keep some sites and materials outside the system. However, with a growing amount of educational information available from commonly blocked sites such as YouTube and even Facebook, access rules must be flexible enough to allow access to material for educational purposes.

- **Teachers, as well as IT departments, should be aware of "work-arounds"** such as using online software tools to allow local downloading and caching of otherwise prohibited or restricted online content for use during classroom instruction. Downloading videos in advance also has the advantage of preventing any network problems or streaming problems from affecting the classroom instruction.

- In addition, simple, free tools such as Skitch (http://skitch.com) allow teachers to take and annotate screen shots of websites, which may often be equally as effective during instruction as having online access to the Internet during a lesson.

List 14.9. New Media Uses That Are Not OK

Like with any tool, new media can be used for good or for, shall we say, less than constructive purposes. This list focuses on some of the least useful and more risky ways to use new media in education.

- **New media tools, such as Google Documents, blogs, or wikis, are not merely online typewriters.** Instead, encourage students to use these platforms to add audio, video, pictures, and illustrations in addition to text to bring deeper meaning to their writing.
- **Don't encourage students to take on alternate personalities online unless it is part of a class project.** Although almost every social network allows people to adopt a user name or "handle," this can allow people to develop online "characters" that allow them to avoid personal responsibility for more antisocial or unacceptable behavior.
- **Do teach students to conceal personal identifying information online.** Allowing students to give too much information about their location, age, birth date, or other material makes this information public and potentially exploitable by others with less than pure motivations.
- **Be cautious when asking students to comment and critique each other's work online.** One of the dangers of online behavior is that it can encourage group-think or other piling-on types of behavior instead of encouraging the value of individual opinions and beliefs. Monitor comments on student blogs, and consider deleting comments that are out of line.
- **Don't encourage students to violate copyrights.** Although copyright law and what's acceptable may be in flux, encouraging students to use popular songs, films, photos, or the like in presentations published online without permission could lead to unexpected legal consequences.
- **Set clear and reasonable limits on online and text relationships with students.** Although a student's occasional text about an assignment or becoming a friend on Facebook is acceptable, remember that teachers are role models, not friends.
- **Don't use your friendship to bully students.** Teachers may be concerned regarding students' online activities outside of school, at least as far as they affect the students' work in the classroom. Avoid the temptation to use social networks as an opportunity to spy on students (checking that they truly are sick, out of town, or otherwise verifying their "stories" or excuses).
- **When troubling behavior pops up accidentally,** don't ignore it, but take reasonable steps to address the situation.
- **Don't use offline relationships with students as instructional opportunities in class.** If you start commenting to a student in class about her poor spelling on Facebook, you are crossing a relationship line that is bound to lead to distrust and be counterproductive.
- **Avoid the PowerPoint syndrome when giving students assignments using technology tools;** remember that the tool has to make sense for the project at hand. If the task can be done better or more efficiently in an analog fashion, don't make the "tech toy" part of the equation just to expose the students to the tool.

List 14.9. (continued)

Example: Mr. G assigned a project in which students were to prepare a PowerPoint presentation about their favorite author. In the rubric, he required each slide to have at least four sentences related to the title on each slide. This lesson essentially requires students to form an outline of their idea, and fails to use PowerPoint for its intended purposes. Slides should not be speaker's notes—we'll assume everyone in the audience can read! Slides should be used to illustrate an oral presentation. In addition, since the brain can only process one form of language input at a time, reading slides and listening to the speaker tend to cancel each other out, ensuring that the audience won't remember either what was said or what was presented on the slides. Slides should be used to illustrate and demonstrate a speaker's points to enrich and enhance understanding. *A better lesson* would be constructed to have students outline their project in writing first, and then create a five-minute oral presentation with at least ten slides with titles, pictures, graphs, diagrams, and more to illustrate the main points made in the outline.

- **Assigning students to use a wiki for a basic report or research project makes more sense when the students are working in groups** and can use the collaborative features, and to help teachers monitor student progress and coach them along the way. Assigning a wiki to a student and asking him or her to use it as a journal makes much less sense and doesn't teach the student very much about the tool at hand.

- **Assigning a podcast project works best if there's a point to recording audio,** such as conducting an interview, recording a small group discussion or problem-solving process, or reviewing presentation styles.

  Example: Ms. Q was excited about podcasts and assigned her fourth-grade class to create a podcast out of their completed book reports. Having students record themselves reading their written book reports may test reading fluency, but it likely doesn't add anything to their report or provide them with an opportunity to demonstrate additional mastery of the material discussed in class. *A better use of podcasting* might be asking students to act out a scene from the book or having several students interview each other, with each assuming the persona of a character in the book. This is more likely to demonstrate additional insight or connectedness to the character and extend meaning and learning for the students than just reading their own writing aloud.

- **Don't discount tools, networks, or new technologies because they are new or foreign.** Each time a tech tool is integrated into the curriculum, both the student and teacher have opportunities to learn and grow.

- **Remember that the best teachers are always learning along with their students.**

Section Fifteen

Special Considerations

Differentiated instruction (DI) is about making sure every student has access to learning. Traditionally, altering lessons or curriculum was mandated only for those who had Individualized Education Plans (IEPs) for special education or gifted education. DI and personalized education are designed to meet the needs of all learners, but it's clear that there are some students who still require additional attention. This section specifically addresses the special needs of these students and how DI strategies can become useful tools in meeting these needs in the normal course of instruction.

List 15.1. Differentiated Instruction and the Gifted Student

Gifted education, like special education, is one of the perennial concerns of parents and teachers alike. This list discusses how to best differentiate instruction for gifted students and provide them opportunities to explore beyond the required curriculum.

- **Balance academic and social needs.** Academically talented (AT) or gifted students can pose a challenge in the differentiated instruction (DI) classroom. Frequently these students may seem intellectually mature beyond their years, but socially and developmentally they remain children. Keeping these students motivated to learn requires teachers to develop a set of activities that are designed not only to keep these students busy but also to feed their curiosity.

- **Don't assume that all gifted students are gifted in every subject or in every area.** Talented students will often surprise their teachers by doing very well in some classes or in one content area and significantly poorer in others. This variance may be due to engagement issues, interest level, motivation, or even subtle learning issues such as ADHD. In the DI classroom, teachers should be able to accommodate the varying needs of these students on an ongoing basis. Rather than pigeonholing them as always needing advanced work, offer advanced work as needed.

- **Gifted students can have disabilities as well.** Perhaps counterintuitively, many bright students can be "twice exceptional" and have learning disabilities, such as ADHD or dyslexia, that affect their classroom performance. These students may struggle with organization or output and seem to be engaged but underperform. Likewise, talented students may do well on some assignments but totally lose concentration and focus on others, causing frustration to teachers, students, and parents alike. Providing scaffold support for students to explore advanced topics while managing basic tasks such as organization, composition, time management, and the like will pay off for both students and teachers in the long run.

- **Gifted students don't need more work, they need different work.** One of the first things teachers notice about gifted students is that they seem to have a quick acquisition rate, they do not need multiple examples to understand the material, and may complete assignments much faster than their peers. However, this fast acquisition rate can frequently mask academic weaknesses that may become problems later on.

Examples

- Students who are facile in mental math will frequently become frustrated when hitting more advanced math courses like algebra, where systematic and stepwise approaches to problems are necessary and their mental shortcuts no longer work so well.

- Students who can make quick intuitive jumps may later rebel when asked to slow down and explain every step of their thinking or to write longer or more detailed prose.

List 15.1. (continued)

- In order to maintain student engagement, additional worksheets and practice won't do it. Students will rapidly figure out that being "smart" just means more work, and will often disengage completely. Instead, developing independent projects that can be worked on alongside their peers and mirror the main curriculum will help these students extend their learning. Students can produce work they can share and help teach to their peers, while still acquiring the necessary information they need to meet curriculum goals.

Project Examples

- In a social studies unit about ancient society, several students already seem to know a lot about the subject matter. The teacher offers these students, who scored highly on the pretest, an opportunity to choose from four independent research projects that included exploring evolution, early societies, and the like. Using a learning contract, the students set due dates for different aspects of the project, and were required by a certain date to complete a website covering their chosen project. A rubric outlining what needed to be included in the final project and applicable points was given to students and their parents. The students were allowed to work on these projects in lieu of completing packets required by the rest of the class. At the end of the unit, the students presented their projects and what they learned to the entire class.
- In a middle school science class, students were learning about the different aspects of the cell. Students already mastering the basic cell anatomy and functions were encouraged to find out all they could about a single aspect of a cell, such as the Golgi apparatus, mitochondria, or the cell membrane, and put together a model and presentation to share the important aspects of this cell feature to their classmates. One student chose to learn more about how things crossed the cell membrane; another chose to explore how the Golgi apparatus made proteins and molecules; yet another investigated how mitochondria where once suspected to be independent organisms and had their own DNA, helping scientists to track how loosely related individuals were across generations.
- In a high school world history class, a student was encouraged to go beyond the text and look at how the geography of the Middle East helped affect trade, sharing of knowledge, and ultimately the political history of one of the countries being studied.
- In a language arts class, a student was asked to help write for the classroom blog, adding additional resources from around the Web that helped explain more about the time period and location of the setting of the book the class was reading together.
- While doing a unit on *Romeo and Juliet,* a group of students were asked to "translate" several scenes into modern English and then perform them in class.

List 15.2. Differentiated Instruction and the Advanced Placement Curriculum

Advanced placement (AP) courses are by nature differentiated as they provide accelerated learning experiences for students who are ready. This list provides further consideration for the AP teacher.

- **Advanced placement courses naturally differentiate along the following lines:**
  - Provide a faster pace of learning
  - Support greater independence in study and thought
  - Directly support the learning needs of advanced students through activities that simulate real-world problems, address multiple perspectives, and result in the development of critical thinking and analytic skills

- **Although AP courses are naturally differentiated for the accelerated learner, this does not mean that the group is homogenous.** AP classes will need consideration for the second language learner, as well as for students who excel in the subject area but may struggle in other areas. For example, students who excel in math and science may struggle in reading and writing and will need strategies to help them when assignments call for these skills.

- **Advanced placement should focus on mastery of the concepts over the score obtained on the test.** To do this, teachers should balance practicing the advanced placement test with a variety of assessments to check for understanding.

- **Teachers of advanced placement classes will need to personalize instruction** as much as classroom teachers. The same principles apply to the AP curriculum as to the regular curriculum.

- **Some students will struggle in the advanced placement class.** Rather than label the student misplaced in the class, teachers will benefit students when they scaffold the learning experience to help students meet the challenge.

- **The temptation in many AP classes is to lecture.** Consider taping lectures and allowing students to listen to them at home so they are able to free up time in class for group work and higher-order thinking projects.

- **Be sure to inform students that all colleges do not accept advanced placement credits.**

List 15.3. Differentiated Instruction and the At-Risk Student

Differentiated instruction (DI) is often presumed to be a way to engage students who are struggling in the classroom or who have Individualized Education Plans (IEPs) for various diagnosed learning disabilities. In fact, however, the U.S. Census Bureau has defined "at-risk" kids as those more likely to drop out of school, have a child outside of wedlock, or have a less than desirable outcome because of having personal, familial, or a combination of both categories of risk factors at play (Kominski, Jamieson, & Martinez, 2001). Although 54 percent of students do not have any risk factors, 36 percent have familial factors, 18 percent have personal factors, and 18 percent have a combination of home and personal factors that put them at risk for failure.

DI is designed to give teachers the tools needed to adjust the curriculum for the individual student's need. Although we address these students specifically in other sections of this book, this list addresses some of the specific issues at play with at-risk kids and how DI strategies may help them overcome these obstacles.

- Students may be classified as being at risk because of familial factors, including absent parent(s); having a foreign-born, non-English-speaking parent; low familial income; or an unemployed parent. These socioeconomic factors tend to disrupt students' home life and, as a result, affect their ability to focus as needed in the classroom.

- Students may also be classified as being at risk due to personal factors, including disability, being retained in school, or by not speaking English "very well," that is, having less than full fluency in English to be able to fully understand and perform at their instructional level.

- Although teachers may not be able to do very much to change familial factors, teachers can do their best to provide an accepting and flexible atmosphere in the classroom to help compensate for some of the less than ideal conditions the student may struggle with outside the classroom.

List 15.4. Differentiated Instruction and Diversity Inclusion

The diversity of learning needs in today's general education classroom continues to grow, especially with non-English-speaking learners. Differentiating for the English language learner involves the same strategies as all other students and will be enhanced with the following strategies.

- **Get to know students.** Ask about their cultural backgrounds. Find out what their parents do and whether or not English is spoken in the home.
- **Show an interest in their cultures.** Select books and class topics that relate to their culture.
- **Determine their overall literacy.** Some nonnative speaking students are also unable to read.
- **Try to speak plainly to them,** avoiding jargon, slang, and contractions.
- **Avoid asking students: "Do you understand?"** They, like almost everyone else, will almost always say "yes" to avoid negative attention.
- **Don't expect them to understand humor** and don't hold it against them if they do find "normal" situations funny.
- **Meet their parents.** Discover how much support for English speaking and learning is available at home or if there needs to be extra support at school.
- **Do not try to coax a hesitant learner out of assumed shyness.** Sometimes being demure is part of the culture. Students from different backgrounds are sometimes discouraged from speaking up.
- **Find alternate ways to reward participation.** Consider points for effective listening. Don't assume they understand things such as raising hands to be called upon or other routines Americans take for granted in the classroom.
- **Find out about students' schooling background.** If your students have not learned in a formal classroom setting before, adjusting to the routines and cultural practices of the American school takes time.
- **Avoid stereotypes** and be watchful for classmates who unwittingly promote stereotypes.
- **Provide written instructions to accompany verbal directions.**
- **Call on students rather than waiting for them to volunteer to participate.** Scaffold their discussion by helping them fill in blanks when they struggle to articulate their thoughts.
- **Don't assume all struggles have to do with language barriers.** When uncertain, seek a translator to help determine the student's level of understanding.
- **When assigning tasks for group work, assign tasks that don't require English-speaking ability for success.** Assign tasks such as preparing the materials and organizing the workspace.
- **Teach the entire class** how to be sensitive to diversity and different types of learners.

References

Section 1

Association for Library Service to Children. Caldecott Medal and Honor Books, 1938–Present. http://www.ala.org/ala/mgrps/divs/alsc/awardsgrants/bookmedia/caldecottmedal /caldecotthonors/caldecottmedal.cfm. Retrieved January 2011.

Association for Library Service to Children. Newbery Medal and Honor Books, 1922–Present. http://www.ala.org/ala/mgrps/divs/alsc/awardsgrants/bookmedia/newberymedal /newberyhonors/newberymedal.cfm. Retrieved January 2011.

Bloom, B. S. (1956). *Taxonomy of educational objectives.* Boston: Allyn & Bacon.

Bruner, J. (1961). The act of discovery. *Harvard Educational Review, 31*(1), 21–32.

Gardner, H. (2006). *Multiple intelligences: New horizons in theory and practice.* New York: Basic Books.

Honolulu Community College. Types of questions based on Bloom's Taxonomy. http:// honolulu.hawaii.edu/intranet/committees/FacDevCom/guidebk/teachtip/questype.htm. Retrieved January 2011.

Hunter, M., & Hunter, R. (2004). *Madeline Hunter's mastery teaching.* Thousand Oaks, CA: Corwin Press.

Moll, L. (1990). *Vygotsky and education: Instructional implications and applications of historical psychology.* New York: Cambridge University Press.

Teacher Tap. Critical and creative thinking: Bloom's Taxonomy. http://eduscapes.com/tap /topic69.htm. Retrieved January 2011.

Wiggins, G., & McTighe, J. (2005). *Understanding by design* (2nd ed.). Upper Saddle River, NJ: Prentice Hall.

Section 2

A to Z Home's Cool Homeschooling. http://homeschooling.gomilpitas.com/weblinks/assets.htm.

Ames, R., & Ames, C. (1990). Motivation and effective teaching. In B. F. Jones & L. Idol (Eds.), *Dimensions of thinking and cognitive instruction.* Hillsdale, NJ: Erlbaum.

Davis, B. G. (1993). *Tools for teaching.* San Francisco: Jossey-Bass.

Davis, B. G. (2009). *Tools for teaching* (2nd ed.). San Francisco: Jossey-Bass.

Devereaux Student Strengths Assessment. [http://www.devereaux.org/site]

Fischer, K. W., & Bidell, T. R. (2006). Dynamic development of action and thought. In W. Damon & R. M. Lerner (Eds.), *Theoretical models of human development: Handbook of child psychology* (6th ed., Vol. 1, pp. 313–399). Hoboken, NJ: Wiley.

Fischer, K. W., & Rose, L. T. (2001). Webs of skill: How students learn. *Educational Leadership, 59*(3), 6–12.

Fleming, G. Learning styles: Know and use your personal learning style. http://homeworktips .about.com/od/homeworkhelp/a/learningstyle.htm. Retrieved January 2011.

Fox, J. (2008). *Your child's strengths: Discover them, develop them, use them—a guide for parents and teachers.* New York: Viking. [http://www.strengthsmovement.com/ht/d/sp/i/191/ pid/191]

Gardner, H. (2006). *Multiple intelligences: New horizons in theory and practice.* New York: Basic Books.

Goleman, D. (1996). *Emotional intelligence: Why it can matter more than IQ.* London: Bloomsbury.

Green, F. R. (1999). Brain and learning research: Implications for meeting the needs of diverse learners. *Education, 119*(4), 682–688.

Guild, P. B. (2001). Diversity, learning style and culture. Johns Hopkins University School of Education New Horizons for Learning. http://education.jhu.edu/newhorizons/strategies/ topics/Learning%20Styles/diversity.html. Retrieved January 2011.

McGreevy, A. (1982). *My book of things and stuff.* Mansfield Center, CT: Creative Learning Press.

Mulroy, H., & Eddinger, K. (2003). *Differentiation and literacy.* Paper presented at the Institute on Inclusive Education, Rochester, NY.

Pomerantz, E. M., Altermatt, E. R., & Saxon, J. L. (2002). Making the grade but feeling distressed: Gender differences in academic performance and internal distress. *Journal of Educational Psychology, 94*(2), 396–404.

Renzulli, J. S. (1977). *The interest-a-lyzer.* Mansfield Center, CT: Creative Learning Press.

Sternberg, R. J. (2006, Sept.). Recognizing neglected strengths. *Educational Leadership: Teaching to Student Strengths* (special issue) *64*(1), [http://www.ascd.org/publications/educational- leadership/sept06/vol64/num01/Recognizing-Neglected-Strengths.aspx]

Strengths Checklist for Parents. [http://www.able-differently.org/PDF_forms/handouts/Strength Checklist.pdf]

Strengthsquest. [http://www.strengthsquest.com/home.aspx]

Thelen, E., & Smith, L. B. (1994). *A dynamic systems approach to the development of cognition and action.* Cambridge, MA: MIT Press.

Tomlinson, C. A. (2001). *How to differentiate instruction in mixed ability classrooms* (2nd ed.). Alexandria, VA: ASCD.

Tomlinson, C. A. (2002). Different learners, different lessons. *Instructor, 112*(2), 21–25.

Valdés, G. (1996). *Con respeto: Bridging the distances between culturally diverse families and schools: An ethnographic portrait.* New York: Teachers College, Columbia University.

Van Geert, P., & Steenbeek, H. (2005). Explaining after by before: Basic aspects of a dynamic systems approach to the study of development. *Developmental Review, 25*(3–4), 408–442.

What's Your Learning Style? http://people.usd.edu/~bwjames/tut/learning-style. Retrieved January 2011.

Section 3

Bloom, B. S. (1956). *Taxonomy of educational objectives.* Boston: Allyn & Bacon.

Donovan, M. S., Bransford, J. D., & Pellegrino, J. W. (Eds.) (1999). *How people learn: Bridging research and practice.* Commission on Behavioral and Social Sciences and Education. Washington, DC: National Academies Press.

Gillespie, M. K. EFF research principle: A purposeful and transparent approach to teaching and learning. National Institute for Literacy. http://www.edpubs.gov/document/ed001932w .pdf?ck=512. Retrieved January 2011.

Herrington, J., & Oliver, R. (2000). An instructional design framework for authentic learning environments. *Educational Technology Research and Development*, 48(3), 23–48. [http://ro.uow.edu.au/edupapers/31]

Honolulu Community College. Types of questions based on Bloom's Taxonomy. http://honolulu.hawaii.edu/intranet/committees/FacDevCom/guidebk/teachtip/questype.htm. Retrieved January 2011.

Pellegrino, J. W. The challenge of knowing what students know. http://bearcenter.berkeley .edu/measurement/docs/Pellegrino_1_1.pdf. Retrieved January 2011.

Renzulli, J. S., & Reis, S. M. (2008). *Enriching curriculum for all students* (2nd ed.). Thousand Oaks, CA: Corwin Press.

Teacher Tap. Critical and creative thinking: Bloom's Taxonomy. http://eduscapes.com/tap /topic69.htm. Retrieved January 2011.

Wiggins, G., & McTighe, J. (2005). *Understanding by design* (2nd ed.). Upper Saddle River, NJ: Prentice Hall.

Section 4

Bromley, K., DeVitis, L., & Modio, M. (1999). *Fifty graphic organizers for reading, writing, and more.* New York: Scholastic Professional Books.

Bulgren, J. A., Schumaker, J. B., & Deshler, D. D. (1988). Effectiveness of a concept teaching routine in enhancing the performance of LD students in secondary-level mainstream classes. *Learning Disability Quarterly*, 11(1), 3–7.

Center for Innovation in Engineering and Science Education. Human Genetics Project, Noonday Project, Square of Life Project. http://www.k12science.org. Retrieved January 2011.

Darch, C. B., Carnine, D. W., & Kammeenui, E. J. (1986). The role of graphic organizers and social structure in content area instruction. *Journal of Reading Behavior*, 18(4), 275–295.

Education Place. [http://www.eduplace.com/graphicorganizer]

Egg Harbor Township Schools. Differentiated instruction: Learning contracts. http://www.eht.k12 .nj.us/~jonesj/differentiated%20instruction/learning%20contracts.htm. Retrieved January 2011.

Flat Stanley. http://www.flatstanley.com. Retrieved January 2011.

Freeology. [http://freeology.com/graphicorgs]

Graphic Organizer. [http://www.graphic.org/index.html]

Herl, H. E., O'Neil, H. F., Jr., Chung, G.K.W.K., & Schacter, J. (1999). Reliability and validity of a computer-based knowledge mapping system to measure content understanding. *Computers in Human Behavior*, 15(3–4), 315–333.

Journey North. http://www.learner.org/jnorth. Retrieved January 2011.

Kagan, S. (1989/1990). The structural approach to cooperative learning. *Educational Leadership*, 47(4), 12–15. [http://faculty.brenau.edu/rchristian/Courses/Articles/CoopStruct.pdf]

Moll, L. (1990). *Vygotsky and education: Instructional implications and applications of historical psychology.* New York: Cambridge University Press.

Roam, D. (2008). *The back of the napkin: Solving problems and selling ideas with pictures.* New York: Portfolio. [http://www.thebackofthenapkin.com]

Rubistar. http://rubistar.4teachers.org. Retrieved January 2011.

A Scaffolding Strategy. http://projects.edtech.sandi.net/staffdev/presentation/scaffolding.htm. Retrieved August 2010.

Teacher Planet. Rubrics for teachers. http://www.rubrics4teachers.com. Retrieved January 2011.

Teachnology. http://www.teachnology.com/web_tools/rubrics. Retrieved January 2011.

Teachnology Learning Contract Maker. http://www.teachnology.com/web_tools/contract. Retrieved January 2011.

Web-Based Inquiry Science Environment. http://wise.berkeley.edu. Retrieved January 2011.

Willerman, M., & Mac Harg, R. A. (1991). The concept map as an advance organizer. *Journal of Research in Science Teaching, 28*(8), 705–712.

Section 5

Goldstein, S., & Brooks, R. B. (2007). *Understanding and managing children's classroom behavior: Creating sustainable, resilient classrooms* (2nd ed.). Hoboken, NJ: Wiley.

Hoffman, W. (n.d.). LD podcast conversations with Rick LaVoie, nos. 67 & 68. [http://www.ldpodcast.com/images/ricklavoie1.mp3; http://www.ldpodcast.com/images/ricklavoie2.mp3]

LaVoie, R. (2005). *It's so much work to be your friend: Helping the child with learning disabilities find social success.* New York: Touchstone/Simon & Schuster.

LaVoie, R. (2007). *The motivation breakthrough: Six secrets to turning on the tuned out child.* New York: Touchstone/Simon & Schuster.

Section 6

Dillion, S. (2010, September 28). 4,100 Students prove "small is better" rule wrong. *New York Times,* p. A1. [http://www.nytimes.com/2010/09/28/education/28school.html]

Williams, W., & Sternberg, R. (2002). Practical issues in parenting. In M. Bornstein (Ed.), *Handbook of parenting.* Hillsdale, NJ: Lawrence Erlbaum.

Section 7

D'Archangelo, M. (2003). On the mind of a child: A conversation with Sally Shaywitz. *Educational leadership: The first years of school.* Alexandria, VA: ASCD. [http://www.casenex.com/casenet/pages/virtualLibrary/Readings/ASCD/el200304_darcangeloASCD.pdf]

Goldstein, S., & Brooks, R. (2007). *Understanding and managing children's classroom behavior: Creating sustainable, resilient classrooms.* (2nd ed.) Hoboken, NJ: Wiley.

Learning Disabilities Association of America. (1999). Speech and language milestone chart. [http://www.ldonline.org/article/6313]

Middenhoff, C. (2008). *Differentiating instruction in kindergarten: Planning tips, assessment tools, management strategies, multi-leveled centers, and activities that reach and nurture every learner.* New York: Scholastic Teaching Resources.

National Institute on Deafness and Other Communication Disorders. [http://www.nidcd.nih.gov/health/voice/speechandlanguage.html]

Quia Online Assessment Tool. http://www.quia.com. Retrieved January 2011.

Tomlinson, C. A. (2001). Differentiation of instruction in the elementary grades. *ERIC Digest.* http://ceep.crc.uiuc.edu/eecearchive/digests/2000/tomlin00.pdf.

Section 8

Association for Library Service to Children. Caldecott Medal and Honor Books, 1938–present. http://www.ala.org/ala/mgrps/divs/alsc/awardsgrants/bookmedia/caldecottmedal /caldecotthonors/caldecottmedal.cfm. Retrieved January 2011.

Association for Library Service to Children. Newbery Medal and Honor Books, 1922–present. http://www.ala.org/ala/mgrps/divs/alsc/awardsgrants/bookmedia/newberymedal /newberyhonors/newberymedal.cfm. Retrieved January 2011.

Charnock, J. (2005). *A non-workbook, non-textbook approach to teaching language arts: Grades 4 through 8 and up.* Tuscon, AZ: Fenestra Books.

MacArthur, C. A., Graham, S., & Fitzgerald, J. (2006). *Handbook of writing research.* New York: Guilford Press.

McGill-Franzen, A., Zmach, C., Solic, K., & Zeig, J. L. (2006). The confluence of two policy mandates: Core reading programs and third grade retention in Florida. *Elementary School Journal, 107*(1), 67–91.

Pressley, M., Wharton-McDonald, R., Allington, R., Block, C., Morrow, L., Tracey, D., Baker, K., Brooks, G., Cronin, J., Nelson, E., & Woo, D. (2001). Strategy instruction for elementary students searching informational text. *Scientific Studies of Reading, 5*(1), 35–59.

Reading Olympics. Elementary school book list. http://readingolympics.cciu.org/resources /2011ESBooklist_ebooks.pdf. Retrieved January 2011.

Reading Olympics. High school book list. http://readingolympics.cciu.org/resources/2011HS Booklist_ebooks.pdf. Retrieved January 2011.

Reading Olympics. Middle school book list. http://readingolympics.cciu.org/resources/2011MS Booklist_ebooks.pdf. Retrieved January 2011.

Tarheel Reader. http://tarheelreader.org. Retrieved January 2011.

Taylor, B. M., & Pearson, P. D. (2000). CIERA school change classroom observation scheme. http://www.ciera.org/news/archives/2001/schoolchange.html. Retrieved January 2011.

Taylor, B. M., Peterson, D. S., Pearson, P. D., & Rodriguez, M. C. (2002). Looking inside classrooms: Reflecting on the "how" as well as the "what" in effective instruction. *Reading Teacher, 56*(3), 270–280.

Section 9

Agruso, S. A., Johnson, R. L., Kuhs, T. M., & Monrad, D. M. (2001). *Put to the test: Tools and techniques for classroom assessment.* Portsmouth, NH: Heinemann.

Andrini, B. (1991). *Cooperative learning and mathematics.* San Juan Capistrano, CA: Resources for Teachers.

Black, J., & Puckett, M. (1994). *Authentic assessment of the young child: Celebrating development of learning.* New York: Merrill.

Clements, D. H. (1999). Concrete manipulatives, concrete ideas. *Contemporary Issues in Early Childhood, 1*(1), 45–60. [http://www.gse.buffalo.edu/org/buildingblocks/Newsletters /Concrete_Yelland.htm]

Del Vicchio, A., Gustke, C. & Wilde, J. (2000). Alternative assessment for Latino students. In J. V. Tinajero & R. A. DeVillar (Eds.), *The power of two languages*. New York: McGraw-Hill.

Deubel, P. Math projects. Computing Technology for Math Excellence. http://www.ct4me.net /math_projects.htm. Retrieved September 2010.

Hancock, C. (1994). *Alternative assessment and second language study: What and why?* [electronic version]. http://www.ericdigests.org/1995–2/language.htm. Retrieved March 2002.

Mabry, L. (1999). *Portfolio plus: A critical guide to alternative assessment.* Thousand Oaks, CA: Corwin Press.

Math Project Journal and Ultimate Math Lessons. [http://www.mathprojects.com/Project Book/Default.aspx]

Moyer-Packenham, P. S., Salkind, G., & Bolyard, J. J. (2008). Virtual manipulatives used by K–8 teachers for mathematics instruction: Considering mathematical, cognitive, and pedagogical fidelity. *Contemporary Issues in Technology and Teacher Education, 8*(3), 202–218. [http://www.editlib.org/index.cfm?fuseaction=Reader.ViewFullText&paper_id=26057]

National Council of Teachers of Mathematics (NCTM). (1991). *Principles and standards for school mathematics.* Reston, VA: Author. [http://www.nctm.org/standards/content.aspx?id=16909]

National Council of Teachers of Mathematics. (2000). *Principles and standards for school mathematics.* Reston, VA: Author. [http://standards.nctm.org]

National Council of Teachers of Mathematics. Illuminations. [http://illuminations.nctm.org]

Nisonoff Ruopp, F., & Poundstone, P. (n.d.) Math with a Laugh Series. http://www .heinemann.com/products/E00931.aspx. Retrieved January 2011.

Peavler, C., DeValcourt, R., Montalto, B., & Hopkins, B. (1987). The mathematics program: An overview and explanation. *Focus on Learning Problems in Mathematics, 9*, 39–50.

Pedrotty Rivera, D. (1996). *Teaching students with learning and behavior problems.* Boston: Allyn & Bacon.

Rubric Bank. [http://intranet.cps.k12.il.us/Assessments/Ideas_and_Rubrics/Rubric_Bank/rubric _bank.html]

Rubric Resources. [http://www.aea5.k12.ia.us/pd/assessment/rubrics.htm]

Willis, D. (2006). *Research-based strategies to ignite student learning: Insights from a neurologist and classroom teacher.* Alexandria, VA: ASCD.

Section 10

BioVision. [http://multimedia.mcb.harvard.edu]

Section 11

Bromley, K., DeVitis, L., & Modio, M. (1999). *Fifty graphic organizers for reading, writing, and more.* New York: Scholastic Professional Books.

Cartoon of the week. [http://www.globecartoon.com]

Editorial Cartoons. [http://unitedfeatures.com/?title=C:Editorial%20Cartoons]

Frandsen, B. (2004). Participation rubric for group development. http://.stewards.edu/cte /resources/grub.htm. Retrieved September 2010.

GoAnimate. http://goanimate.com. Retrieved January 2011.

Parr, J. (2003). Group discussion rubric. http://www.mashell.com/~parr5/techno/group.html. Retrieved September 2010.

Politically Correct Cartoons. http://www.conservativecartoons.com/index.php.

Teachnology. http://www.teachnology.com/web_tools/materials/timelines. Retrieved January 2011.

ToonDoo. http://www.toondoo.com. Retrieved January 2011.

XtraNormal. http://www.xtranormal.com. Retrieved January 2011.

Section 12

Osterwalder, A., & Pigneur, Y. (2010). *Business model generation: A handbook for visionaries, game changers, and challengers.* Hoboken, NJ: Wiley. [http://www.businessmodelgeneration.com]

Roam, D. (2008). *The back of the napkin: Solving problems and selling ideas with pictures.* New York: Portfolio. [http://www.thebackofthenapkin.com]

Section 13

Harrison, C. (1997). Differentiation in theory and practice. In J. Dillon & M. Maguire (Eds.), *Becoming a teacher: Issues in secondary teaching* (pp. 140–150). Philadelphia: Open University Press.

Section 14

Classroom 2.0. [http://classroom20.com]

PB Wiki. [http://my.pbworks.com]

Wetpaint. [http://www.wetpaint.com]; [http://wikisineducation.wet paint.com]

Wikispaces. [http://www.wikispaces.com]; [http://educationalwikis.wikispaces.com]

Section 15

Kominski, R., Jamieson, A., & Martinez, G. (2001). *At-risk conditions of U.S. school-age children.* Working Paper Series No. *52.* Washington, DC: Population Division, U.S. Bureau of the Census. [http://www.census.gov/population/www/documentation/twps0052/twps0052.html]

Index